The Bicycle Racing Guide

The Bicycle Racing Guide

Technique and training for bicycle racers and triathletes

Rob Van der Plas

Bicycle Books – San Francisco

Published by:
Bicycle Books (Publishing), Inc.
1282a – 7th Avenue
San Francisco, CA 94122

Distributed to the book trade by:
(USA) Kampmann & Co, Inc., New York, NY
(Canada) Raincoast Book Distribution Ltd., Vancouver, BC
(UK) Fountain Press Ltd., Tolworth, Surrey

Printed in the United States of America

Library of Congress Catalog in Publication Data

Van der Plas, Robert, 1938–
The Bicycle Racing Guide
Technique and training for bicycle racers and triathletes
Bibliography: p. Includes index
1. Bicycles and bicycling – Manuals, Handbooks, etc.
2. Cycling – Physiological Aspects
3. Sports – Training and Coaching
4. Authorship – Manuals, Handbooks, etc.
I. Title
Library of Congress Catalog Card Number 85-73276

ISBN 0-933201-13-3

Table of Contents

Part I
Getting ready to race

1
Discovering Bicycle Racing

Quite suddenly the English speaking world has rediscovered the sport of bicycle racing. Yes, it is a rediscovery: though few of today's active cyclists are aware of it, bicycle racing has been popular before, both in Britain and on the American continent. Between the turn of the century and the late 'thirties the US were the scene of some of the world's most spectacular bicycle track races. And British bicycle racers were quite dominant in Europe during much of the nineteenth century.

Today's re-emergence of bicycle racing does not build on this earlier tradition. As recently as 1980 it seemed the French, Italians, Belgians and Dutch had divided up the big pie of professional cycling amongst themselves, with the East Germans and Russians dominating the amateur scene. Then, out of the blue, appeared English speaking stars – both amateurs and professionals. The US team so dominated the 1984 Olympics, that the coach of one traditional cycling nation's team was reported to privately admit he was sorry his country hadn't joined the Soviets' boycott of the Games.

An even bigger surprise was the performance of the English speaking professionals in the 1985 Tour de France. Though Bernard Hinault won this world's toughest stage race for the fifth time, his American teammate Greg LeMond did more than become

The American bicycle racer Steve Hegg, one of the world's fastest track time trialists, on his specially built track bicycle and wearing an aerodynamic helmet. (Photo courtesy Raleigh USA)

second: he became the instant favorite for many years to come. LeMond kept this promise by winning the 1986 Tour. And other English speaking cyclists dominated professional racing in 1985 and 1986, with men like the Canadians Stieda and Bauer, the Americans Hampsten and Knickman, the Irishmen Kelly and Roche, the Australian Anderson and Scotland's Robert Millar, not to mention the excellent performance of the American women.

Scientific Training

Great successes don't come overnight. Clearly, the intensive and scientific training techniques largely developed – or at least practiced – in the US and other English speaking countries are paying off. The scientific approach was not new: researchers at American, European and Australian institutes had long been active in the field. But such methods had in the past been insufficiently used by racers and coaches alike. Most of the European bicycle racing experts relied largely on the lore of traditional methods, some of them right, but many outright counterproductive.

By contrast, much of the scientific research into the matter was not merely conducted at training centers and colleges in the US and other English speaking countries, but it was also put into practice by coaches and sports physiologists in these countries. Their sudden successes proved them correct. It was a shock to the smug European cycling world, which for generations had been outright anti-scientific, a world in which old wives' tales and superstition abounded.

A similar shock should have been recorded ten years earlier when the Eastern European amateurs started chalking up one success after the other. Their training and motivation was in similarly capable hands as is the case for many of today's 'Anglophobes'. But at that time professional racing was not affected, and it was simply assumed the scientifically trained Easterners, though good amateurs, couldn't measure up to the tough and race-bred Western European professionals.

Recently, the English speaking amateurs and professionals started to demonstrate to the rest of the cycling world that scientific training practices pay off at any level. In fact, it has been a great help to the international scene, because the scientific work long in progress at European institutes was finally given a chance to prove its worth. Up to that time any scientific work had been simply ignored by the racing establishment. As a reaction to the successes from elsewhere, several racers and coaches became more willing to take scientific methods seriously.

Of course, some European racers and coaches had already found their way in the search beyond conventional training and racing methods. Scientific training and motivation is what – even before the 1984 Olympics – allowed Francesco Moser to shatter the World Hour Record, and as this book goes to the press it is rumored a competing team is coaching an obscure but strong rider to try and beat that record in turn. And even if they don't succeed, someone no doubt soon will.

Clearly, bicycle racing has reached the stage of great advances and drastic changes. More has been researched and written on the subject of training, monitoring and motivation for the racing cyclist in the years since 1980 than during the half century that preceded. Today, there is no excuse for relying on tradition, superstition and old wives' tales: to the diligent researcher, the facts can be found in any university library.

But let's not get too complacent. Probably at least ninety percent of those who start racing in the US and the other English speaking countries never get the benefit of scientific training either, and perhaps as high a percentage of trainers and club officials here is not much better informed than are their European colleagues. The few racers who excel early may be fortunate. Once chosen to an sponsored team that is scientifically accompanied, they will get all the help needed to train and race consciously and correctly. Unfortunately, much of the serious work has in the past been applied only at the top level of sports. Little has been written specifically for the non full-time athlete.

The vast majority of bicycle racers, however, are as likely as not caught in the same mire as are most of the Euro-

Some of the great men of professional road racing hard at work: Bernard Hinault, flanked by Panizza and Pollentier. (Photo H. A. Roth)

pean racers. Many are in the hands of trainers who know little of scientific training methods, and even more of them start out unaccompanied, and stay so throughout their career. As mentioned above, the information needed to train scientifically and to race intelligently is available. However, only too few racers and coaches know where to look; or they may not know how to apply the available information. That's why this book was written: it will help the beginning or experienced racer understand how to reach an optimal performance without the aid of a million dollar support project.

What is most intriguing to me is that people for whom bicycle racing is more a hobby than a way of life are perhaps in the best position to benefit from scientific training methods. These are the people who have previously been left out on a limb, without famous experts to care for them – the vast majority of bicycle racers for

whom this book is written. With the old established training methods the key to success was presumed to be the number of miles ridden and the hours spent in the saddle. Today it will be possible to reach an optimal performance in perhaps half the time, clocking up less than half the mileage.

Of course, there is another side to the coin: success isn't based on theory alone. Much of what the hard-working and race-toughened Europeans have been doing for generations has helped, even though these people didn't know the theory behind their training and racing methods. Many an American racing cyclist can still pick up lots of useful methods that have been practiced by their less literate European peers. Only a blend of theoretical knowledge and proven practical methods will carry the day.

Finally, in this regard, I should stress that not everybody can be a winner – much though this seems to contradict the American dream of success as the obvious reward for hard work. Some people have the genetic makeup to be great bike racers, others do not. But that should not discourage the less well endowed from practicing and competing, if that's what they enjoy. Participation in an exciting sport and improvement of one's own performance over time, or the maintenance of health and fitness into the age where others are sedentary, is perhaps more rewarding than fame, which is short lived and often followed by disappointments.

Triathlon and the Role of Cycling

This book is not only aimed at bicycle racers, but also at triathletes. In triathlon, bicycling is generally the most time-intensive discipline. For that reason, serious progress in bicycling will provide a dramatic opportunity for overall improvement. A recent survey showed that the vast majority of triathletes come from the ranks of the army of runners that has been trotting America's pavements for many years in search of fitness. Most of these people have little or no bicycle training experience. That in itself offers reason enough for these athletes to take bicycle training more seriously than the way it can be covered in most of the general texts on triathlon.

There is another good reason for triathletes to maximize bicycle training: the cross training effect. Briefly, this can be described as the benefit to other muscle groups and the improvement in other disciplines, derived when particular muscle groups and disciplines are trained. This phenomenon contradicts long-held training theories and practices, which propounded the need for training specificity and held that e.g. swimming would be bad for an athlete's cycling performance.

At the level of top competitive single-discipline sports the old practice is probably valid. Not so at the level of 'spare time' sport, nor can it possibly be upheld in multi-discipline sports like triathlon. In fact, triathlon is an open invitation to a method of training one discipline in order to improve performance in the others. Much of the potential for improvement is to be found in overall physical fitness, as expressed in aerobic cardio-respiratory capacity. Though technique in the various disciplines must be adequately fostered, it is only part of the whole picture. The heart and lungs, the maximum power and the endurance to maintain high output levels largely determine an athlete's overall performance in this field.

To train heart and lungs, to maximize power output and endurance, bicycling is the optimal sport. Bicycling allows hard training without the damage to muscles, joints and tendons that is associated with hard running training. Nor is it subject to the physical and practical disadvantages that limit swimming as the universal training discipline. It does not involve the jarring shocks of running, nor does it excessively expose the body to the elements, reducing its resistance due to constant soaking. Cycling can be practiced starting at the front door, it can be simulated indoor and can be done more conveniently, practically and enjoyable than any other form of training.

Probably at least one half of a triathlete's total training effort should go into overall fitness work, the rest into discipline-specific training of technique and style. Virtually all of the basic fitness training can be absolved on the bicycle, leaving swimming and running training to more manageable portions. Thus a triathlete who has 15 hours weekly available for training may spend perhaps 10 hours on the bike, three hours running and two hours swimming. This way the running and swimming sessions can be reduced in number. More overall benefit and fewer physical risks will result than by dividing up the time more evenly over the various disciplines. In addition, since cycling (if done correctly) is not rough on bones, joints, tendons and muscles, it will be possible to train relatively hard right up to the day before a competitive event without fear of injury.

All this is not meant to downplay discipline-specific training. On the contrary: it should be an encouragement to make running and swimming training more specific with regards to the refinement of technique and style. When most overall fitness, power and endurance training is done on the bike, the (fewer and shorter) swimming and running sessions can be geared virtually entirely to refining style and technique and strengthening the specific muscles needed for

those disciplines. Just don't go overboard, seeing cycling only as a means to improve your endurance and your heart-lung capacity: don't forget to work on cycling technique as well.

About this Book

This book does not pretend to be yet another original contribution to the growing pool of scientific information about training for bicycle racing. Instead, it is merely a convenient and accessible summary of material that could otherwise only be found out through extensive search of the literature on training as it applies to the non full-time cycling athlete. In addition, it covers much of the knowledge that could be gained in practice by several years of direct experience in coaching or being coached, racing and watching, experimenting and observing. Here, in one simple volume, is most of the essential information needed to train and prepare for optimal performance in bicycle racing.

It also tries to emphasize the practical side of bicycle riding — whether in competition or during training rides. I have observed that many bicycle racers who may have plenty of strength and endurance fail dismally because they lack practical technique. This does not merely mean technique in the sense of posture and leg movement, but the whole complex relationship between bike and rider under all conceivable conditions. The book will explain in detail how to obtain the superb technique that allows you to make the most of your strength and ability.

The book is divided into three parts and an appendix. In the first part the reader is made familiar with the most basic information about bicycle racing and the necessary equipment. Here is covered the choice of material and a brief summary of the various disciplines of bicycle racing on the road, on the track and cross-country. Furthermore, it lays the foundation for proper and effective cycling techniques needed for fast and predictable performance.

The second part is perhaps the most essential (and not for nothing the most voluminous) section of the book. Here is explained what determines the cyclist's performance and how to improve it. It outlines in great detail how the human body and the bicycle interact and how to improve the performance with the aid of training and other methods. Also covered in this section are the subjects of diet, doping and motivation.

In the third part we will look at the practice of bicycle racing. Here you will learn about the techniques, skills and tactics required in actual racing practice, ranging from conventional criterium road racing to track racing and from time trialing to cyclo-cross. Also included is valuable advice for triathletes, who may be thought of as 'incidental' bicycle racers.

Choice of Words

Let me conclude this chapter with some remarks on the subject of language. First, there is the predicament of masculine and feminine forms of speech. Though bicycle racing has always been largely a man's sport, great feats have been achieved by women. I for one hope to see an increase in popularity of this sport amongst women, since a duration sport like cycling matches the female constitution perfectly. Nevertheless, I have chosen to generally use only the masculine forms he, him and his.

Then there is the subject of cycling and racing jargon. I have kept the book as much free from such specialized expressions as possible. In the first place, many of the terms of this jargon are mere fashion buzz words, often lacking any precise definition of meaning, which makes them at best mean different things to different people, perhaps meaning nothing at all to many people at the worst.

Secondly, various words and expressions are in use in different parts of the world. What is plain to the American makes no sense at all to the Englishman and leaves the Canadian merely confused. In fact, in many cases they don't even mean the same to readers in different parts of the same country. As much as possible, I have therefore chosen to use plain English, which may not sound very 'in', but is at least understandable to all. Wherever special terms are unavoidable, because there isn't a term in your Webster (or for that matter in your Oxford) dictionary to cover the concept, I have made an effort to explain the term the first time it is used. The alphabetical index in the back of the book will help you find these explanations in various places in the text.

Finally, there is the problem of the difference between British and American usage. This question goes beyond mere spelling differences: sometimes, different words and phrases are used either side of the Atlantic to say the same thing, or the same word may have two different meanings. As much as humanly possible, I have selected neutral expressions and the most moderate form of American spelling.

Thus, British readers will be confronted with words like center, fiber and tire, where they would perhaps expect to read centre, fibre and tyre. On the other hand, wherever American spelling leaves two or more options, I have chosen the one that differs least from the form that conforms to British usage.

2
An Overview of Bicycle Racing

Internationally, bicycle racing in its various forms is one of the most popular sports, both in terms of participation and of spectator interest. Though you may never notice much of either form of popularity if you spend all your life on the North American continent, or for that matter in one of the other English speaking countries, it may be rewarding to know that your chosen sport has more than esoteric appeal elsewhere.

In recent years bicycle racing has received enough exposure in the English speaking world to have become less of an 'odd' pursuit. Just the same, most people will still think of young kids travelling at walking speed, rather than of healthy athletes zipping by at 25 mph when they hear you call yourself a cyclist. To be a bicycle racer means to be exposed to lots of misunderstanding and often a hefty dose of derision. In fact, some of the general unfamiliarity with cycling as an athletic pursuit may even be present in many of those who decide to take up the sport. Cycling is indeed more than even some active racers realize. In this chapter you will find a brief introduction to the sport in its various forms.

Organization

Bicycle racing is more formalized than long distance running, though still less so than most other sports: to participate in bike races you usually needn't be a member of a team, but you must hold a license from your

Close pack racing in a criterium stage of the 1985 Coors Classic. Tom Broznowski leading Alex Stieda, the eventual winner of this stage at San Francisco's Fisherman's Warf. (Photo John Swanda)

national cycling organization. No big deal: in most countries you send in your money and you get your license. Theoretically, you'll be ready to race. I'd suggest you do a little more by way of preparation, but this is the essential first step.

In the US the national organization is the USCF (United States Cycling Federation), in Canada it's the Canadian Cycling Association, in Britain the British Cycling Federation. Internationally, the bicycle racing scene is supervised by the UCI (Union Cycliste Internationale), to which all the various national organizations are affiliated. The license from one country's organization will also entitle you to compete in (many) races in other countries. The addresses of the various national cycling organizations may be found in the Appendix.

With the license, the prospective racer will receive a schedule of races (generally only those in his district and the major national ones) and a rule book. The latter explains which equipment requirements apply and what to wear for races. It will also outline how to register for races and it will give details of the accident insurance that covers the participants of sanctioned races (and in many countries also while training). Generally, it will also warn you that you may lose your license for participating in unsanctioned races. The rule book makes dull but useful reading, which I recommend not to skip – if only because it will save me the trouble of including much of that type of information in this book.

Most bicycle racers will join a team or club. Highly recommended, since it makes life a lot easier and generally makes training and racing more enjoyable and effective. However, in a country the size of the US or Canada, there are lots of potential racers who live a hundred miles or more from the nearest cycling club. In that case it may still be useful to join, but you'll not be able to get many of the benefits (nor the work, if that should be any consolation). Most races are organized by individual clubs and may be open to anybody with a license, although there are exceptions either way: some club races may be open to non-license holders or they may be exclusively for members only.

If you're getting into this game for triathlon or mountain bike racing, different rules will generally apply. Both sports have their own organizations, and though licensed riders will not jeopardize their status by participating in triathlon events, the situation with mountain bike racing is still up in the air in the US. Depending on the interpretation of the rules, licensed riders may risk their status by participating in some of such events if they are not sanctioned by the USCF (which, indeed, to date most are not).

The new racer will be granted a license for the lowest category of the class that corresponds with his age. These classes are defined differently in various countries; for the USCF they are summarized in Table 2–I.

Table 2–I   USCF Classes

Class	Ages (incl.)
Midget	8–11
Intermediate	12–14
Junior	15–17
Senior	18–34
Veteran	35–44
Master	45–54
Grand Master	55 and over

The great majority of licenses are held in the Senior classification, and the number of races offered in this class is correspondingly high. Within the senior class, distinction is made between several categories of experience and competence. The new racer is assigned to category IV and may move up to the next category only after qualifying by finishing amongst the top six in six, or amongst the top three in three qualifying races in his category. Similarly, it's possible to move up to Category II and eventually I, where the real racing takes place: only Category I racers are selected for the national teams and international events.

Types of Bicycle Racing

There are three basic types of bicycle racing and any number of sub-categories: road racing, track racing and cyclo- cross. The major features of the various types of racing shall be explained below. In this summary I have followed the general classification into road, track and cyclo-cross racing. In addition, wherever appropriate, I will describe the most important individual disciplines in some detail. Further information on the practice of these disciplines can be found in the chapters of Part III of this book.

Road Racing

Road racing is by far the most popular form, and consequently this book must emphasize this type of racing. Road racing itself can be divided into several different disciplines, namely the mass-start events (criterium races, road or point-to-point races and stage races) and time trials, where the riders start individually.

Time Trialing:
The time trial is a race against the clock. Individual racers start separated by intervals of usually one minute. No exciting finishing sprints between several racers, just calculated plodding along at maximum endurance

speed for the distance. The circuit is generally a measured section of open road, which has to be ridden once out and back. It is a real test of cycling strength, most typically over a distance of 25 miles on mainly level roads, though especially in Britain other distances, as well as special hill climbs, are frequently ridden as well. In addition, there are team time trials, usually ridden by teams of four riders, staying very close together in order to maximize the advantage of reduced wind resistance to those following. The lead position, where the hardest work is done, is frequently changed, and generally the time recorded is the one for the third rider of the team.

The individual time trial was the British racing cyclists' response to the early governmental edicts that outlawed mass start racing as *furious riding*. These made it illegal to organize or participate in the form of road racing that was practiced in the rest of the world. Time trials have the advantage of being relatively easy to organize. They appeal to the beginning racer who has reservations about participating in mass-start events, since the latter demand more bike handling skill and may show up weakness of form rather dishearteningly. In recent years the time trial has received a new lease of life with the emergence of triathlon, the cycling leg of this discipline being essentially a time trial.

Time trials needn't even be organized: set up your own to monitor your private progress as you become better, especially during your first season of training. The world record for 25 miles lies below 50 minutes, but you need not fear the competition in Senior Category IV races if you get down to 65 minutes. There's a lot more to successful participation in mass-start races than basic riding speed alone, but you don't get anywhere without it.

Long Distance Time Trials:
This is a sport for hardy loners. In Britain individually ridden time trials over such distances as Land's End to John O'Groats, covering the full length of England and Scotland, have long been contested. In the US the spectacular Race Across America, in which several participants compete in a monster ride from the West Coast to the East Coast, has done a lot to capture the public's interest for our sport. Such rides require enormously complex and expensive preparation, supervision and accompaniment for the participants. This makes this discipline a purely commercial venture. On the other hand, it's also possible to do it on a bootstrap, providing you are not aiming for a record or national recognition.

Criteriums:
Perhaps as many as 90 % of all sanctioned races in the US, and 70 % in the rest of the world, are criteriums: races of numerous laps around a road circuit that is closed to traffic. Generally, the circuit is less than 3 miles long, with American races often exceeding the absolute lower limit, not infrequently getting down to less than a mile per lap. This form of racing brings both the racers close together and the spectators close to the racers. More fun to watch and more exciting to participate in, it is little wonder that this is such a popular form of racing. It does require rather formidable skills in bike handling, since you'll be cycling fast amongst a close pack (if you keep up the pace) around many tight corners.

Different distances, i.e. different numbers of laps, will be scheduled for the riders in various categories. Shorter distances will be scheduled for the younger classes and lower categories, as well as for women. The latter is unfortunate, since in general the female metabolism is better suited for longer distances at slightly lower, rather than for short distances at maximum output levels. Typical distances vary from 20 miles for midgets and intermediates to 40 miles for Senior IV and women to 60 miles for Senior I and II racers, though longer distances are possible.

Point-to-Point Races:
This form of race, also simply called road race, usually doesn't emphasize bike handling skills and tight pack racing as much as does criterium racing. Not all races of this type truly finish at a different point than where they started. Often a course is traversed several times, but this course is considerably longer and has fewer curves than that of a criterium. Many other races of this kind consist of a long ride from one town to another or a single loop, returning to the point of departure. They are often less hairraising than criterium races. On the other hand, they usually require more formal preparation, including support vehicles.

Distances are generally quite a bit longer than they are in other types of events. The most famous races of this kind are the European *classics*. These are five races in Belgium, France and Italy which (together with one of three slightly less prestigious events in Switzerland, Germany and Holland, included every third year) count towards the annual individual and team awards for professionals. Each of these classics exceeds 130 miles in length. In the US there are not as many events like this, perhaps largely due to the great distances and vast emptiness between towns: whereas the course of Paris–Roubaix or Liege–Bastogne–Liege will be lined with spectators from nearby towns, Colorado mountainsides, Nevada deserts and Iowa corn fields don't make good places to drum up crowds of enthused spectators.

Both the national and the international road racing championships (e.g. for the World and Olympic titles) fall in this category. They are rarely true point-to-point races, virtually always consisting of several laps around a circuit of anywhere from 5 to 20 miles. In professional as well as amateur events, sponsored teams play a major role these days. That makes it difficult in such championships, when riders who customarily ride for different teams must adjust to entirely different allegiances.

The whole business of individual competition with teams is somewhat baffling to the beginner, both as a racer and as a spectator. It may even seem unreasonable that tactical games are played to lure members of the opposing team into unfavorable positions, or that riders ride at the head of a group and then reduce the speed in order to enable a team mate to catch up. In the chapters on the practice of racing in the third part of the book this phenomenon will be treated in more detail.

Stage Races:
In principle, the stage race is a sequence of several other road races on consecutive days with the same participants. The American Coors Classic and the British Milk Race fall in this category, as well as their more famous counterparts on the European continent, such as the Tour de France and the Giro d'Italia. Originally, each stage consisted of a point-to-point race, but time trials and criterium type stages are now also included, especially in the US, where the criterium stages often predominate.

Both stage races and point-to-point events tend to be open to teams rather than to individual riders. Just the same, the major winner is always an individual, even though there are prizes for the best team and though special team time trials may be included in a stage race. At the end of each

Neither gears nor brakes: custom built track bicycle, built by Hans Mittendorf, one of Europe's premier frame builders.

day, the individual rider's time is added to that same rider's cumulative total through the preceding stages. In addition, time bonuses may be granted (or rather deducted) for first, second and third places, as well as for particular achievements – be they sprints or climbs – along the way.

The major US stage race is the annual Coors Classic, which has in recent years grown to be an international event of some repute. Due to the great distances between towns and the American predilection for blood and guts, this race misses the character of the true stage race. Rather, it may be called a series of criterium races on very tight courses, separated by a few point-to-point and time trial stages.

Track Racing

There are even more different disciplines on the track than were mentioned for road racing. But, since track racing is so much rarer than road racing, I shall treat the subject here rather summarily. A racing track or velodrome may be constructed outdoor or indoor, though the vast majority are outdoor structures. The track is a compact oval with steeply banked curves. The Olympic size is 333.33 m (about 1111 ft), but most indoor tracks are quite a bit smaller. Smaller tracks require even steeper banking in the curves, which is pretty hair-raising at first. Special track racing bikes are used, which have neither gears nor brakes. Details of the track and the equipment are given in Chapter 28 in Part III of this book. Here is a brief description of some of the most popular track disciplines.

Time Trials and Pursuit:
Track time trials are relatively short, namely usually 1000 m as the short distance, and 3000, 4000 or 5000 m (depending on the category of the participants) as the longer distance. More interesting to watch is pursuit racing, which is generally combined with the longer time trial distance to stage direct contests between the best placed time trialists. Essentially, the time trial is then a qualification run for the pursuit race. Here two racers start at opposite points on the track and race the set distance both against the clock and against one another. Since each rider has the distance to his competitor as a gauge to his own performance, high speeds and exciting racing take place. A rider who closes up the half lap gap has won at that point, otherwise the full length is ridden and whoever covers it in the shortest time is the winner. Both time trials and pursuits may be offered as individual events or as team events. The teams generally consist of four riders, though two-man team races are often ridden in Europe. In addition, tandem races are offered.

The granddaddy of all time trials is a track event: the World Hour Record, invariably ridden on an outdoor track. This is purely a record ride, not a regular feature in any race schedule. It's perhaps the most demanding and certainly the most difficult athletic achievement, requiring a perfect knowledge of one's own abilities, momentary condition and available reserves. For nearly twelve years the Belgian racer Eddy Merckx held this record, until in 1984 he was dethroned by the Italian time machine Francesco Moser, who set it at 50.51 km with the help of scientific training and monitoring, as well as aerodynamically improved equipment.

Match Sprint:
This is the most curious discipline to the uninitiated. Though the race is held over 1000 m, covering several rounds of the track, only the time for the last 200 m is recorded, but even

there the time is (at least in the finals) not what matters most. This is purely a race between two riders and even more a battle of wits than one of speed. The riders may often stand still several minutes trying to force the opponent into the less favorable front position lower down the banked track. Then, quite suddenly, one of the two charges off, taking advantage of the height difference, and it's almost always the one in the rear who wins.

Motor paced racing:
In motor paced racing the cyclist rides in the slipstream of a motorcyclist. There are two basic forms of motor paced racing. In the race behind big motors heavy motorcycles with a roller mounted behind the rear wheel are used, in combination with specially built bicycles with a smaller front wheel and with a front fork that seems to be turned around to increase directional stability. The motorcyclists wear special padded suits to maximize the wind shelter they provide to the cyclist following. In derny or joco racing the pacemaker rides a light motorcycle with auxiliary pedals to regulate the speed. The cyclist follows on a normal track bicycle.

Mass Start Track Races:
Though the masses are never as great as they are in road events, track mass-start races are quite popular. They can take several different forms, some of them being more geared towards entertainment than serious racing. Most popular is the points race. In this kind of race decreasing numbers of points are awarded to the first through fifth placed riders every fifth lap. The points are added at the end of the race and the rider with the highest cumulative number of points is the winner.

In the elimination race the rider whose rear wheel crosses the line last

at the conclusion of each lap is taken out of contest. Finally, when only two riders remain, the rider whose front wheel crosses the line first is declared the winner. Sounds like a children's game, and that is indeed the way some of cycling's great track racers manage to play it, much to the spectators' delight.

Madison Racing:
This is the peculiar form of spectator-oriented duration racing that was introduced in the US towards the end of the 19th century. It forms the backbone of the six-day races that are to this day offered on many European indoor tracks each winter. Here two-man teams race against one another, but the two members of each team do not race together. Rather, they take turns in what amounts to a relay event. At any one time only one rider is racing, while his teammate is resting, either in the dressing room or by slowly cruising around high up on the track. The riders of the team take turns, pushing one another off as they do so.

Omnium:
In principle, the omnium is merely a combination of any number of the preceding disciplines, with points awarded for the performance in each race. Since the late sixties, this same principle has been more and more used to make the potentially deadeningly dull six-day races more lively. No longer do the racers merely go around in circles, but the show is frequently interrupted by any of the other disciplines.

Keirin:
This is a kind of greyhound racing on bicycles that is popular amongst the betting public in the land of the rising sun. Up to nine cyclists start, preceded by a motorized pacemaker, whom the racers may not overtake during the initial rounds. With two rounds

remaining, the pacemaker stops and the cyclists are on their own, racing the remaining last two rounds as an extended sprint. Since the Tokyo Olympics this has been an Olympic discipline, a status it deserves about as much as wife beating and pogo stick jumping. My guess is that it will soon lose its Olympic status, lest every nation insist on having its local form of circus entertainment included in the Olympic program.

Cyclo-Cross

This is the conventional form of off-road racing and is practiced mainly in what amounts to the off-season for road racing. The course consists of mainly unpaved surfaces, which may include anything from ploughed fields to snow drifts and from sandy banks to rock-strewn mountainsides. The start must be on a wide clear section and at least two thirds of the course must be suitable for riding the bike, whereas it may have to be carried over tricky sections and special obstacles.

The course is usually about one to two miles long and is traversed repeatedly for a set period of time, whereby not all riders manage the same number of laps. After the time limit is up, the bell tolls for the last round and the winner is the one (of usually several riders) with the greatest number of laps who comes in first.

Equipment replacement has developed into a fetish in this discipline, especially in the US, where many riders appear with three or four differ-

ent bikes, choosing another one not only for each lap, but even for different sections of each lap. In the meantime assistants and mechanics divide their time between cleaning the last bike used and scurrying the next one to the rider wherever he thinks he needs it.

Partly as a reaction to this ludicrous bike scuttling, the new type of mountain bike, with fat tires and super low gearing, has found quite a number of users in this sport. In fact, an entirely new type of off-road cycling has developed around these bicycles with the understanding that the same bike will hold up throughout the race and that the rider maximizes riding, rather than carrying the bike.

Cycling for Triathletes

Cycling is probably the most important discipline in any triathlon event, being quite simply the one that takes the longest. A mediocre swimmer and even a plodding runner can place well in many triathlons, but a poor cyclist doesn't stand a chance. Cycling is therefore the one discipline that justifies the most intensive training effort for anyone ambitious in this fascinating sport. Triathlon as such can not be addressed in this summary of bicycle racing events, and throughout this book the triathlete may at times wonder whether he really needs to know all this. Indeed, you may forget or skip some of the peculiarities of bike racing. Yet only a full understanding of the many varied training and technique aspects of cycling will assure an optimal performance in triathlons.

3
The Racing Bicycle

In this chapter the racing bicycle will be described in some detail. The emphasis will be on the selection of components to reflect the particular requirements of training and racing in the various disciplines. The scope of this book does not permit a very detailed technical treatment of the subject. You will be shown the most essential things – for the rest, get more familiar with your bike by riding it consciously and giving it the maintenance it deserves.

Becoming thoroughly familiar with the bicycle by doing your own mainte-

nance will probably help you race more effectively. For that reason I suggest you get one of the many general bicycle books on the market, such as my *Bicycle Repair Book*. The more complex and delicate maintenance work, on the other hand, should probably be left to a competent bicycle mechanic.

The following sections also contain some criteria for the selection of high-quality bicycles and components. There is a danger to this approach, in that it is only too tempting to go overboard. Particularly Americans have a way of putting too much money into their equipment and too little work into their legs. Any well-heeled idiot can buy a bicycle that's fancier than what European professionals ride, but he

Typical high quality road racing bike, based on a custom built frame by the British frame builder Bob Jackson.

can't make it go any faster than a $400 basic racing bike.

Races can be won on very basic equipment. Especially in the beginner categories such as Senior IV and III, as well as triathlon, an expensive bike with the lightest components will not bring you any advantage whatsoever. Your super bike is just going to get damaged and will be out of adjustment most of your first racing season, and will cost another fortune to replace or repair. Start off on a basic bike and don't move up to a better machine until you have absolved at least two seasons of training and one season of racing. Only then will you have developed the abilities that will allow you to benefit from more sophisticated equipment.

Parts of the Bicycle

Fig. 3.1 shows the major components of a ten-speed racing bicycle as it is used for at least 99% of all bicycle races. Upon first sight it distinguishes itself in very little from the run-of-the-mill derailleur bicycle as it has been rusting away in every suburban gar-age since the seventies. The difference lies in the details of construction and the quality of the materials used, and I shall be explaining the essential differences in the sections that follow.

The labels in Fig. 3.1 refer to the major components. Each of these is built up of several individual parts. It is most convenient to treat the two dozen components shown (and the more than a thousand minor bits and pieces) that make up the modern bicycle by component or function groups: frame, steering system, seat, wheels, drive-train, gearing system and brakes.

There are many different manufacturers of complete bicycles and of the individual components. In addition, many smaller outfits make individual frames in small series or to the individual customer's requirements. Generally, a bicycle manufacturer only builds the frame and fits the standard components made by specialized component manufacturers. It is impossible to state which make of bicycle, or even which make of components, is the best in all cases.

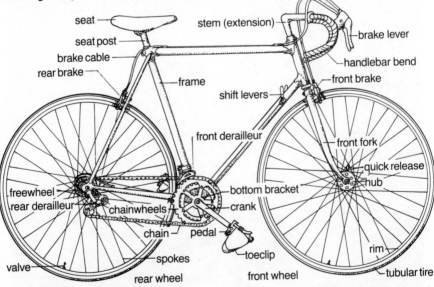

Fig. 3.1 Parts of the racing bicycle

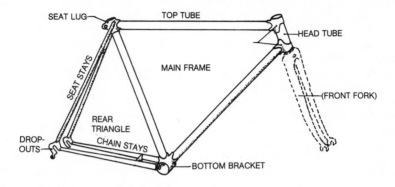

Fig. 3.2 The frame

Most manufacturers make products in several different price categories and quality levels. Though e.g. Campagnolo is generally considered to make the highest quality of many components (they make cranksets, wheel hubs, derailleurs, pedals, head sets, seat posts, freewheels, brakes and rims), some articles by another manufacturer may well be better for a given purpose or offer better value for money than one of the lower Campagnolo series. And, if you're less than a meticulous mechanic, or ride a bicycle that is even slightly off-tune, you may find that the cheaper components of any make will work better for you than the things built for professionals and top amateurs.

But the question need not even be asked: what matters more is whether you can afford the product you choose and whether it is good enough for its purpose. To answer that question I suggest you listen carefully to the advice of the competent mechanic or sales person in the bike shop. But ask carefully, without putting the words in the sales person's mouth. If you suggest a particular product must be the best, he will probably not contradict you and gladly sell you such an item, even if he knows it's much more expensive than what you really need.

The Frame

Think of the frame as the bicycle's backbone. Most racing frames are constructed of steel tubes that are brazed (soldered) into hollow lugs. As shown in Fig. 3.2, the main frame consists of top tube, seat tube, down tube and head tube. The rear triangle consists of double chain stays and seat stays, connected by means of tubular bridge pieces.

The frame's major lug is the bottom bracket shell, in which the crank axle is mounted. The other lugs are referred to as seat lug and upper and lower head set lugs. At the points where chain and seat stays join are flat plates called drop-outs, in which the rear wheel is mounted. A stiffener bridge connects the chain stays and a similar item, referred to as brake bridge, connects the seat stays. In addition, minor parts may be brazed directly onto the frame tubes: bosses for the gear levers, tunnels for brake cables, guides for the derailleur cables, bosses to mount a water bottle cage, a lug to install a front derailleur.

High strength steel tubing is generally used for racing bicycles. Special steel alloys with small percentages of other metals have been developed for this purpose. In combination with special forming operations (referred to as cold drawing) and sometimes with special heat treatment processes, these materials can be made so strong that wall thicknesses as little as 0.5 mm (0.02 in) and even less give adequate strength. Note that the racing frame's low weight is not due to the use of lighter materials (the density or specific gravity of steel alloy is not less than that of any other steel), but to the use of reduced wall thicknesses.

The large diameter tubes of the main frame are generally made of butted tubing. This means that the wall thickness of these tubes increases towards the ends, while the rest of the tube has a very small wall thickness. This is done to better take the local forces and to prevent weakening due to the heat of brazing, while still maintaining most of the weight savings of minimal wall thickness in the central section of the tubes.

Butted and straight (or plain) gauge alloy tubing is made by a number of specialized manufacturers. However, each of these makes quite a number of different versions, using various steel qualities and wall thicknesses. Therefore, saying a frame is made with e.g. Reynolds tubing means very little: it may be anything from Reynolds 453, which is not a spectacularly strong steel and therefore comes with a relatively hefty wall thickness, to Reynolds 753, which is so strong that it is made with absolutely minimal wall thicknesses and in consequence also rather fragile. And when someone tells you a frame is butted throughout, you have it on my authority that he is lying: only the main tubes are ever butted – not the head tube, nor the rear stays.

Not that it matters much: you will do just as well on the more reasonably priced frames made with the lesser steel alloys like Reynolds 453 and Columbus Aelle. And it doesn't have to be butted tubing either: several

manufacturers make very suitable tubing with constant wall thicknesses. You may be better off checking to make sure the frame is made with reasonable care and especially that the lugs and drop-outs are of satisfactory quality. Drop-outs must be quite thick and the right hand one should include a derailleur eye.

In recent years more and more frames made with aluminum tubes that are glued to aluminum lugs have become available. Of even more recent vintage are similarly constructed (very expensive) models with tubes made of epoxy-embedded carbon fibers. All these frames are indeed very light and quite nice to ride under many conditions, since they absorb road shock. Slightly less suitable for sharp cornering at the high speeds typical of criterium racing, they are nevertheless highly suited for other forms of racing, training and triathlon use, being both light and comfortable to ride. In addition, different frame constructions, using either welded aluminum or combinations of steel and aluminum, are becoming available.

Frame Dimensions

Fig. 3.3 shows the major dimensions of the frame. The nominal frame size, and with it the size of the bicycle, is de-

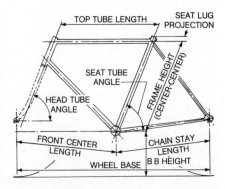

Fig. 3.3 Frame dimensions

termined by the length of the seat tube. It may be measured one of two ways: from the center of the bottom bracket to the top of the seat lug or from the center of the bottom bracket to the center of the top tube. The latter method will result in a nominal size that's 15 mm (⅝ in) less for the same frame – make sure with a measuring tape which method is used.

Determine the right frame size by straddling the frame with wheels mounted: there should be 3–5 cm (1¼–2 in) crotch clearance when the feet are flat on the ground, wearing cycling shoes or other shoes with thin flat soles. It is usually possible to buy a production frame to fit any adult rider from about 1.50 m (5 ft) up to about 1.90 m (6 ft 4 in) with normal proportions. Shorter or taller riders and those with very unusual propor-

tions may have to get a custom frame specially built to fit their particular physique.

Of the other dimensions, the wheel base, i.e. the distance between the wheel axles, is often quoted. It can only be determined when the fork is installed. Frames for racing bikes tend to be short: 38–39 in. The other dimensions and clearances also tend to be on the low side for a racing bike, in order to keep the bike rigid, predictable to steer and free from swaying. For the same reasons, the angles of seat tube and head tube relative to the horizontal plane tend to be steeper than they are for touring bicycles: 73–74 degrees.

Most manufacturers use the same seat tube angle for all sizes, while the smallest frames will have shallower head tube angles than the larger models, to allow a short top tube with enough clearance between pedals and front wheel. For long races on rougher roads, especially when the bike must not be steered in very tight

Nowadays, components are frequently offered in complete sets, also called gruppos. This Ofmega gruppo is designed and priced for the highest requirements.

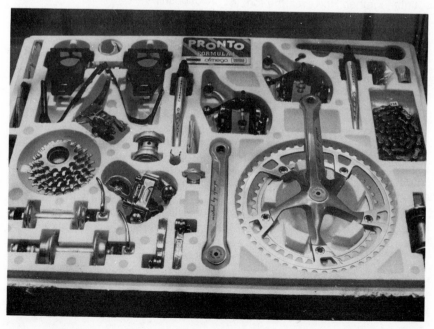

curves, slightly longer frames with shallower angles are more comfortable, whereas track racing bikes are built very short and steep.

The position of the bottom bracket may vary somewhat. It can be expressed either as bottom bracket drop, relative to the position of the wheel axles, or as height above the ground with the wheels installed The normal range is a drop of 6.5–8 cm, resulting in a height of 26.5–28 cm (10.25–11 in). A higher bottom bracket increases ground clearance and prevents pedal scrape in tight corners at the expense of some slight stability loss. Good for cyclo-cross and criterium racing.

The Steering System

The bicycle's steering system is shown in Fig. 3.4. It consists of front fork, handlebar stem, handlebar bend and the headset bearings on which the fork pivots in the frame's head tube. The fork must match the frame used and the two are generally bought together. However, the fork is more likely to get damaged later and may have to be replaced, at which time the two must be matched for size.

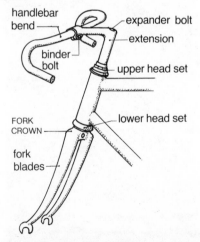

Fig. 3.4 The steering system

handlebar bend — expander bolt — extension — binder bolt — upper head set — FORK CROWN — lower head set — fork blades

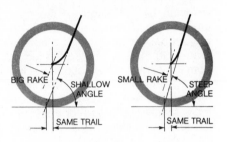

Fig. 3.5 Steering geometry

BIG RAKE — SHALLOW ANGLE — SAME TRAIL

SMALL RAKE — STEEP ANGLE — SAME TRAIL

The fork consists of a fork shaft or steerer tube, a fork crown, two fork blades and fork-ends, or drop-outs, into which the front wheel will be mounted. Critical dimensions are the shaft length, blade length and rake – that's the distance over which the blades are bent forward. This rake together with the incline of the fork with respect to the vertical determines the bicycle's shock absorption and steering characteristics. The rake should match the frame's head tube angle: the steeper this angle, the smaller the rake should be. Fig. 3.5 shows these relationships.

The steerer tube must match the particular frame size, as shown in Fig. 3.6. The correct size is determined by adding the head tube length to the headset's stacking height and then deducting 2 mm (about ¹⁄₁₆ in). High quality forks are made of the same materials as high quality frames. Cheaper forks look similar but are quite a bit heavier and less springy than an expensive fork of the same dimensions, since the wall thickness is greater.

The headset, shown in Fig. 3.7, consists of a double set of ball bearings. The upper one is adjustable and must be set so that there is neither noticeable slop, nor any tightness in the steering movement. These bearings are always lubricated with bearing grease, in which the bearing balls are embedded inside the bearing

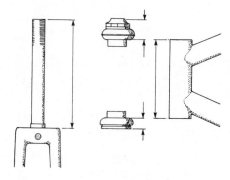

Fig. 3.6 Steerer tube length

To get the handlebars at a different distance from the saddle, the stem can be replaced by one of a different size. Stem and bend will be of aluminum alloy and the bend is wrapped with cloth or plastic handlebar tape. For triathlon use, or for that matter any cycling on less than perfectly smooth road surfaces, shock-absorbing foam plastic sleeves are a good alternative.

The Drivetrain

This is the complex of components that transfers the rider's input to the rear wheel: pedals, cranks, bottom bracket, chainwheels and chain. The gearing system, which may be considered part of the same functional group of components, will be treated separately below.

cups. Adjustment is achieved by unscrewing the locknut, lifting the lock washer and then tightening or loosening the adjustable cup, after which the locknut must be tightened again.

On racing bikes, the handlebars are fully adjustable due to their two-part construction, comprising the handlebar bend and a separate stem, also referred to as extension or gooseneck. The height is adjustable by means of the expander bolt, which clamps the stem inside the steerer tube by means of a wedge or cone shaped device. The angle of the handlebars is adjusted by means of a binder bolt on the part of the stem which clamps around the handlebar bend.

On most racing bicycles cranks, chainwheels and bottom bracket bearings are matched components from the same manufacturer and are referred to as crankset (in the US) or chainset (in Britain). Aluminum alloy cranks with separately interchangeable chainwheels or chainrings are used. Make sure the attachment spider for the chainwheels is one integral forging with the RH crank, to guarantee adequate strength and rigidity. The pattern of attachment holes varies quite a bit, with more different dimensions showing up every time a new model is introduced. The choice of the number of teeth for the various chainwheels is a matter of gearing, which will be covered in Chapter 7.

The cranks on racing bikes are attached to the bottom bracket axle by means of a cotterless system, illustrated in Fig. 3.8. The cranks have square, tapered holes, and the spindle or axle has matching square, tapered ends with internal screw threads. Recessed bolts hold the cranks onto the axle. These bolts are hidden by

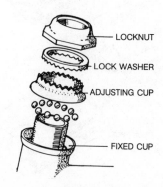

LOCKNUT

LOCK WASHER

ADJUSTING CUP

FIXED CUP

Fig. 3.7 The upper headset

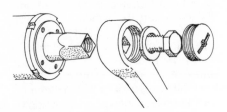

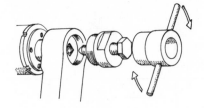

Fig. 3.8 Cotterless crank attachment   Fig. 3.9 Crank extractor tool

means of screwed-in dust caps. From time to time the bolts must be checked and tightened with a special crank tool (Fig. 3.9), especially during the first 50 miles or so after initial installation. The bolts which attach the chainwheels to the RH crank, shown in Fig. 3.10, must also be checked and tightened occasionally.

The bottom bracket axle is mounted in a set of ball bearings in the bottom bracket shell. One of two systems may be used: the adjustable BSA bearing, or a unit with fixed non-adjustable bearings. The latter is generally referred to as sealed bearing unit and is lubricated for life. It must be replaced in its entirety if it does develop play or fails to run smoothly. The BSA type bearing can be adjusted by means of the lockring and adjustable cup on the LH side. This item would be best lubricated with thick mineral oil – if only oiling nipples would be provided, as used to be the case up to the early sixties. Instead, they are nowadays merely packed with grease,

making it necessary to overhaul and repack them with grease once or twice a year.

The pedals are mounted in the ends of the cranks. The RH pedal is attached with normal RH screw threading, while the LH pedal has LH threading, so it must be turned to the left to install, to the right to remove. Two different threading standards are in use, French and international; make sure to get the right kind if the pedal has to be replaced. Fig. 3.11 shows quill and platform type racing pedals; the latter type are getting increasingly popular.

Toeclips are attached to the pedals. These come in several sizes to correspond to the shoe size. Generally

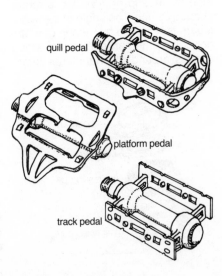

quill pedal

platform pedal

track pedal

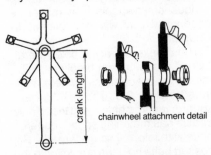

crank length

chainwheel attachment detail

Fig. 3.10 Crank and chainwheel attachment   Fig. 3.11 Pedal types

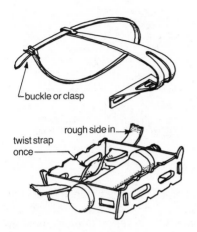

Fig. 3.12 Toeclip and strap

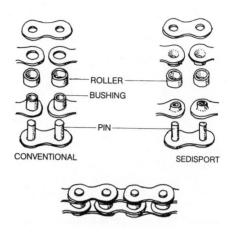

Fig. 3.13 Chain construction

speaking, the smallest size is used with shoes up to size 6½, medium up to size 8, and large for bigger feet. See the illustration Fig 3.12 for the correct way to install the toeclip strap, so it does not slip through when pulled to tighten. In recent years patented special pedals with built-in clips and easily operated releases have become available. Though they cannot be ridden with any other than the matching shoes, they have proven to be very effective and comfortable.

The chain is built up as shown in Fig. 3.13. For road and cyclo-cross bikes it must be the type for derailleur gearing, which has an inside width of ³/₃₂ in and a link length of ½ in. The ends are joined with a special chain extractor tool. The same tool is used to set the chain to the correct length. To minimize friction of the entire drivetrain, select the chain length as follows: Place the chain around the smallest chainwheel, around the derailleur as shown in Fig. 3.14 and around the smallest sprocket. In this position there must be just the tiniest bit of spring tension in the rear derailleur mechanism. Finally, check whether the chain still fits around the biggest

chainwheel and the biggest sprocket without completely tightening it. You'll need a rear derailleur with a wider range if these two extreme situations cannot both be accommodated.

The chain must be cleaned in kerosene or other solvent with a little mineral oil mixed in and subsequently dried, then lubricated with a special chain lubricant after every ride in the rain or once a month in dry weather. After about 5000 miles, or whenever it has seemingly stretched so far that it can be lifted off the chainwheel as shown in Fig. 3.15, the chain must be

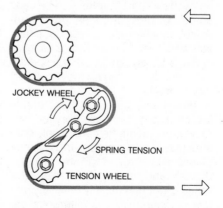

Fig. 3.14 Chain routing at derailleur

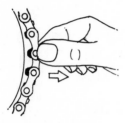

Fig. 3.15 Chain wear check

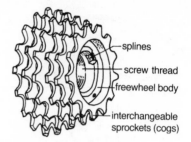

Fig. 3.16 Freewheel block

replaced. This will probably also be necessary whenever the freewheel or one of its sprockets is replaced, since an old chain tends to skip off the teeth of a new sprocket. Conversely, you may have to replace the smallest sprocket or the entire freewheel whenever the chain is replaced.

The Derailleur System
A derailleur gearing system is used on all road racing bikes to adapt the transmission ratio to the terrain and the rider's ability. It consists of a front changer, a rear derailleur and a set of shift levers, with which the chain can be literally derailed from one sprocket to another (at the rear wheel) or from one chainwheel to the other (at the crankset). The derailleur system and its components will be described in some detail in Chapter 7. The rear sprockets are contained on a freewheel mechanism, which is either screwed on to the rear hub, as shown in Fig. 3.16, or forms part of a special rear hub, depending on the make and model used.

Almost any rear and front derailleurs will be quite satisfactory for road racing, providing they are solidly constructed: models made up of flimsy pieces of bent metal will not work predictably and reliably. For racing, the range of gears is usually relatively narrow compared to the difference between the gears used in touring. Just the same, I feel the beginning racer or triathlete should beware of the extreme narrow range gearing used by top racers. See chapters 7 and 14 for further suggestions.

The Wheels
Perhaps the biggest difference between a racing bicycle and any run-of-the-mill derailleur bike is in the wheels. Superficially they look alike, but the wheels on the racing bicycle ride incredibly much better. Low rolling resistance and minimal rotating mass is the secret of good racing wheels. Even a quite mediocre bicycle can be turned into a nimble racer by merely installing well trued, light wheels with narrow high pressure tires.

As illustrated in Fig. 3.17, each wheel consists of a central hub with ball bearings and a quick-release to hold the wheel in the frame, a metal

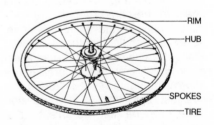

Fig. 3.17 Parts of the wheel

rim on which the tire is mounted and a set of usually 36 spokes. The spokes keep the whole structure of the wheel under balanced tension, held at the hub with a bent section and a thickened head, and at the rim with a screwed-on nipple. On racing bikes, hubs and rims are made of aluminum alloy; stainless steel is generally used for the spokes.

Tires come in two types, illustrated in Fig. 3.18: conventional wired-on tires (often incorrectly referred to as clinchers in the US) and special tubular racing tires. The latter are referred to as tubs in Britain, as sew-ups in the US. Each type of tire requires a matching rim: sprint rim for the tubular tire or Westwood rim for the wired-on tire. For the same allowable pressure, riding comfort and rim rigidity, the combination of Sprint rim with tubular tire will be lighter than the combination of Westwood rim with wired-on tire.

Amongst racers, tubular tires are used almost exclusively. However, modern narrow high pressure wired-ons are only a little heavier (as are the matching rims) and have an equally low rolling resistance. If you're on a budget and suffer punctures with any regularity, I suggest you choose wheels with wired-on tires at least for your training rides, since they can be

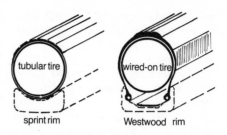

Fig. 3.18 Tubular and wired-on tires

easily repaired, unlike the tubular tire. Repairing the latter takes lots of time and patience, and even more experience. When a new or repaired tubular tire is mounted on the wheel, the cement must be allowed to dry overnight before the wheel can be used. All in all. tubular tires are a lot of hassle.

If you want to change from one type of wheel to the other, choose wired-ons of the French size 700C. These fit 622 mm rims, and are properly designated by the ETRTO size 20–622, 23–622 or 25–622, depending on their nominal width in mm (see Fig. 3.19). The rims for these tires have the same diameter as the Sprint rims used for 27 in tubular tires, allowing quick changing from one kind of wheel to the other for training and racing, respectively. Of course, this assumes you use adult size wheels: for younger and smaller riders 26, 24 and 22 in

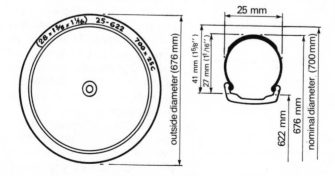

Fig. 3.19 Tire size designation for wired-on tires

wheels are also available in both tubular and wired-on versions, though both
types are hard to find outside France
and Italy.

Tire inflation pressure and spoke
tension are the secrets of good racing
wheels. Inflate your tires of either kind
to at least 90 psi (6 bar). This will
minimize rolling resistance and protect both tire and rim against damage.
Making sure the spokes are taut and
equally tensioned will keep the wheel
round and true. If the wheel should get
out of round, it can usually be sal-
vaged by retentioning some of the
spokes. If frequent problems of this
type occur, I suggest getting the rear
wheel spoked in a four cross pattern,
as shown in the illustration Fig. 3.20.
Instructions for this kind of work can
be found in any general bicycle book,
such as my *Bicycle Repair Book*; the
same goes for the repair of tubular
and wired-on tires. To keep the wheels
trued and avoid spoke breakage, the
spokes should be so tight that even
the bottom spoke is under some tension when the rider's weight is resting
on the bike.

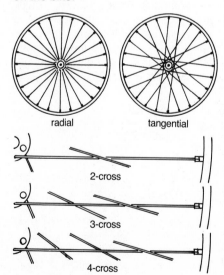

Fig. 3.20 Spoking patterns

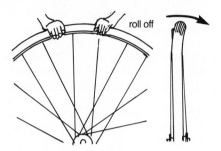

Fig. 3.21 Removing tubular tire

As regards tire design, the lightest
and most flexible tires and tubes offer
noticeably better riding qualities. That
usually also means these tires will be
quite narrow: 25 mm or less. Formerly, the black rubber tread area was
given a complicated pattern, supposedly to give more traction. Recently, it has become apparent that smooth
tires, referred to as slicks, offer better
traction, lower rolling resistance and
longer wear on any road surface,
whether wet or dry.

Tubular tires and matching rims
come in different weights and qualities. I suggest you don't choose the
lightest: the time lost due to damage
of too flimsy a tire or wheel can never
be made up, and the differences in
performance are not enough to matter
in most races. For time trials on good
roads you may choose the lightest
equipment you can afford, but for
criterium and general road racing I
recommend 280 gram tubulars,
mounted on rims that weigh around
300 gram each. Those are minimal
weights, suitable for racing. I prefer to
use 350 gram tubulars or wired-ons
for training. Most triathletes also use
wired-ons in competition, though I
would prefer tubulars.

If a tubular tire goes flat in a race
you may get a replacement wheel, if
there is a general equipment van or
you have given off your own pair of
spare wheels. In training you'd better
carry a spare tubular – or, if you use

wired-ons, a tire patch kit for a five-minute repair (yes, that's all it takes once you have developed some practice). How to fold a spare tubular in order to take it along is shown in Chapter 4.

The tubular tire is cemented onto the rim and should be allowed to set for at least 24 hours before being ridden. When a punctured tubular has to be replaced, pull off the old tire as shown in Fig. 3.21 in a rolling movement, starting opposite the valve. Put the spare on starting at the valve and center it carefully, once before and once after inflating. This tire will not adhere to the rim cement as well as it should for tight cornering, so ride carefully and cement it on as soon as possible. Avoid the use of smooth anodized rims, since they don't allow adequate adhesion of the tire, so it is likely to twist off, especially on long descents.

The wheel hubs for road racing bicycles, shown in Fig. 3.22, are held in with quick-release mechanisms. To remove the wheel, unlock the lever to put it in the open position. It may be necessary to open up the brake with its quick release lever a little to move the wheel through. On the rear wheel, the derailleur must first be set for the chain to engage the smallest sprocket. Hold back the derailleur with the chain while pushing the wheel forward out of the slot in the drop-out, as shown in Fig. 3.23. Proceed similarly to install the wheel, taking care to

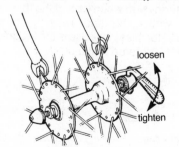

Fig. 3.22 Quick-release hub

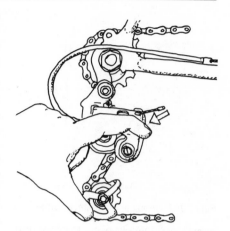

Fig. 3.23 Hold back derailleur

center the wheel between the fork blades or seat and chain stays.

The hub bearings must run smoothly without noticeable play. Adjustment procedures are covered in any general bicycle book. The best way to lubricate them is with a thickish mineral oil (e.g. SAE 60), which must then be replenished after every ride to flush out any dirt. This only works on models with an oiling hole and can't be recommended if your bike has to be brought into the living room. If you have neither a garage nor oiling holes, the hub must be lubricated with bearing grease. In the latter case, disassemble and repack the bearings with grease about twice a year.

The Brakes

All road and cross-country bikes are equipped with rim brakes, whereas track bikes do without brakes altogether. Fig. 3.24 shows the most commonly used types: the sidepull brake for road racing and the cantilever type for cyclo-cross and other off-road use. The former consists of a self-contained calliper unit, the latter has separate brake arms that are mounted on pivots, permanently attached to the front fork and the seat

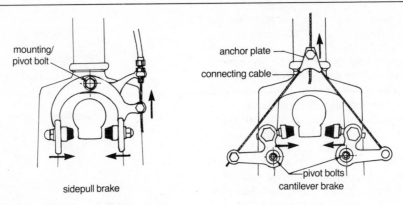

sidepull brake   cantilever brake

Fig. 3.24 Sidepull and cantilever brakes

stays, respectively, of cyclo-cross and other off-road frames.

The critical dimensions of a sidepull brake are the width over which the brake blocks can be separated to clear the rim and the height adjustment range between the brake blocks and the mounting bolt. Racing brakes tend to be small and narrow to match these dimensions on high-quality racing bikes – on a simpler frame, you may have to choose slightly more mundane brakes which have longer brake arms, though they may work quite adequately.

The brake handles, shown in Fig. 3.25, must be installed so that they can be easily reached and contracted with the brakes applied fully when there is about 2 cm (¾ in) clearance between the lever and the handlebars. If required, modify the position before handlebar tape is installed,

and adjust the tension with the adjusting barrel at the end of the cable (see Fig. 3.26). The cables must be run in gradual curves, yet kept as short as possible consistent with that requirement. It is wise to lubricate the inner cable before installing it, and to replace the cable as soon as individual strands start to break. Also make sure the brakes are mounted solidly and that the brake arms move back freely under the spring tension when the levers are released.

The brake shoes must be so adjusted that they exactly match the sides of the rim. However, especially on cheaper (i.e. less rigid) models, the front of the brake shoe should contact the rim slightly before the back to compensate for the twisting of the brake arms under the effect of the braking force. If you also race or train in the rain, you will need brake shoes that perform even when wet: at the time of this writing, far and away the best model for this kind of use is the Modolo D-0015 sintered brake block.

Fig. 3.25 Brake lever

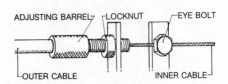

Fig. 3.26 Cable adjustment

Triathlon Bicycles

This section can be kept very brief because, whatever you may have been told elsewhere, triathletes don't really need very special bicycles. The models offered specifically for the purpose by some manufacturers differ in very little except the name from other models. They are a good choice, but not the only choice. Since triathlon cycling is essentially time trialing, without tight curves to be ridden amidst equally tight packs of racers, you can get away with less direct (and bone jarring) steering. Consequently, slightly shallower frame angles and a longish frame may be in order, and these are indeed the characteristics of most special triathlon bikes.

As for other components, most triathletes can get by admirably well with the same equipment as beginning racers use. Most triathlon bikes come equipped with wired-on tires. The benefits of high quality tubular tires with matching light rims will not be lost on triathletes either, but they require a lot more care, for which reason I suggest you only choose tubulars if you are so close to the top in your sport that the extra care will pay off. Since comfort is perhaps a primary consideration, I'd look around for a very comfortable saddle. Brazeons to mount two water bottles will be nice too.

There has been a trend amongst top competitors to make the most of

Sylviane Puntous of Canada, one of the world's strongest triathletes, at the 1985 USTS Los Angeles Regional championship. (Photo courtesy Bud Light – USTS)

the fact that the USCF and UCI equipment restrictions, which apply to sanctioned bicycle races, are not enforced in triathlon. Besides, since triathlon does not involve the closely packed tight maneuvering work typical of regular (criterium) road racing, some factors that would inhibit the road racer can be ignored by the triathlete and other time trialists. Thus, enclosed disk wheels, supposedly reducing air resistance, have been used here. It may be a slight advantage, but it is not going to make more than a few seconds difference on a 40 km ride (25 miles): not worth the hassle for anyone who is not in contention for first place.

Recently, several manufacturers have introduced special pedals and fitting shoes that work like ski bindings. They are safer and more convenient than the conventional toeclips, except when you have to walk.

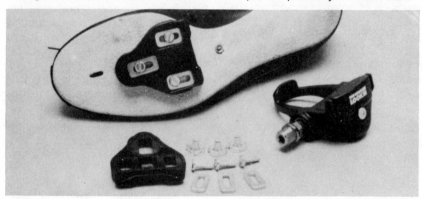

4
Clothing and Equipment

Though clearly the most important, the bicycle is not the only equipment needed for bicycle racing. In this chapter all other such essential and useful items will be covered. We'll start with clothing, followed by a variety of mechanical gadgets that will make your cycling more effective or convenient.

Bicycle Clothing

For years I have preceded any discussion of this subject with an apologetic remark about the ridiculous appearance of cycling clothing, being barely offset by its effectiveness. Not any more. Today cycle clothing and body clinging triathlon suits are high fashion in some circles. Unfortunately perhaps, because it introduces the danger of buying for style, rather than for function. Even though the styles have changed a bit, the shapes are still as shown in Fig. 4.1.

The bicycle racer wears cycling shoes, white cotton socks, cycling shorts, a cycling shirt or jersey, cycling gloves and head protection. If you

are a triathlete you may wear the unique garb designed for that sport in an actual race. At least on training rides, even the triathlete should keep in mind that your seat is your tenderest asset and that consequently the remarks about cycling pants apply to you as well. Similarly, cycling shoes are a must in triathlon, as they are in any other form of high-speed cycling.

Cycling Shoes:
Special cycling shoes, shown in Fig. 4.2, should be worn whenever racing or training. These items have a very stiff sole to distribute the pedal force over the entire foot. In addition, they have a cleat or shoe plate with which the foot is positioned correctly over the pedal. Most cycling shoes sold nowadays have adjustable cleats, though some models require the installation of separate non-adjustable cleats with nails or screws. This is a job I'd leave to a good bike store, where it should be done in your presence, to make sure the things get installed in the right position.

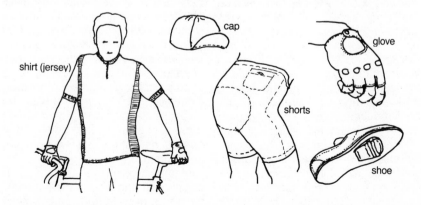

Fig. 4.1 Bicycle racing clothing

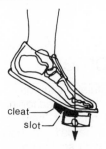

cleat
slot

Fig. 4.2 Cycling shoe and cleat

Whether adjustable or not, the slot must be lined up with the upper ridge at the back of the pedal. In addition, it must be aligned so that the foot is not twisted as it goes through the crank revolution. It has been estimated that at least 30 % of all cyclists don't have perfectly aligned feet, and these people would probably be better off with an orthopedic shoe insert, which unfortunately doesn't fit in any cycling shoe. Instead, you may inquire about special adjustable pedals (*Biopedal*), if you notice an irregular or twisting foot pressure.

The shoes must be generously cut near the toe and be laced high. Keep the lacing tight at the instep. This prevents the foot from slipping too far into the shoe, which would crush the toes and soon result in so much discomfort that you would be forced to choose an inefficient pedalling style or give up altogether.

Socks:
Wear white cotton (or in winter woollen) socks without seams that have a thick sole and heel area. The rule book requires white, the other requirements will improve wearing comfort. The modern special socks that do not slip inside the shoe seem to be an excellent solution for cyclists as well. I find tennis shops the best places to buy these and other socks suitable for cycling.

Shorts:
Cycling shorts fit tightly but elastically, reaching above the waist and at least halfway down the upper leg. They should have a piece of soft and smooth chamois sewn inside the seat area, to prevent chafing and saddle soreness, and to absorb perspiration as much as possible. These things are worn directly over the bare skin and must be washed out without soap after every longer ride. Obviously, you therefore need at least two pairs.

They come in various materials, ranging from wool to polypropylene and other synthetic fibers. Being old fashioned, I prefer the feel of wool, but there is little doubt that the synthetics generally fit and look better and are judged to be more comfortable by many racers. The great advantage of the synthetics shows up in rainy weather, when they don't absorb as much water as wool, which seems to weigh a ton when wet. The chamois liner can be replaced when it is worn out, taking care to put the new one in as smoothly as the original liner was.

Shirt:
The cycling shirt or jersey is a tight fitting knitted garment with a very long bodice, short sleeves, a zipper opening in the front and pockets in the back. Long sleeve models are available for cold weather cycling. Choose a model with three pockets, so that you can put any heavy item you may want to carry, be it an extra water bottle, a tool pouch or a sandwich, in the middle pocket, where it will not drag sideways. The zipper should be nylon, since you may hurt yourself on a metal one, which also gets hard to operate once it has got wet from perspiration.

Materials galore, and again I find closely knit fine wool unbeatable for comfort – even in hot weather. Wool not only absorbs the sweat as it is produced, it also gives it off gradually. This means that optimal cooling is achieved while you are perspiring. When you are still perspiring after very intensive work, the body temperature is reduced gradually this way. None of the synthetics masters this trick better than wool, whatever the advertising claims. However, cycling clothing is now fashion wear and synthetics offer the prettiest colors and the sexiest designs.

Under their cycling shirt many riders wear a sweat shirt. That's because they choose a synthetic shirt, which doesn't do a proper job of absorbing and transmitting the essential body juices. Wearers of woolen shirts can do without.

Gloves:
Though not required by the rule book, all bike racers wear leather gloves with cut off fingers and an open top. The palms should be padded to absorb road shock and to protect the hand in case of an accident, when the rider tends to put out his hand to brake the fall. The closure should be by means of Velcro tape.

Training Clothing:
Good training clothing is not very different from good racing wear. There's no place for warm-up suits and other bulky air traps in bicycle training. While training, you will be moving even between peak efforts. And when you are moving, you do not want any loose garments that trap layers of air around your body. Just wear the same garb as you use to race in, except that you should choose long sleeved shirts and long pants (or separate add-ons which serve the same purpose) if the outside temperature calls for it: anything below 18 degrees C (65 degrees F). The only time to wear a track suit or warm-up suit is before or after a race, not while riding a bike.

Bad Weather Wear
Some of us hardy ones even train in the rain, by sleet, snow and ice. It's not only necessary to get enough real-life cycling experience around the year, it can be enjoyable if the right clothing is worn and distances are kept down to something reasonable. Fig. 4.3 shows suitable cold weather garb. This is the stuff to wear while training, but even in races you may need more than the sleek summer clothing. Many races are also held if the weather is less than perfect; in Europe most races are never cancelled, whatever the weather.

As for your training rides, even if the weather is reasonable when you leave, it may rain before you get back. On days like that you may be well advised to take some kind of rain gear. A Goretex jacket and, if it is also cold, perhaps spats or long pants with coated front panels are quite effective. There are also rain proof covers for shoes and socks, though I prefer to put plastic bags around my socks inside the shoes.

In really cold weather you may wear a woollen long-sleeve shirt with a tightly knitted woollen sweater over

— wool cap

long wool pants —

long wool socks —

lined shoes with thick soles —

wool sweater jacket with waterproof front and shoulders

lined gloves

water-proof front

shoe covers

Fig. 4.3 Cold weather clothing

the top, long pants, full finger gloves, a helmet liner that covers the ears, long woollen socks and winter shoes with extra thick soles to provide maximum insulation. A winter jacket with impregnable front and shoulder panels and similarly designed pants will keep a cold wind out quite effectively. It is possible to get a wind breaker apron to be worn under the shirt, but I still prefer to stuff a folded newspaper under the outer layer of clothing. The latter solution has the advantage of being easily installed and removed without loosing time and undressing in public.

Head Protection

For the participation in USCF sponsored races you are required to wear head protection. The various types are illustrated in Fig. 4.4. To prevent fatal injuries in an accident you will not be served well by the equipment racers generally wear to satisfy this requirement. Obviously, what used to be euphemistically referred to as a racing helmet and is more appropri-

ately dubbed a 'hairnet', consisting of a few padded strips of leather, won't do the trick. What you need is an energy absorbing hard shell helmet, which may or may not have openings, but which must be of integral expanded foam construction of significant thickness.

It is my firm opinion that non-integral, open models (which I grant to be much more comfortable to wear when it is very hot) do not provide adequate protection. This is an opinion shared by virtually all who have investigated the nature of cycling induced brain damage. A helmet that does not meet ANSI Z-90.4 will not be adequate protection, and I think it a crying shame the UCI has not seen fit yet to require head protection that meets this standard, as the USCF finally has after a widely publicized spree of cyclists' deaths in recent years.

In addition to requiring a thick layer of impact-crushable (i.e. permanently deformable, non-flexible) foam and a hard integral outer shell, the helmet must stay in place on the head when you fall off the bike. To do that you'll need a three point attachment of the chin strap, and you must fasten it tightly enough to stop it from sliding back and forth, without becoming uncomfortable.

European professionals don't wear any kind of head protection other than a cotton cap, while the amateurs combine that garment with the leather hairnet. Advantage of the cap is that it lends itself to the imprinting of advertising texts. It also has a handy flap that keeps the sun out of your eyes or off your neck, depending which way round it is worn. Combine a real helmet with a sun shield to achieve the same effect, in addition to reasonable head protection.

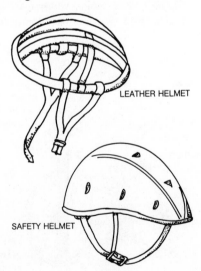

LEATHER HELMET

SAFETY HELMET

Fig. 4.4 Head protection

Bicycle Equipment

In this section only the most essential mechanical aids to effective bicycle riding and training will be covered. These are the items that can be taken along or mounted on the bike to advantage for one purpose or the other: water bottle, pump, spare tire, tools, speedometer, fenders, lights and perhaps a warning device. Though I use all of these, I'm aware that most (American) cyclists consider most of these items superfluous. They don't need fenders because they don't ride in the rain, no lights because they don't ride at dark, they take no tools because they consider them too heavy.

I do not have the missionary zeal, so I shall not attempt to reform those who argue that way. It is up to you to join the rest who (quite differently from what they say) neglect their training when it might rain, get caught in the dark on suicide trips without lights and hitch hike back from a training ride because they lack the simple tool or the pump that would have kept them going. Just the same, in the hope that my words are not lost on all who read them, here are some remarks that may help those who are prepared to equip themselves better for the task at hand, in addition to some remarks about the less controversial accessories.

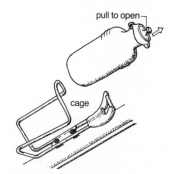

Fig. 4.5 Water bottle and cage

Water Bottle:
Take one along on any ride, certainly if it is hot and you'll be staying away more than an hour. The bottle cage may either be mounted on bosses permanently attached to the frame, or by means of metal clips installed around the frame's down tube. In the latter case, first wrap the locations where the clips will go with e.g. handlebar tape to protect the paintwork and to avoid slipping. The bottle itself should be the type with a spout shown in Fig. 4.5, which is easiest to operate while cycling. You drink not by sucking it, but by holding it an inch away and pushing the bottle, neatly squirting some liquid into your mouth.

There are special insulated bottles, as well as insulating covers for ordinary bottles. These seem to keep cold

Simplicity and ease of operation are the essential criteria for a good electronic speedometer. This IKU instrument has only two conveniently shaped and positioned buttons.

Fig. 4.6 Bicycle tire pump

drinks cool better than hot ones hot. Another way to keep a drink cool is by wrapping the bottle with a cloth (e.g. an old sock), which you keep wet by squirting water on it from time to time. The evaporation of this will keep the contents quite cool. It's no luxury to take two bottles, preferably one with water and the other one perhaps with fruit juice. You may refer to Chapter 20 before you get tempted to fill the second bottle with one of those miraculous energy drinks or electrolyte replacement liquids you've seen advertised.

Pump:
Even if you take no other tools, carry a pump on your training rides. In addition, you may want to get a stand pump and you definitely should get a pressure gauge to check the tire pressure before you set out on a race or a training ride. Depending on the terrain and the type of tire used, any pressure over 80 psi will be called for: 7 bar (100 psi for a tubular tire on a smooth road is not excessive. Turn the wheel until the valve is up, unscrew the round nut on the (Presta) valve before inflating; hold the end of the pump straight and steady on the valve with one hand while inflating. Pump and

Fig. 4.7 Tire pressure gauge

gauge are shown in Fig. 4.6 and Fig. 4.7, respectively.

Portable bicycle pumps are designed to fit between the frame tubes along the seat tube. Most manufacturers make two or three different sizes to match a range of frame sizes. I prefer the pumps made by the French Zefal company, which deliver a very high pressure and have a good closing fit at the valve. In general, a long pump with a small diameter will allow a higher pressure than large diameter models. Definitely no use are hand pumps with a tubular connector, since they can not deliver a high enough pressure to the valve.

Speedometer:
Together with a simple wrist watch, this device can make all the difference between effective and ineffective training, especially for the racer who has to ride alone. The benefit lies in the performance monitoring function known in sports physiology as KOR (knowledge of results), which will be explained in Chapter 21. Nowadays, electronic speedometers are used, mounted on the handlebars and driven from an induction pick-up point at the front wheel hub. These are powered by battery or by either a solar cell or a built-in generator, which avoids all sorts of problems.

There are now numerous such devices on the market, some of them giving a lot more information than speed and distance alone. Pedalling speed and even pulse rate may be monitored. The most important functions are momentary and average trip speed and trip distance. More impor-

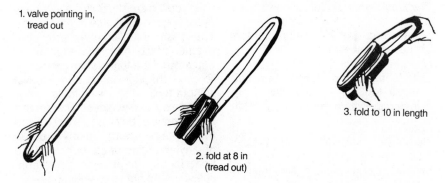

1. valve pointing in, tread out

2. fold at 8 in (tread out)

3. fold to 10 in length

Fig. 4.8 Rolling up tubular tire

tant than any number of additional functions will be the ease of operation. Providing the most important functions listed above are available, the device with the least number of knobs will prove the most useful.

Spare Tire:

If you use tubular tires you should carry at least one spare on all training rides. And if you often need it you shouldn't be riding tubulars, but sturdy high-pressure wired-on tires with separate inner tubes and tools to fix them. Carry the tire in a tire pouch attached behind the saddle, folded as illustrated in Fig. 4.8. Release it from its cramped position at least overnight once a week, placing it slightly inflated around an old rim so it does not deteriorate when stored. I prefer to carry the tire in a saddlebag, but you can also get a special spare tire pouch. Choose one that has a separate compartment to take some tools, and attach it so that it does not sway. If you should wish to take a wired-on tire along on a training ride, Fig. 4.9 shows you how it can be folded to take up minimal space.

Tools:

Take along the most essential tools on all training rides. Use the spare tire pouch or a separate little bag, secured under the saddle. I suggest carrying the following items:

☐ small screwdriver
☐ Allen wrenches to fit the hexagonal recess bolts on your bike
☐ 6-in crescent wrench
☐ set of open-end or box wrenches in sizes 8–13 mm
☐ small pair of needle nose pliers

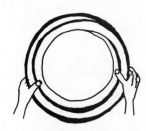

1. fold into three loops   2. fold outer loops in to center

3. tie three loops together to form 9-in ring

Fig. 4.9 Rolling up wired-on tire

□ enough change for a few phone calls
□ wrench part of crank extractor tool
□ spoke nipple wrench
□ chain rivet tool
□ if you use wired-on tires: puncture repair tools (tire irons, called tire levers in Britain, and tire patch kit)

Fenders:
Here we get into the realm of the disputed: I prefer to train, even though it might rain, and I prefer to stay tolerably clean and comfortable when it does. For that I need fenders or mudguards, but you are free to do without. If you choose to install them on your training bike, choose light plastic ones and make them easily removable.

The top bracket that attaches the fender to the brake bolt can easily be removed and installed if you replace the (thick) brake bolt attachment nut by two (thin) locknuts, as shown in Fig. 4.10. These thin nuts must both be tightened, even when the fender is not installed, to provide enough hold. The stays will be installed at the fork-ends or drop-outs. Some bikes have drop-outs with screw eyes for fender stay installation. Though the weight of these eyelets is negligible, they seem to be out of fashion.

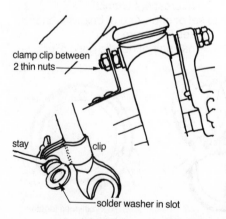

clamp clip between 2 thin nuts

stay   clip

solder washer in slot

Fig. 4.10 Removable fender attachments

If your bike doesn't have screw eyes, you may use little metal clamps. These are installed over protective patches of e.g. handlebar tape, wrapped around the fork blades and stays. To allow the installation and removal without tools, make wing bolts by soldering a sizable washer in the slot of a fitting screw or bolt with a slotted head (usually size 5 mm). Attach a rubber or vinyl mud flap at the bottom of the front fender to prevent water from splashing up right into your shoes.

Saddle Bag:
The best place to carry any items like extra clothing, food, spare tire and tools on a training ride is in a saddlebag, mounted directly behind the saddle. In Britain this is the universal way to carry things on any bike, and it is unfortunate that so few saddlebags are used in the US. However, they do exist and are a worthwhile investment that should be carried on any longer training ride. Its presence distracts a little bit from the professional racing cyclist look so desired by many of the would-be champions, but it is better than trying to look like a champ only by being a fool.

Lights:
Like the preceding items, lights are useful on a training bike: they can extend your days, and perhaps your life. Get at least an easily removable battery light, powered by two D-cells, for installation on the handlebars. For protection from overtaking vehicles, use either a rear light or a particularly big red or amber reflector in the rear, mounted low enough not to be obstructed and to be picked up by a car's low beam. Pedal reflectors in the rear are useful, spoke reflectors are no use and a white front reflector is no substitute for a headlight. The removable lights can be carried in the saddlebag whenever there is a chance your trip might extend into dusk or darkness.

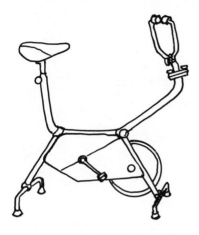

Fig. 4.11 Bicycle ergometer

Check bulbs and batteries at least once a week to make sure they will be operating properly.

Warning Devices:
As long as you ride in normal traffic on regular roads, you will probably never need a bell or a horn. But if you use bike paths or other recreational facilities, where you have to mingle with joggers, dogs and roller skaters, you will have to be prepared for disaster unless you can warn them of your speedy approach. Similarly, you will need one on very narrow winding mountain roads, where opposing traffic can not always be seen.

A bell, prescribed for cyclists in many countries, won't do the trick. The intended recipient may not even hear it over the sound of his Walkman if he's a jogger or dog walker, not to mention the situation with an approaching truck on a mountain pass. Even if the signal is heard, the reaction may be minimal, because you'll probably be thought of as a mere cyclist, who travels at crawling pace and seems to be no threat to the recipient of the signal. Only a powerful handheld signal horn, operated by pressurized gas, will have the desired effect. Either keep it in your back pocket or mount it on the bike.

Training Equipment
Although the most effective way of bicycle training is by means of riding a bicycle on the road, some modern gadgetry can be useful. The most suitable device would be one that most closely simulates the experience of riding a bicycle. Use either a windload simulator or a bicycle ergometer. Both are preferable to the conventional bicycle rollers on which racing cyclists used to spend many hours spinning away in winter. Unlike the rollers, ergometers and wind-load simulators can provide a resistance similar to that encountered when riding.

The bicycle ergometer, shown in Fig. 4.11, is a fixture with a heavy flywheel driven via the pedals. Most of these provide all the discomfort of a cheap children's tricycle, though it should be possible to install pedals with toeclips, racing saddle and racing handlebars. This device has its uses in accurately determining the body's response to a given workload, since the resistance can be set to a certain force, and the corresponding speed is indicated to allow calculating the power output as the product of force and speed.

The windload simulator, shown in Fig. 4.12, is more useful for actual training purposes, since it provides a resistance that is quite similar to the one encountered when cycling on the road, namely increasing rapidly with increasing speed. It is a frame with rollers and a set of wind turbines, on which you can place your own bicycle, thus providing a familiar environment. Some models actually guide the air that is moved by the turbines back to cool the rider, which makes them more comfortable for longer training periods.

Use the windload simulator in combination with at least a speedometer, possibly with added functions to monitor pedalling rate and pulse. In combination with your own understanding of training theory, as explained in chapters 16–18, this set-up should allow you to carry out quite sophisticated training and monitoring, especially if you also remain conscious of your body's own responses, as evidenced by your pulse and the way you feel.

Weight training equipment is another item that has recently entered the torture chambers of many training athletes. I remain skeptical of their value. Though they can have their uses, they are no good for what most people have in mind. Don't use this kind of training to try and develop or strengthen your leg muscles, because that can only be done correctly

wind turbine

use own bike

Fig. 4.12 Windload simulator

on a bicycle, a bicycle ergometer or a windload simulator. Instead, use it to strengthen the muscles that are used mainly isometrically in cycling: those of the arms, stomach, back and shoulders. Chapter 13 will explain why, while Chapter 18 shows how it is done.

More style than protection: Cinelli 'hairnet' type racing helmet.

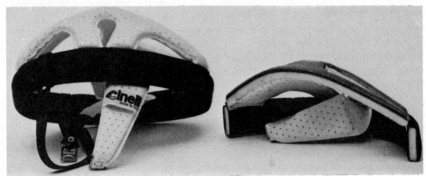

5
What Makes a Winner?

It is of course not possible to give a patent recipe for success in bicycle racing or any other pursuit. In fact, you may never win a race, even if you read the smartest book and follow the advice of the most competent coach. But every cyclist can benefit from knowing why certain individuals win races. It will probably help you be more successful yourself. Even if you don't beat others, you may consider yourself a winner if you improve on your own earlier performance.

Athletes Born and Athletes Made

Any athlete's performance potential has an upper limit, beyond which even the strictest training regimen can't lead. It's in your genes. If you should have inherited the genetical complex that makes great long distance racers, you may be another Greg LeMond, if not an Eddy Merckx. If you don't, you may never win a race or break a record.

But that's only the upper limit. The genetic star who doesn't train correctly will never make it, and there is adequate evidence to suggest top class performances are within the grasp of even the averagely genetically endowed. Road racing cyclists

Bernard Hinault, in the center, is one of cycling's great winners. Small but muscular, he is both a great climber and a superb time trialist. (Photo H. A. Roth)

are fortunate in a way. Their chosen discipline is probably more subject to improvement through effective training than any other sporting discipline. This is because road racing depends more than virtually any other sport on sustained sub-maximal performance, which is perhaps the ability most subject to improvement through training.

There is hope for all, even though certain forms of cycling are largely reserved for the genetically blessed. The sprint – whether as a distinct track discipline or as the finish of a road race – is such a skill. But there are many ways to excel in cycling without being a born sprinter. Several of the world's greatest cyclists can't beat lesser athletes in a sprint finish. They just have to win on their terms, which may be a sustained solo run, a fast climb or a superior tactical maneuver. Nothing shady about the latter, as will be explained in the chapters of Part III. Bicycle racing is not a contest to establish who has the strongest quadriceps and hamstrings, but one to establish who can reach the finish line first, a contest in which skill, endurance and brains figure as much as force.

Thus it should be clear that the greatest latitude of performance potential lies, not in the genetic endowment, but in the complex of activities aimed at the improvement of overall cycling. Training is the word. And training means more than riding many miles or exercising the muscles with weights. Effective training is a vast complex of activities that includes these techniques as well as many more methods which shall be covered briefly below and in much more detail in the chapters of Part II.

Athletic pursuits can be absolved in one of two ways – or rather, any gradation between two extremes: associative or dissociative. The dissociative cyclist quietly turns the cranks around, while his mind is somewhere else. The associative one pays maximum attention to what he is doing and what is going on around him. Successful athletes in any sport tend to be of the associative type, people who race with their whole body and their whole mind. Though this attitudinal difference is largely predetermined by temperament, it may well be possible to become more associative, and thus increase one's chances of improvement. Force yourself to pay maximum attention to the activity of cycling, whether in training or while racing.

Cardio-respiratory Fitness and Endurance

To be an effective bicycle racer, endurance and the ability to deliver a considerable power output over a long period of time – whether in racing or training – must be developed. This is primarily done with the kind of training that has been on everybody's mind since it has become popular to be fit. It aims at improving the capacity of heart and lungs for sustained activity. This is perhaps the basis of all bicycle performance, since it is simply not possible to effectively train for any of the other important aspects of cycling without having reached a state of basic fitness. In cycling it is particularly essential because the overwhelming majority of all bicycle racing miles are ridden under just such conditions.

It amounts to doing sustained exercises of the kind of work that taxes the heart and the breathing apparatus enough to enlarge the heart muscle and the lung capacity. This is also known as aerobic work, i.e. exercise at any level of output that can be performed without getting out of breath. But it is not right to expect that any kind of aerobic work also has a training effect: for that, you must reach and sustain at least a certain proportion of your maximum aerobic capacity.

The fitter you become as a result of earlier training, the higher this level will be, so the faster you'll have to ride to achieve further improvement. This is indeed a very summary description: in subsequent chapters we'll take a closer look at this and all the other techniques mentioned here. To allow exercising at the high level, training methods have been developed that are more effective than merely plodding along at whatever speed can be maintained for many hours.

Anaerobic Power

Maximum level performance, particularly for brief periods, such as in a sprint or a sudden acceleration, demands a temporary power output that very much exceeds the sustained power output potential that can be handled aerobically. This is known as anaerobic work and will be described in some detail in Chapter 12. Though anaerobic capacity can be increased, it is largely limited by the distribution of particular muscle fiber types, which is indeed genetically predetermined.

Cyclists with high anaerobic potential will always outsprint those who have a lower percentage of such particular muscle fibers. That does not mean sprinting speed cannot be improved, but it does mean that the level to which it may be improved is limited to a genetically predetermined point that cannot be exceeded with any kind of training.

Basic Cycling Style

The repeated movement of cycling must be learned and practiced to become truly effective and to take minimal effort. Though not quite as significant as it is in e.g. swimming, style is a very important aspect of bicycle racing. The successful racer has to constantly work on making his move-

ments fluent. This is important if the cyclist's motions are to be really efficient, since the less fluent movement means that a significant proportion of the effort goes into merely overcoming the body's internal resistances, without delivering any effective work to move the bicycle forward.

This is perhaps best illustrated when an inexperienced cyclist rides a bike on rollers. Even though there will be no resistance, theoretically allowing almost unlimited pedalling speeds, the novice will find it very hard to pedal faster than say 80 revolutions per minute (RPM). The trained racing cyclist can reach 180 RPM under the same conditions. But even the experienced cyclist will have to work on it: after a three month interruption of training I measured a reduction of 20–30 RPM in maximum pedalling speed for several trained racers.

Cycling Technique

Bicycle road racing requires more than sitting on a bike and pedalling. Handling the bicycle and all its mechanisms, holding and moving the body correctly, gearing and braking, steering and accelerating are all basic cycling skills that must be mastered to race (or even train) effectively. Then all those skills must be performed in the midst of a crowd of perhaps a hundred others, some of whom don't handle their bikes as well as they should and may well get in your way. Tricky, to say the least.

Though there are mechanical substitutes that allow you to develop your muscles, improve your pedalling style and increase your endurance in a gym or even in the comfort of your own home, there will be no substitute for real life cycling when it comes to developing these skills. Much of your bicycle training must therefore be done on the road, preferably under varying conditions and often in the presence of other cyclists.

Muscle Strength

You can't hope to become a powerful cyclist without first developing strong muscles. It is particularly needed in climbing, accelerating and sprinting. Unfortunately, the typical long duration cycling performance is not in itself a very effective way of increasing muscle strength. Consequently, some other way of training has been sought that develops the muscles – primarily those of the legs, though arm and torso muscles may need additional strengthening as well.

This kind of training effect can be achieved either on or off the bike. On the bike it is achieved with short powerful bursts of power output, such as in climbﬁng or sprinting; off the bike this effect can to a limited extent be simulated with weights and special muscle exercising devices. Here the problem occurs that the visible effect does not necessarily coincide with the actual effect. Whereas with actual sprint or climbing training the muscles become more specifically suited for doing just the kind of work demanded of them, weight training only serves to produce bulky muscles that may look good but aren't optimally efficient when applied to propel a bike.

Racing Skill

Even if you are the strongest and best trained cyclist, you may not win if you are not also familiar with the way races operate. This implies more than just understanding tactics, difficult enough in itself. It also requires sensitivity to messages sent by your own body and mind, as well as judging the powers and tactics of others around you, and a correct interpretation of the characteristics of the racing course. You must know yourself and you must

pick up the vibes around you. In short, you must be alert to all the complex events that are taking place during a race.

You learn to race by racing, and even if you are that one in a million whose genealogical make-up seems predestined for bicycle racing, you will have to ride many races just as alert to the events around you as to your own efforts to do well. Successful racers are above all experienced racers. Only too many natural talents who received early recognition have been fooled into thinking talent could make up for experience, and were soon forgotten. A case in point is the West German professional Didi Thurau, a born cyclist with great endurance, a powerful sprint and a beautiful riding style, who became an instant celebrity in the 1978 Tour de France. Hailed instantly as the next generation's Eddy Merckx, he maintained his fine riding style, but never learned to race like a winner.

Mental Attitude

Unconventionally, perhaps, I would suggest considering this together with physical wellbeing, since the two cannot be separated as easily as is generally assumed. To be a successful racer you will have to develop the mental attitude to work your physical body effectively. Your mind must govern the body, yet at the same time, your mind will have to learn to understand the body. The difference between associative and dissociative involvement, mentioned elsewhere in this chapter, is an attitudinal factor that can be influenced to some extent: remain fully conscious of what is going on around you, and stay alert to your own performance.

It's not done with plain determination, toughness or spartan asceticism alone. Nor am I proposing you hype yourself into thinking you can do more than you can. It is just as dangerous to misuse the mind as it is to abuse the body. For the mind to govern the body, it also has to take on the functions for which you have a mind in the first place: to sense, interpret and understand what your body requires.

Full confidence in your training technique, your own condition, the course of the track and the state of your equipment will greatly enhance your chances of success. Again, don't fool yourself, because it's not enough to pretend such confidence if it is not justified. To give just a material example, having the ultimate equipment will probably not help one bit. Yet understanding that your equipment, even if it's less sophisticated than what many others use, is adequate

Multiple world champion Jeannie Longo of France, women's winner of the 1986 Coors Classic, demonstrating perfect riding style and posture during the 3000m pursuit race. (Photo H. A. Roth)

and reliable will provide the confidence needed to be successful.

Perhaps this can all be summed up best with the word consciousness: stay attuned to your body, your cycling technique, your equipment and the world around you. Think about what you are doing and what is happening in the race field. Be prepared at all times to take in information from all sources and to revise your plans if necessary – whether that concerns training, equipment choice, feeding habits, life patterns or racing practices.

General Physical Fitness
The successful athlete must be at ease with his body. It's not enough to have developed enormous cycling muscles, a brutish endurance and the mental alertness described above. You must be fit in the simplest sense of the word. To achieve that, you may use any of a number of different exer-

cises, ranging from breathing to yoga, from stretching to massage and warm-up. The most useful of these techniques will be described in the chapters of Part II.

Knowledge of Results

Hardly anything seems to be more effective in the improvement of physical performance than the athlete's awareness of his own progress. That's why a speedometer and a wrist watch, regularly followed performance tests, and a detailed training and racing log will be essential tools and methods to reach a peak performance. Early and frequent participation in races and training with others are further methods to derive such benefits.

Diet and Lifestyle

Overrated as the emphasis on the athlete's diet has been in recent years, there is no doubt that a careful selection of foods and beverages – or at least the avoidance of the wrong ones – will improve your chances to race and train effectively. In addition, it will be wise to adapt your lifestyle to the demands of your training and racing regimen. You needn't live a life of cy-cling only, but you may have to limit yourself to a less hectic and extravagant lifestyle than some people are reputed to enjoy.

The other aspect of this latter suggestion is that you may have to set your limits in accordance with what is possible and desirable with a given lifestyle. You can't expect to train like a professional if you also have to study, hold a job, care for a family or merely have social or cultural interests outside of cycling. You may still combine any or even all of these interests with cycling. Though you will probably never reach your full potential as a bicycle racer, you may do well enough and enjoy a fuller life.

The limited choice of training techniques open to the person with a varied lifestyle may well help make both his racing and training practice more conscious and effective in terms of total time spent relative to the effect. The restraint of time will force you to choose the most time-effective training methods. Just the same, these restrictions may limit your maximum cycling performance, and the training schedule must be fitted around your other interests and activities.

6
Bike Set-up and Riding Posture

This chapter contains all the information necessary to set up the bike and start pedalling effectively for high speed cycling. Sounds simple enough and perhaps superfluous. Yet it is so fundamental that I suggest you follow this advice even if you feel you have been cycling long enough to have established the requisite position and style. Incorrect set-up can severely limit a cyclist's development and training progress.

The material contained here is by no means all that can be said about

effective cycling technique. It is merely the essential foundation that allows the cyclist to start bicycle training and to develop style and technique effectively. Besides this chapter, refer to Chapter 4 regarding the correct adjustment of the cleats on your cycling shoes. The finer points of riding technique, including bike handling and gearing, will be covered in subsequent chapters.

Frame Size
The racing bicycle and its components have been developed to their present form to meet the essential ergonomic requirements of fast cycling. But that only works effectively if the

Eric Heiden, 1985 US professional champion, shown here during a road race in Beverly Hills, California. (Photo David Nelson)

correct frame size consistent with the rider's physique is chosen. Here is a list of the requirements that must be fulfilled by the frame:

☐ It must allow placing the seat at such a height above the pedals and at such a distance behind them as to allow smooth and effective pedalling when seated.
☐ It must allow a handlebar position in which the upper body is virtually horizontal for minimal air resistance, another point far up and forward to allow effective pedalling when standing up with all the weight on the pedals, and a position for relaxed riding with the upper body moderately inclined.
☐ The top tube must be so high as to provide adequate rigidity while still allowing the rider to straddle it with both feet on the ground while standing still.

It may be obvious that all these conditions can not be met without varying the frame size in accordance with the rider's physiognomy. Just the same, the vast majority of riders will not require a custom-built bicycle, since the design of various components allows adequate flexibility to accommodate a range of rider physiques with a given leg length. Custom-built bike frames are therefore far less critical for effective racing than is generally assumed. A standard racing frame, equipped with fitting components that are adjusted correctly, will serve all but the physiognomically exceptional rider.

My impression is that most beginning cyclists choose a frame one or two inches larger than they should. This may not be a serious disadvantage for casual riders, but in racing it will prohibit developing a really effective riding style and limit your maximum performance. A higher than optimal frame does not allow lowering the handlebars enough for the nearly horizontal posture required to beat the wind at maximum speed and to work some of the body's strongest muscles.

To establish the correct frame size it is little use to consult standard frame sizing tables, if only because not all manufacturers measure the frame by the same method. I suggest you determine the correct size in several stages. First establish the maximum size consistent with your leg length. Do that by straddling the top tube of a complete bike or a frame with wheels installed. Both feet must be flat on the ground, wearing thin-soled cycling shoes or in stocking feet. At least one to two inches clearance must remain between the top tube and your crotch.

The preceding test has suggested one frame size that may fit. Another frame design with the same nominal size, e.g. with a higher bottom bracket, may not provide the same fit. You have found a likely candidate, but not necessarily the ultimate frame. Continue with this bike by adjusting seat and handlebars in accordance with the procedures below before making up your mind firmly: you may need a still smaller frame or in rare cases a bigger one.

Seat Height

Here I shall describe three methods of seat height adjustment that are good enough for preliminary set-up and the first thousand miles of cycling. Your ultimate seat positioning may require individual experimental fine-tuning that can not possibly be described in any manual. On the other hand, in the vast majority of all cases, each of these techniques will lead to a satisfactory seat position without need for further adjustments.

The first method is referred to as 109 % rule. It was developed at Loughborough University in England and is illustrated in Fig. 6.1. To use it, first

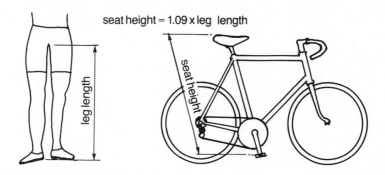

seat height = 1.09 x leg length

Fig. 6.1 Seat height – 109 % rule

measure your inseam leg length by standing with your back against a wall with your legs straight, the feet about 5 cm (2 in) apart. Make a pencil mark for the location of the crotch on the wall, e.g. with the aid of a drawing triangle (oddly enough referred to as a square in Britain) pushed up between the legs, perpendicular to the wall. Measure the vertical distance between this mark and the floor.

Now multiply the figure so found, be it in inches or in cm, by 1.09. That is presumed to be the optimal distance between the top of the saddle and the pedal axle when the pedal is down, crank in line with the seat tube. Measure it out and set the seat accordingly with the top horizontal. How the saddle is raised or lowered will follow under *Seat Adjustments* below.

The second method is used by many coaches and riders and is illustrated in Fig. 6.2. Since it is a trial-and-error method, it is not as easy to carry out without help. You must again wear cycling shoes with flat heels. Place the bike next to a wall or post for support when you sit on it. Move the seat up or down (following the adjustment procedure below) until it is set at such a height relative to the pedal that the heels of your cycling shoes rest on the pedals when your knee is nearly straight but not strained with the pedal

in its lowest position, crank in line with the seat tube.

Sit on the bike and place the heels on the pedals. Symmetrical pedals can be merely turned upside down, on platform models the toeclips must be removed. Pedal backwards this way, making sure you do not have to rock from side to side to reach the pedals. Now raise the saddle 12 mm (½ in) above this height and tighten it there. This heels-on-pedals style only applies to adjusting the seat height, not when you are cycling, as described below.

The third method is illustrated in Fig. 6.3. It was developed by the American coach Mark Hodges and is

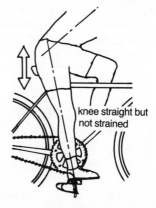

knee straight but not strained

Fig. 6.2 Seat height – conventional method

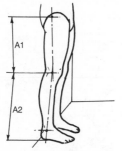

Fig. 6.3 Seat height – Hodges method

probably the most reliable method. You will need a helper to establish the correct height. Stand upright with your back against a wall, the feet 15 cm (6 in) apart. Now measure the distance from the floor over the ankle joint and the knee joint to the greater trochanter. That's the outwardmost bump on the femur or hip, which coincides with the hip joint's center of rotation: when you raise the leg this point does not move.

Establish the optimal saddle height, measured between the top of the saddle and the center of the pedal axle (crank pointing down in line with the seat tube) by multiplying the dimension so found by 0.96. If appropriate, add an allowance for thick cycling shoe soles, thick cleats or unusually shaped pedals.

With any of these methods, you will probably have to do some fine-tuning to achieve long-time comfort. Riders with disproportionately small feet may want to place the saddle a little lower, those with big feet perhaps slightly higher. This should not be treated with fetishism: raise or lower the seat in steps of 6 mm (¼ in) at a time and try to get used to any position by riding several hundred miles or several days before attempting any change, which must again be in the order of about 6 mm to make any real difference.

When cycling, the ball of the foot (the second joint of the big toe) should be over the center of the pedal axle, with the heel raised so much that the knee should never straighten fully. Not all cyclists incline the foot equally much, as suggested by Fig. 6.4, where the foot orientations of several European professionals are illustrated as they go through the pedal cycle. Consequently, the amount by which the saddle is moved relative to the point determined by this or any of the other rules given here will eventually vary a little for different riders – a matter of 6 mm (¼ in) one way or the other.

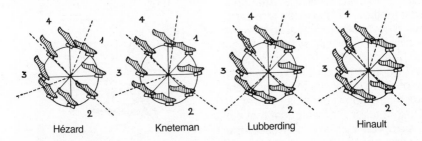

Hézard   Kneteman   Lubberding   Hinault

Fig. 6.4 Foot orientation

Fig. 6.5 Saddle forward position

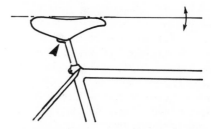

Fig. 6.6 Saddle horizontal position

Saddle Forward Position and Angle

The normal preliminary saddle position is such that the seat post is roughly in the middle of the saddle. For best results with a conventional frame geometry, adjust the saddle forward or backwards after it has been set to the correct height. Sitting on the bike with the foot under the toeclip and the crank placed horizontally, the knee joint, i.e. the bony protrusion just behind the knee cap, must be vertically aligned with the spindle of the forward pedal, as shown in Fig. 6.5.

The angle of the saddle relative to the horizontal plane should initially be set so as to keep the line that con-

nects the highest points at the front and the back level, as illustrated in Fig. 6.6. After the handlebars have been set to the correct height, as described below, it may be necessary to modify this angle to prevent slipping forward or backwards. This too will not become apparent until after some miles of cycling. Adjusting procedures for both forward position and angle are outlined below under *Saddle Adjustments*.

Handlebar Height

In bicycle racing, the highest point of the handlebars should always be lower than the top of the saddle. Just how low will be determined by the shape of the handlebars and the rider's physiognomy, depending on torso height as well as upper and lower arm length. That's why only experiment can tell what will eventually

Former world champion Beate Habetz of Germany, riding the 3000 m pursuit. The supposedly aerodynamic helmet kept slipping forward over her eyes during this race for the 1981 world championship, which probably cost her the title.
(Photo H. A. Roth)

be right for any particular rider. Here I shall merely tell you how to determine the initial position for a frame size check, followed by the adjustment for a relaxed initial riding style. After about a thousand miles of cycling you should be able to fine-tune the handlebar height and stem length to match your needs perfectly.

In order to make sure the frame is not too high, the first check should be whether the fully crouched position can be achieved. Place the handlebars in their lowest possible position and, sitting on the saddle, hold them in the lowest part of the bend (below the brake levers). With the lower arms horizontal and the upper arms close to vertical, the upper body should now lie almost horizontally. This is the full tuck position, illustrated in Fig. 6.7. It may be necessary to choose a longer or shorter handlebar stem for comfort in this position. If this full tuck is not possible with any handlebar stem available, a smaller or (rarely) a larger frame may be required.

To set the handlebars for a relaxed initial riding style, without sacrificing the advantages of the full tuck when conditions call for it, proceed as follows. First set the top of the bars about 5 cm (2 in) lower than the saddle. Sit on the bike and reach forward for the part of the bends between the

Fig. 6.8 Relaxed riding posture

straight top and the position of the brake handle attachments. In this position your shoulders should be about midway between seat and hands, as shown in Fig. 6.8. The arms should feel neither stretched nor heavily loaded and run parallel.

If they don't satisfy the last criterion, your handlebar bend is too wide or too narrow; if you can not find a relaxed position, you will need a longer or shorter stem. If you should have a particularly long combination of lower arms and torso in relation to your leg size, you may not be comfortable even with a long stem. In that case, a slightly larger frame, which has a longer top tube as well as a longer seat tube, may be in order. Conversely, long legs, combined with short arms and torso may require you use a shorter frame to achieve the right top tube length. In extreme cases of either variety, when the right top tube length just cannot be achieved with a bike that fits in height, a custom made frame will be required.

Finally, grab the handlebar bend at the ends, leaning forward on them while seated. The handlebar angle relative to the horizontal plane should be such that in this position the hands don't tend to slip either into the bend

Fig. 6.7 Full tuck body position

or off towards the ends. Consistent with the low handlebar position used in racing, this angle will be nearly horizontal for most riders, whereas it becomes steeper as a higher position is used. Initially, beginning racers may find it preferable to place the handlebars somewhat higher for comfort; in that case, the ends must also point down slightly. Just don't forget to straighten them out as you develop the style that allows you to ride with the lower handlebar position after some practice.

Saddle Adjustments

To do the actual mechanical adjusting work on the saddle, first take a close look at the saddle and compare it with Fig. 6.9. The saddle height is adjusted by loosening the binder bolt behind the seat lug, raising or lowering the saddle with the attached seat post in a twisting motion and then tightening the binder bolt again in the correct position, making sure it is straight.

To change the forward position, undo the adjustment bolts (only one bolt on some models) on your adjustable seat post. These bolts are usually reached from under the saddle cover, though some can be reached from below. Once loosened, push the

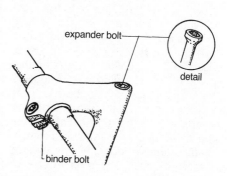

Fig. 6.10 Handlebar adjustments

saddle forward or backwards until the desired position is reached; then tighten the bolts, making sure the saddle is held under the desired angle relative to the horizontal plane.

Handlebar Adjustments

You are referred to the accompanying illustration Fig. 6.10. To vary the height of the handlebars, straddle the front wheel. Undo the expander bolt, which is recessed in the top of the stem. If the stem does not come loose immediately, you may have to tap on the head of the expander bolt with a hammer, which will loosen the internal clamping device. Now raise or lower the handlebar as required. Tighten the expander bolt again while holding the handlebars straight in the desired position.

To change the angle of the handlebar ends with respect to the horizontal plane, undo the binder bolt that clamps the handlebar bend in the front of the stem. Twist the handlebar bend until it is under the desired angle and then tighten the binder bolt again, holding the bar centered. To install a longer stem or a different bar design, you are referred to any bicycle maintenance book or your friendly bike store.

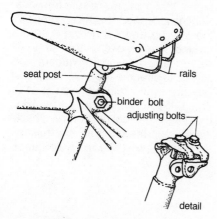

Fig. 6.9 Saddle adjustments

Basic Bike Handling

Now it will be time to take to the road on your bike. In case you are not yet familiar with the racing bicycle and the rest of your equipment, here's just a suggestion for getting on and off the bike. All other riding and handling techniques involve long learning processes that will be treated in separate chapters, but the simple act of starting the bike should be mastered immediately. Simple though this may seem, it is worth practicing, if only to avoid embarrassing and time wasting mishaps when cycling with others, especially in your first training rides and races.

Before you start off, make sure your shoe laces are tied and tucked in, or short enough not to run the risk of getting caught in the chain. Make sure the bike is set in a low gear, e.g. with the chain on the small chainwheel and an intermediate or big sprocket. Of course, the bike should have been checked to make sure it will be operating properly and that the tires are well inflated.

Start off at the side of the road after having checked to make sure no traffic is following closely behind. Straddle the top tube by swinging the appropriate leg either over the handlebars or the saddle. Hold the handlebars with both hands in the top bends. Tap with the toe of your starting foot against the pedal to turn it around, so the toeclip is on top, and immediately place the foot under the toeclip with the slot of the cleat over the ridge of the pedal. Move the foot until the pedal is in the top position. Pull the toe strap, but not quite so tight as to cut off circulation in the foot, then pedal back three quarters of a revolution to bring the pedal to 2 o'clock, i.e. just above the horizontally forward.

Look behind you to make sure the road is clear, then check ahead to establish which course you'll want to follow. Place your weight on the pedal, leaning on the handlebars. Put the other foot on its pedal as soon as it is in the top position. The first few revolutions will be cycled with this second pedal upside-down, either standing up or seated. When you have gained some momentum, tap the toe against the back of the free pedal to turn it over, and right away push the foot in under the toeclip. Pedal a few more strokes, then pull the loose toestrap to secure the second foot to its pedal as well.

To slow down, whether just to stop or to get off the bike, first look behind you again to make sure you are not getting in the way of cyclists or motorists following behind. Aim for the position where you will want to stop. Change into a lower gear, appropriate for starting off again later. Push against the buckle of the toestrap for whichever foot you want to have free first, meanwhile pulling up the foot slightly to loosen it when that pedal is up.

Slow down by braking gently, using mainly the front brake to stop. When you have come to a standstill, or just before that point, make sure the pedal with the loosened strap is up, then pull the foot up and out. Place it on the ground, leaning over in that same direction and moving forward off the saddle to straddle the seat tube. Now you are in the right position to start again. If you want to get off the bike, bring the other foot up, pedalling backwards, pull the toestrap and release the foot. Now you're ready to get off the bike.

7
Using the Gears

The road racing bicycle is equipped with a sophisticated derailleur system for multiple gearing. To change gear the chain is shifted onto any chosen combination of chainwheel and sprocket with the aid of two derailleur mechanisms. This system allows minute adaptations of the gearing ratio to the cyclist's potential on the one hand, and the terrain, wind or road conditions on the other hand. All that is mere theory, because in reality the vast majority of cyclists, including most triathletes and beginning racers, plod along in the wrong gear for the work load. Indeed, learning to select the right gear may well provide the biggest single step towards improved cycling speed and endurance.

There is a sound theory behind the principle of gear selection, based on the optimal pedalling rate, which shall be covered extensively in Chapter 14. Interesting though this theory is, one need not wait with applying the technique until it is thoroughly understood. That's why I shall outline the

correct use of gearing to the extent you will need it as a beginning racer at this point. Once you do reach the explanations in Chapter 14, you will be the more likely to appreciate the theory if you have already experienced the benefits of the technique in practice.

The Derailleur System

Fig. 7.1 shows and names the mechanical components of the derailleur system. The chain runs over one of two chainwheels, called chainrings in Britain, mounted on the RH crank and any one of five, six or seven sprockets mounted on a freewheel block at the rear wheel. While pedalling forward, the chain can be moved from one chainwheel to the other by means of the front changer, or from one sprocket to another by means of the rear derailleur.

Because the various chainwheels and sprockets have different numbers of teeth, the ratio between pedalling speed and the speed with which the

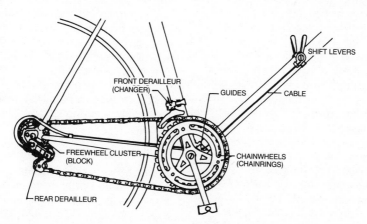

Fig. 7.1 Derailleur system

rear wheel, and with it the whole bike, is driven is changed whenever a different combination is selected. Bigger chainwheels in the front and smaller sprockets in the rear result in higher gears, smaller chainwheels and bigger sprockets give lower gears. Higher gears are selected when cycling is easy so the speed can be high; lower gears when higher resistances are to be overcome, e.g. when starting off, riding uphill or against a head wind.

The front and rear derailleurs are controlled by means of shift levers mounted on the frame down tube (the only correct position for road racing purposes). Most shifts are made with the rear derailleur. With the usual racing set-up, all the highish gears are reached by means of shifts of the rear derailleur, while the front derailleur remains on the larger chainwheel; all the lower gears are reached by shifts of the rear derailleur after the front derailleur has been moved once to engage the smaller chainwheel. Though it is also possible to select chainwheel and sprocket sizes in such a way that intermediate gears between rear derailleur shifts are always reached with a front changer shift, the above reflects the gearing as installed on essentially all bikes used for racing.

The rear derailleur is controlled from the RH shift lever. To put the chain on a different sprocket in the rear, move the RH shift lever while pedalling forward with reduced force. Pull it back to change to a larger sprocket, giving a lower gear; push the lever forward to reach a smaller sprocket, resulting in a higher gear.

The LH shift lever controls the front derailleur or changer, which simply shoves the cage through which the chain runs to the left or the right, moving it onto the smaller or the bigger chainwheel. Pulling the lever back engages the bigger chainwheel for the

higher gear on most models, pushing it forward engages the smaller chainwheel to obtain the lower gearing range.

The Need for Gears

The reason for gearing lies in the possibility it provides to pedal at an efficient rate with comfortable force under a wide range of different conditions and riding speeds. If the combination of chainwheel and sprocket size were fixed, as it is for the single-speed bicycle, any given pedalling speed invariably corresponds to a certain riding speed. The rear wheel will be turning at a speed that can be simply calculated by multiplying the pedalling rate with the quotient of chainwheel and sprocket size (expressed in terms of the numbers of teeth):

$$V_{wheel} = V_{pedal} \times T_{front} : T_{rear}$$

where:
V_{wheel} = wheel rotating speed (RPM)
V_{pedal} = pedalling rate (RPM)
T_{front} = number of teeth, chainwheel
T_{rear} = number of teeth, sprocket

The actual riding speed depends on this rotating speed and the effective wheel diameter. The effective diameter of a racing wheel is about 680 mm. This results in a riding speed in MPH that can be determined by multiplying the wheel speed in RPM by 0.08. These two calculations can be combined to find the riding speed in MPH directly from the pedalling rate and the chainwheel and sprocket sizes as follows:

$$MPH = 0.08 \times V_{pedal} \times T_{front} : T_{rear}$$

where MPH = riding speed in MPH and the other symbols are as defined above. To express riding speed in km/h, use the following formula instead:

$$km/h = 0.13 \times V_{pedal} \times T_{front} : T_{rear}$$

To give an example, assume you are pedalling at a rate of 80 RPM on a bike geared with a 42 tooth chainwheel and a 21 tooth rear sprocket. Your riding speed, expressed in MPH and km/h respectively, will be:

$0.08 \times 80 \times 42 : 21 = 13$ MPH

or:

$0.13 \times 80 \times 42 : 21 = 21$ km/h

Depending on the prevailing terrain conditions, that may be too easy or too hard for optimum endurance performance. If you are riding up a steep incline, this speed can require a very high pedal force, which may well be too exhausting and damaging to muscles, joints and tendons. On a level road this same speed will be reached so easily that you don't feel any significant resistance. All right for cruising, but not for training, let alone racing.

The derailleur gearing system allows you to choose the combination of chainwheel and sprocket sizes that enables you to operate effectively at your chosen pedalling speed for optimal performance. You may of course also vary the pedalling rate, which would appear to have the same effect as selecting another gear. Indeed, pedalling slower will reduce riding speed and therefore demand less power, whereas a higher pedalling rate will increase road speed and requires more power.

However, power output is not the sole, nor indeed the most important, criterion. Performing work at a given power output may tax the body differently, depending on the associated forces and movement speeds. It has been found that to cycle longer distances effectively without tiring or hurting excessively, the pedalling speed must be increased well above what seems natural to the beginning cyclist.

Whereas the beginner tends to plod along at 50–60 RPM, efficient long distance cycling requires pedalling rates of 100 RPM and more. That doesn't come overnight, because the cyclist first has to learn to move his legs that fast, but it is an essential requirement for bicycle racing. Much of early training work must therefore be aimed at simply practicing the art of pedalling faster. That must be done in a rather low gear to ensure the factor to be developed, namely muscle speed, limits training intensity, rather than power output or muscle strength.

Gearing Practice

Once you know that high gears mean big chainwheels and small sprockets, it's time to get some practice riding in high and low gears. First do it 'dry': the

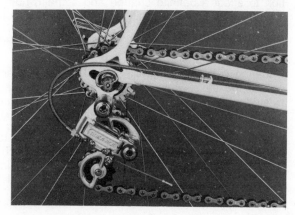

Rear derailleur with the typical road racing set-up for narrow range gearing. You may find it desirable to choose a freewheel with more widely different sprockets, which also give lower gears, especially early in your racing career and for hilly terrain.

bike supported with the rear wheel off the ground. Turn the cranks by hand and use the shift levers to change up and down, front and rear, until you have developed a good idea of the combination reached in any one shift lever position. Listen for rubbing and crunching noises as you shift, realizing a shift has not been executed correctly until the noises have subdued.

Now take to the road. Select a stretch of quiet road where you can experiment around with your gears without risk of being run into the ground by a closely following vehicle or get in the way of other cyclists. Start off in a low gear and shift the rear derailleur up in steps. Then shift to the other chainwheel and change down through the gears with the rear derailleur. Get a feel for each gear and try to imagine which gear you should select for given conditions. Practice shifting until it goes smoothly.

Reduce the pedal force, still pedalling forward as you shift. Especially shifting with the front derailleur will not work as smoothly as it did when the cranks were turned by hand. You will notice that the noises become more severe and that some changes just don't take place as you had intended. To execute a correct change, you may have to overshift slightly first: push the lever a little beyond the correct position to affect a definite change and then back up until the chain is quiet again.

It will often be necessary to fine-tune the front derailleur position after a change with the rear derailleur. That will be the case when the chain is twisted under an angle that causes it to rub against the side of the front changer. Some people never learn, and they'll never be successful racers. Others learn to shift predictably and smoothly within a week. These are the ones who take the trouble to practice it consciously. Half an hour of intensive practice each day during one week, and the continued attention required to do it right during regular riding is all it takes to become an expert very quickly.

Gear Designation

Just how high or low any given gear is may be expressed by giving the number of teeth on chainwheel and sprocket, respectively. However, this is not a very good measure. It may not be immediately clear that a combination designated as 42 X 16 has the same effect as the one designated 52 X 21 (actually, these would be more correctly referred to as 42 : 16 and 52 : 21 respectively). It will be clear that it becomes nearly impossible this way to compare gears on bikes with different wheel sizes, as used in the youth classifications.

To allow a direct comparison between the gearing effects of different gears or bikes, two different methods are in use, referred to as gear number and development, respectively. Gear number is a somewhat archaic method, used only in the English speaking world. The gear number is the equivalent wheel size in inches of a directly driven wheel that corresponds to any given combination of wheel size, chainwheel and sprocket. It is determined by multiplying the quotient of chainwheel and sprocket sizes with the wheel diameter in inches:

$$N_{gear} = D_{wheel} \times T_{front} : T_{rear}$$

where:
N_{gear} = gear number in inches
D_{wheel} = wheel diameter in inches
T_{front} = number of teeth, chainwheel
T_{rear} = number of teeth, sprocket

Returning to the example for a bike with 27 inch wheels, geared with a 42 tooth chainwheel and a 21 tooth sprocket, the gear number would be:

27 x 42 : 21 = 54 in

This is what happens when you change gear with the rear derailleur: the chain is shifted sideways onto another sprocket.

This is the customary, though rather quaint, method used in the English speaking world to define bicycle gearing. The rest of the world expresses the gear in terms of development. This is the distance in meters covered by the bike with one crank revolution. Development is calculated as follows on the basis of the wheel size:

$$Dev. = 0.00314 \times d_{wheel} \times T_{front} : T_{rear}$$

where:
Dev. = development in meters
d_{wheel} = wheel size in mm
T_{front} = number of teeth, chainwheel
T_{rear} = number of teeth, sprocket

The development for the same example would be:

$0.00314 \times 685 \times 42 : 21 = 4.30$ m

Fig. 7.2 illustrates the concepts of gear number and development. In practice, you will not be expected to figure this kind of thing out yourself. Instead you may refer to the tables in the Appendix. Just remember that a high gear is expressed with a high gear number or a long development. For racing purposes, very low gears in terms of gear number are in the forties or around 3.5–4.5 m in terms of development; high gears are those above 90 in or with a development of more than 7.20 m.

Gear Selection
Possibly the biggest problem for the beginning racer is to determine which is the right one out of the bewildering array of available gears. To generalize for normal road racing and time trialing conditions, I would say it's whichever gear allows you to

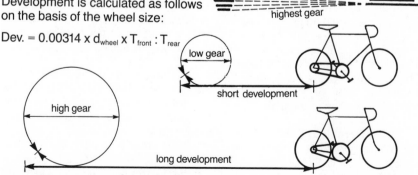

Fig. 7.2 Gear number and development

maximize your pedalling rate without diminishing your capacity to do effective work.

Perhaps you start off with the ability to pedal no faster than 80 RPM. That'll be too low once you have absolved some training, but for now that may be your limit. So the right gear is the one in which you can reach that rate. Count it out with the aid of a wrist watch frequently until you develop a feel for your pedalling speed. If you find yourself pedalling slower, change down into a slightly lower gear, and speed up the pedalling rate at the same riding speed. If you're pedalling faster, keep it up until you feel you are indeed spinning too lightly, and then change into a slightly higher gear.

Gradually, you will develop the capacity to pedal faster. As that happens, increase the limiting pedalling rate along with your ability, moving up from 80 to 90, 100 and eventually even higher pedalling rates. When riding with others, don't be guided by their gearing selection, since they may be stronger or weaker, or may have developed their pedalling speed more or less than you have.

It should not take too long before you learn to judge the right gear in advance, without the need to count out your pedalling rate. You will not only know to change down into a lower gear when the direction of the road changes to expose you to a headwind or when you reach an incline, you will also learn to judge just how far to change down, and up again when the conditions become more favorable. Change gear consciously and frequently in small steps, and you will soon enough master the trick.

Derailleur Care

For optimal operation of the derailleur system, several things should be regularly checked and adjusted if necessary. The derailleurs them-

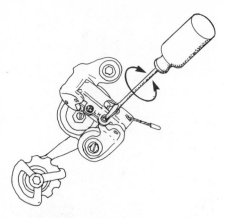

Fig. 7.3 Derailleur adjustment

selves, as well as the chain and the various sprockets, chainwheels and control cables, must be kept clean and lightly lubricated. The cables must be just taut when the shift levers are pushed forward and the derailleurs engage the appropriate gear. The tension screw on the shift levers must be kept tightened to give positive shifting without excessive tightness or slack.

When the chain gets shifted beyond the biggest or smallest chainwheel or sprocket, or when certain combinations can not be reached, the derailleurs themselves must be adjusted. For this purpose they are equipped with set-stop screws, which can be adjusted with a small screwdriver, as illustrated in Fig. 7.3. If necessary, place the chain back on the sprocket or chainwheel in an intermediate gear, and proceed as follows:

1. Establish where the problem lies: front or rear derailleur, shifted too far or not far enough, on the inside or on the outside (or, put differently, high or low gear).

2. Determine which of the set-stop screws governs movement limitation in the appropriate direction. On many models these screws are marked with

an H and L for high or low gear, respectively. If not, establish yourself which is the appropriate screw by observing what happens at the ends of the screws as you shift towards the extreme gears. The high range set-stop screw is the one towards which an internal protrusion moves as you shift into the highest gear with the appropriate derailleur shift lever.

3. Unscrew the set-stop screw slightly (perhaps half a turn at a time) to increase the range if the extreme gear could not be reached. Tighten it if the chain was shifted beyond that last sprocket.

4. Check all the gear combinations to establish whether the system works properly now, and fine-tune the adjustment if necessary.

The Victory set of components by Campagnolo set the trend in component design with sleek and simple styling, soon followed by several other major component manufacturers.

8
Controlling the Bicycle

There is more to riding a racing bicycle than merely setting it up and manipulating the gears as was outlined in the two preceding chapters. Before you even begin to think about training, let alone racing effectively, you must learn to handle the bicycle under all conceivable situations. This is the subject of the three remaining chapters of Part I.

The present chapter deals with learning to ride the bicycle efficiently with proper control over the steering and braking mechanisms. This will help you cycle with minimal effort and maximum confidence. In the next chapter you will be introduced to the peculiarities of effective riding techniques for racing and training. Chapter 10, finally, will explain how to prevent falls and accidents, as well as how to avoid injuries from any cause in this fast and demanding sport.

The Steering Principle

Contrary to popular belief, a bicycle is not steered most effectively by merely turning the handlebars and following the front wheel, as is the case for any two-track vehicle, such as a car. Though bicycles and other single-track vehicles also follow the front wheel, they also require the rider to lean the bike into the curve to retain their balance at the same time. Fig. 8.1 shows how this looks in a high speed turn.

If you were to merely turn the handlebars, the lower part of the bike would start running away from its previous course in the direction in which the front wheel is then pointed. Meanwhile, the mass of the rider, perched high up on the bike, would continue following the original course due to in-

ertia. Thus, the center of gravity would not be in line with the supporting bike, and the rider would come crashing to the ground. Due to the effect of centrifugal force, the tendency to throw the rider off towards the outside of the curve increases with higher speeds, requiring a more pronounced lean the faster you are going.

It is possible to steer by turning the handlebars and then correcting lean and steering to regain balance. In fact, many older people, especially women, seem to do it that way, succeeding quite well at low speeds only. As soon as the imbalance becomes imminent, they have to make another correction in the other direction. After some more cramped and anxious movements, they finally get around the corner. This accounts for the tensioned and apparently impulsive riding style typical for such riders, even if they have practiced it so long that they

Fig. 8.1 High-speed turn

Curve radius, speed and body lean are inter-dependent. The higher the speed, the more the bike leans in the direction of the turn. The figure in the center follows the natural curve. To force a tighter curve at a low speed, lean the bike further than the body. To force a tighter curve at a high speed, lean the body more than the bike.

Fig. 8.2 Turning and body lean

don't realize their movements are awkward.

The effective technique for riding a curve at speed depends on placing the bike under the right angle, where the centrifugal force is offset by a shift of the mass center of gravity to the in-side, before turning off. Two methods may be used, depending on the amount of time and room available to carry out the maneuver. I refer to these two methods as natural and forced turn, respectively. To under-stand either we'll first take a look at the intricacies of balancing the bike when riding a straight line, after which the two methods of turning can be ex-plained.

Bicycle Balance

What keeps a bicycle or any other single track vehicle, whether a hoop or a motorcycle, going without falling over is the inertia of its moving mass. Rolling a narrow hoop will show that it is an unstable balance: once the thing starts to lean either left or right, it will just go down further and further until it hits the ground. That's because the mass is no longer supported in line with the force. Try it with a bicycle wheel if you like. If your front wheel could not be steered around the steer-ing axle, and the rider couldn't move

sideways, he'd come down the same way very soon.

On the bicycle, the rider feels when the vehicle starts to lean over. Theoretically, there are two ways out of the predicament: either move the rider back over the center of the bike or move the bike back under the rider. In practice, the latter method is used for high speed cycling. When the bike begins tp perceptably lean to the side, the rider steers the front wheel a little in the same direction, which places the bike back in such a position that balance is restored. In fact, this point will be passed, and the bike will start leaning over the other way, and so on.

This entire movement is relatively easy to notice when you are cycling slowly. When standing still, the balancing motions are so extreme that only a highly skilled cyclist can keep control. The faster the bicycle, the less perceptible (though equally important and therefore harder to master) are the requisite steering cor-rections to retain balance. To get an understanding of this whole process, I suggest you practice riding a straight line at a low speed. Then do it at a higher speed and see whether you agree with the explanation, referring also to Fig. 8.2.

Clearly, both riding a straight line and staying upright with the bike are merely illusions. In reality, the bike is always in disequilibrium, following a more or less curved track, and the combination bike-and-rider leans alternately one way or the other. At higher speeds the curves are longer and gentler, while the amount of lean can be perceptible; at lower speeds the curves are shorter and sharper, with less pronounced lean angles for any given deflection.

The Natural Turn

Under normal circumstances, the rider knows well ahead where to turn off, and there is enough room to follow a generously wide curve. This is the situation of the natural turn. It makes use of the lean which results from normal straight path steering corrections. To turn to the right, one waits until the bike is leaning over that way.

Instead of turning the handlebars to that same side, as would be done to get back in balance to ride straight, you just leave the handlebars alone for a while. This causes the bike to lean over further and further in the direction of the turn. Only when the lean is quite significant do you steer in the same direction, but not as abruptly as you would do to get back up straight. Instead, you will fine-tune the ratio of lean and steering deflection to ride the curve out.

When the turn is completed, you will still be leaning over in the direction of the turn and would ride a circle without some other corrective action on your part. You get back on the straight course by steering further into the curve than the amount of lean demands. This will put your mass center of gravity back straight over the bike or even further over. This allows you to resume the (nearly) straight line, putting you back into the normal curved course with which you approach the straight line.

You probably learned to do this when you were a kid, but never realized that you were doing all this. You could perhaps continue to ride a bicycle for ever without understanding the theory. However, to succeed as a bicycle racer, you will be much better off when you have the theoretical knowledge and have learned to ride a calculated course, making use of this information. Ride around an empty parking lot many times, leaning this way and that, following straight lines and making turns, until it is both second nature and something you can do consciously, knowing the relevant limitations.

Notice, as you are practicing this technique, as well as when riding at other times, that speed, curve radius and lean are closely correlated. A sharp turn will require more lean at any given speed. Similarly, at high speed any given turn will require much greater lean angles than the same turning radius at a lower speed. As you practice this technique, learn to judge which are the appropriate combinations under different circumstances.

The Forced Turn

Especially in bicycle racing, you will often be confronted with situations which don't allow you to wait until you are conveniently leaning the appropriate way to make a gradual turn. You may be surrounded by a pack of eager competitors with only a few inches to move sideways. Or, whether in a race or on a training ride, a sudden obstacle may force you to divert suddenly. You will often have to get around a sharp curve that can not be taken naturally at speed.

These situations often require the second method of turning, which I call the forced turn. In this case, the turn

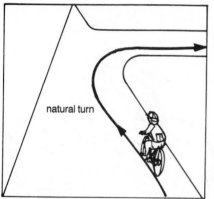 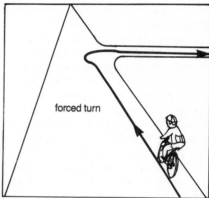

Fig. 8.3 Path taken in natural and forced turn

must be initiated quickly, regardless which way the bike happens to be leaning at the time. You have to force the bike to lean over in the appropriate direction and under the right angle consistent with the direction and radius of the turn. And it has to be done quickly.

Do that by steering away from the turn sharply just before you get there. You and the bike will immediately start to lean over in the direction of the turn. You would risk a disastrous crash as your bike moves away precipitously from the mass center of gravity, if you were to continue in a straight line. You have very quickly achieved a considerable lean angle in the direction of the turn. This must be compensated by steering quite abruptly in this same direction. Since this is the direction of the turn, you are set up just right to make a sharp turn. Once completed, steer back into the turn just a little further, to get the lean for regaining the straight course, as explained for the natural turn.

The forced turn technique must also be practiced intensely and consciously, since it by no means comes naturally. Initiating a left turn by steering right will probably require most beginning cyclists to overcome all sorts of reasonable inhibitions and de-

mands lots of practice. Take your bike to the empty parking lot again a few days in a row, wearing protective clothing in case you fall: helmet, gloves, jacket and long pants.

Practice and experiment until you've mastered the trick, and refresh your skill from time to time, until this instant turning technique has become second nature. Fig. 8.3 compares the paths taken in the natural and forced turn, respectively. The latter one will not only be helpful when taking a tight turn, but will prove of equal benefit when you need to temporarily divert from your straight course for one reason or the other. In Chapter 9 you will be shown how to apply it to the difficult task of avoiding a suddenly appearing obstacle while riding fast.

Braking Technique

In racing and training, you will often have to use your brakes, though not to make a panic stop. In fact, the sensible cyclist should hardly ever have to brake to a standstill. Instead, you will be using the brakes to control your speed. That may be necessary under racing conditions more frequently than otherwise, since you will want to maintain the highest possible speed as long as possible, and go through the situation which demands a lower speed as quickly as possible.

Effective braking means that you can ride up fast close to the turn or the obstacle which requires the reduced speed, brake to reach the lower speed quickly, and accelerate immediately afterwards. So you will be using the brakes to get down in speed from 30 to 20 MPH to take a turn, or from 30 to 28 MPH to avoid running into the racer ahead of you. Or you may have to get down from 50 to 10 MPH to handle a switchback or hairpin curve on a steep descent. To do that effectively without risk requires an understanding of braking physics. Though you may often have to reduce speed quickly, you should also develop a feel for gradual speed reduction to prevent skidding and loss of control. In fact, inexperienced cyclists are more often in danger due to braking too vigorously than due to insufficient stopping power.

Braking amounts to deceleration, i.e. speed reduction, which can only take place gradually. The rate of deceleration can be measured and is expressed in m/sec^2. A deceleration of $1\,m/sec^2$ means that after each second of braking the travelling speed will be 1 m/sec less than it was at the beginning of that second. A speed of 30 MPH corresponds to 13 m/sec. To get down to standstill would take 13 sec if the braking deceleration is $1\,m/sec^2$; you'd reach 9 m/sec or 20 MPH after 4 seconds. At a higher rate of deceleration it would take less time (and a shorter distance) to reach the desired speed.

Racing bicycles have remarkably effective brakes, providing it's not raining. A modest force on the brake handle can cause a deceleration of 4–5 m/sec^2 with just one brake. With both brakes the effect is even more dramatic, enabling you to slow down from 30 to 15 MPH within one second. There

Fig. 8.4 Transfer of weight while braking

are some limitations to braking that have to be considered, though.

In the first place, rain has a negative effect on the bicycle rim brake's performance, as the build-up of water on the rims reduces the friction between brake block and rim drastically. This applies especially if it is equipped with rubber brake blocks, as offered by most manufacturers as standard, especially on most of their expensive racing brakes. For any rubber brake blocks, I measured a reduction from 4.5 to 1.5 m/sec^2 for a given hand lever force (and to half that figure for bicycles with chrome plated steel rims, which should therefore not be used, even on the cheap bicycles on which they are installed). Lately, some special brake block materials have been introduced that are less sensitive to rain. The presently best example is Modolo's type D-0015 brake block which displays far less difference between wet and dry performance.

The second restriction is associated with a change in the distribution of weight between the wheels as a result of braking. Because the mass center of the rider is quite high above the road, and its horizontal distance to the front wheel axle rather small, the bicycle has a tendency to tip forward while decelerating. Weight is transferred from the rear to the front of the bike, as illustrated in Fig. 8.4. When the deceleration reaches about 3.5 m/sec^2, the weight on the rear wheel is no longer enough to provide traction. Braking harder than that with the rear brake just makes the bike skid, resulting in loss of control.

When a deceleration of about 6.5 m/sec^2 is reached, whether using both brakes together or the front brake alone, the rear wheel actually starts to lift off the ground, dumping the rider over the handlebars. Consequently, no conventional bicycle can ever be decelerated beyond this limit. This is a very high deceleration, which you should not often need, but it is good to realize there is such a limit and that it can not be avoided by using the rear brake in addition to the front brake. During a sudden speed reduc-

tion or panic stop such high decelerations may be reached. On a downslope the effect will be even more pronounced. In such cases, reduce the toppling over effect by shifting your body weight back and down as much as possible: sit far back and hold the upper body horizontally.

Since about twice the rear brake's deceleration is possible with the front brake, the latter should be preferably used under most conditions. Under most circumstances short of a panic stop, you can brake very effectively using the front brake alone. When both brakes are used simultaneously, the front brake can be pulled quite a bit harder than the rear brake. If you notice the rear brake is less effective if pressed equally far, I suggest you adjust, lubricate or replace the brake cable.

Freddy Schmidke of Germany, one of the world's strongest short distance time trialists and track sprinters, in the more favorable position, awaiting his chance to jump out of this sur-place or track stop during the 1981 World Championships. (Photo H. A. Roth)

Of course, not all braking will be done abruptly. Gradual braking must also be practiced. In particular when the road is slick, in curves or when others are following closely behind, gradual deceleration and the ability to control the braking force within narrow limits is of vital importance. Practice braking consciously with utmost attention to the relationship between initial speed, brake lever force and deceleration, to become fully competent at handling the bike when slowing down under any conditions.

Braking becomes a different kettle of fish in hilly terrain. On a steep downhill, the slope not only increases the tendency to tip forward, it also induces an accelerating effect, which must be overcome by the brakes even to merely keep the speed constant. A 20 % slope, which is admittedly rarely encountered, induces an acceleration of about 2 m/sec^2. Obviously, on such a downhill stretch you will encounter big problems in wet weather if you don't keep your speed down to start with. So it will be necessary to reduce the speed by gradual, intermittent braking. This will tend to wipe most of the water from the rims, retaining braking efficiency a little better, and will not overtax brakes when you do have to reduce the speed suddenly, e.g. to handle an unexpected obstacle or sharp turn.

Effective braking must be learned to achieve complete control of the bicycle under normal and difficult cycling conditions. In particular, the dramatic difference between the bike's behavior when braking on the straight and in a curve must be experienced to be appreciated. Again, this is a matter for conscious practice on an empty parking lot. Include braking in your regular exercises during the first weeks of cycling preparation. Even after you have been training for some time, you may be well advised to repeat practice sessions, as outlined for steering and braking control in this chapter, from time to time. It will pay off during competition.

9
Basic Riding Techniques

Riding a racing bicycle fast and effectively requires hands-on experience. That is one good reason to ride lots of training miles before you try your hand at racing. But some of the associated skills can be learned faster and more thoroughly when you understand the principles that will be applied. Building up on the information about posture, gearing, steering and braking provided in the preceding chapters, you will be shown here what to do under various typical riding situations.

Bike handling turned nightmare at the section known as the Wall of Geeraardsbergen of the Belgian one-day road race Omloop van Het Volk. (Photo H. A. Roth)

During much of your racing and training you will probably be surrounded by others. Even though this is not a problem in conventional time trialing, the skills to master this situation should be learned by all racers and triathletes, whatever they regard as their preferred discipline. In this respect the most basic advise is to ride consciously, with your eyes wide open and your mind on the road ahead, also paying attention to those around you. Especially in the beginning categories, many falls and injuries are caused by inadequate alertness, and are entirely avoidable.

There is more to it than taking care of yourself, because many crashes are caused by others. The trick is not so much avoiding the wrong action

yourself, but rather learning how to compensate for the errors that others make. This advise is not restricted to accident risk alone, but applies to the entire spectrum of activities around you. Missing an escape, accelerating at the wrong time, exposing yourself to a headwind, and taking a wrong turn are just a few of the mistakes to guard against. Be alert, and you will be able to avoid most errors.

Many of the techniques used in group riding should be counted as tactical maneuvers and will be treated as such in subsequent chapters, particularly those of Part III. Some techniques are so elementary that they must be treated here, so you can start practicing them early in your career as a bicycle racer. In addition to these practices for fast group riding, the basic techniques needed to train effectively will be covered in the present chapter.

Reaching Speed
In Chapter 6 you have been shown to get on the bike and start off smoothly. The next trick is to reach the ultimate riding speed as quickly and efficiently as possible. The idea is to waste as little precious time and energy as possible during this process of getting up to speed Tricky, because accelerating demands disproportionately high levels of power and consumes energy correspondingly. And the faster it's done, the more demanding it is.

Clearly, you have to strike a balance here. Accelerating faster than necessary wastes energy that will be sorely needed later. Done too slowly, it may put you behind far enough to lose touch with the other contestants. It will be your decision to find the right balance between speed and power, but the way to reach it is easy to describe: start in a low gear and increase speed gradually but rapidly. No fast and slow spurts but a gradual build-up.

Either keep pedalling faster and faster in the low gear, changing up only as you reach a significant speed, or be prepared to do some short duration hard work, standing out of the saddle, pulling on the upstroke of the pedals as well as pushing on the downstroke. The latter method may be required to keep up with a fast pack that surges away from the start. As soon as speed is reached, sit in the saddle and select a good gear for spinning at your comfortable high pedalling rate.

Riding a Constant Speed
With a small measuring device called accelerometer one can follow the changes in riding speed of a cyclist travelling at speed. It has been found that the most successful riders tend to be those whose speed varies least over time. Not only does a good cyclist ride the same number of miles one hour as the next, he travels as many yards one minute as the next, as many feet with one crank revolution as the next, and indeed ideally as many inches during each section within any revolution. If you slow down during one short section, you will find it takes disproportionately long to make up for the loss.

Pay attention to this while you cycle at all times. As long as the external conditions don't change drastically, you should make every effort to keep a very constant movement. Gauge your speed by comparing it to that of your companions, or use your watch and count out pedal revolutions and milestones when cycling alone. It will be most important to pay attention to it whenever you are out on a training ride.

Accelerating
However efficient a constant speed may be, sometimes you will still want to accelerate to a higher speed. This

may be necessary to catch up with riders ahead, so you can take advantage of the wind-breaking effect by riding immediately behind them, or to avoid getting dropped. On a training ride you need acceleration e.g. to get across an intersection before the light changes or to avoid running into another vehicle.

As with getting up to speed in the first place, it will again be most efficient to increase the speed as gradually as possible. Unless you are already spinning at the highest possible rate, you will find accelerating by increasing pedalling speed more effective than by increasing pedal force in a higher gear. In other words, it will often be best to shift down into a slightly lower gear and increase the pedalling rate vigorously. Once you are gathering momentum and are getting close to your maximum spinning speed, shift up and continue to gain speed in the slightly higher gear.

You will be going quite fast already and are generally not in a position to take advantage of the drafting effect (called pacing in Britain) provided by a rider whom you can follow closely. Therefore you must minimize your

Fig. 9.2 Group riding with cross wind

wind resistance by taking on the most aerodynamically favorable position: chest pulled horizontally close to the bike, head down as much as possible, while retaining vision ahead, arms and legs tucked in close to the rest of your body.

Against the Wind

Especially when there is a head wind, the effect of air drag on the power needed to cycle at high speed is quite significant, as will be outlined more fully in Chapter 11. Economize on your effort by avoiding the wind effect as much as possible. When riding alone, try to seek out the sheltered parts of the road wherever possible without exposing yourself to danger or becoming too uncomfortable.

Keep your profile as low as possible when cycling against the wind. When you ride in a group, try to exploit the wind shelter effect of riding immediately behind another rider, or staggered appropriately when there is a crosswind. Figures 9.1 and 9.2 show the resulting configuration for situations without and with crosswind, respectively. The methods used for exploiting this principle to the fullest will be covered in the section *Paceline Riding* below.

Fig. 9.1 Group riding against the wind

Climbing

Hill climbing is not merely a special skill that can be learned by all, it also requires a certain physique for greatest effectiveness. Everybody's climbing skills can probably be improved up to a point, but some riders will be born climbers, while others may never do very well in that discipline. What it takes is a high power to weight ratio. To put it differently, you need a big heart and voluminous lungs relative to the total body mass, and in general, a low body weight will be advantageous.

Clearly, big bulky riders like the legendary Eddy Merckx and Francesco Moser are at a disadvantage here, despite their phenomenal power. Conversely, it is no accident that so many of the small-boned Spanish and Columbian racers are amongst the world's strongest climbers. Just the same, it is an ability that can be learned and developed well enough by the average rider to at least keep up with the pack.

Again, a regular motion is most efficient, and that is best mastered by staying seated in a rather low gear. For a hilly course, you should take the trouble to equip the bike with wider ratio gearing than for level riding. Just what sizes of sprockets should be installed is up to you, but I'd say 90 % of all beginners tend to pick gearing ratios that are too high (or, to put it differently, sprockets that are too small). There should be nothing embarrassing about a 26 tooth rear sprocket in the back for a hilly course.

Climbing out of the Saddle

When the lowest available gear is too high to allow a painless spinning leg motion, it will be time to shift to another technique. Some riders at this point will try to increase the length of the power stroke by means of some hefty ankle twisting, really pushing the

Fig. 9.3 Honking or climbing out of the saddle

leg around. As we shall see in Chapter 13 about muscle work, this is a very tiring technique, requiring long muscle work phases and short recovery periods. A better method of high-gear, low pedalling speed climbing is referred to as honking in Britain, and seems to be a mystery to many Americans.

Honking makes use of the rider's body weight to push down the pedals, whereas the body is pulled up after each stroke very quickly by standing up. This motion can be compared to climbing stairs. In this case the muscle work is done each time the body is raised, rather than when pushing the pedal down and around. To do it effectively, hold the tops of the brake handle mounts in the front of the handlebars. You can either take quick snappy steps or throw your weight from side to side in a swinging motion, as illustrated in Fig. 9.3.

These climbing techniques are effectively used by European and Latin American riders, while they are inadequately known in many circles in the US. Too many cyclists here do neither one nor the other: their gearing is too high for spinning, yet they don't master the snappy honking technique, instead trying to grind their way up the hill. I suggest you take a close look at the illustration and practice honking as well as spinning: the one in a high gear at pedalling speeds below 55 RPM, the other in a low gear at 65 RPM or more. Avoid pedalling rates of 55–65 RPM by choosing your gear to stay within either the one range or the other.

Avoiding Obstacles

Oftentimes, you will be confronted with some kind of obstacle right in your path. This may be anything from a pothole to a dropped bicycle pump or even a crashed cyclist. Even when travelling at speed and with little room to maneuver, you can learn to avoid running into such things by using the

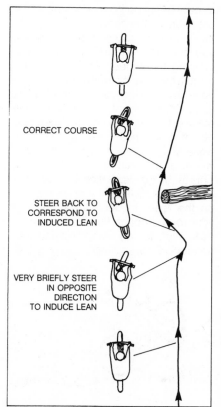

CORRECT COURSE

STEER BACK TO CORRESPOND TO INDUCED LEAN

VERY BRIEFLY STEER IN OPPOSITE DIRECTION TO INDUCE LEAN

Fig. 9.4 Diverting around obstacle

technique of the forced turn described in Chapter 8. This maneuver is illustrated in Fig. 9.4.

As soon as you perceive the obstacle ahead of you, decide whether to pass it on the left or the right side. Ride straight up to it and then, before you reach it, briefly but decidedly steer into the direction opposite to your chosen avoidance (i.e. to the right if you want to pass on the left). This will make the bike lean over towards the other side (to the left in this case). Now just as quickly steer into that direction, which will result in a very sharp turn. As soon as you've passed the obstacle, oversteer a little more to cause a lean that helps you put the bike back on its proper course.

These are some more things to practice on an empty parking lot, wearing a helmet and two long sleeved shirt (the double layer of textile is much easier on the skin, since the one layer will just slip off the other, rather than removing chunks of your flesh). Mark phoney obstacles with chalk or place foam pads or sponges on the road which you'll practice passing abruptly on both sides until you've mastered the trick.

Jumping the Bike

Another useful circus act for hard training and racing situations is the skill of making first the front, then the rear wheel jump over or through an obstacle. It's a matter of shifting your weight back or forth to lift the appropriate wheel off the ground. First throw your weight backwards, while pulling up on the handlebars to unload and lift the front wheel. At the same time, accelerate vigorously by pushing hard on the forward pedal. With some practice, you'll soon be able to lift the front end of the bike at least a foot up in the air.

Next, try to do the same with the rear wheel by throwing your weight

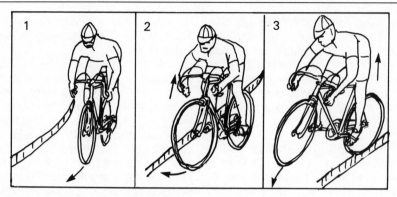

Fig. 9.5 Jumping sideways over obstacle

forward and pulling up on the pedals with the toeclips at the same time. This is harder, but it too can be learned. Finally practice coordinating the two shifts so that you first lift the front and then as soon as you've reached the highest point start lifting the back. After some time you will be able to actually make the bike fly, when you lift both wheels in such short sequence that the rear wheel comes off the ground well before the front wheel comes down.

One variant of this technique is the art of jumping up sideways, e.g. onto the curb or across a ridge or railway track, parallel to the road. To do this, the bike has to be forced to move sideways in a short and snappy diversion just preceding the jump. Do that by combining the diversion technique described above under *Avoiding Obstacles* with the jump. Fig. 9.5 shows how this can be done.

Get close to the ridge you want to jump, riding parallel to it. Then briefly steer away from it. This will immediately cause the bike to lean towards the obstacle. Now catch yourself by steering sharply in that same direction, lifting the front wheel when you are close to the obstacle, immediately followed by the rear wheel. Practice is all it takes, and the empty parking lot with a chalk line as a sub-

stitute ridge will be the best place to practice it long before you risk it in a race or a fast group ride.

Sometimes you will have to ride through a big pothole or any other depression in the road surface. To do that with minimal risk to bike and rider, you can use something akin to the jumping technique. First unload the front wheel by throwing your weight back and pulling up the handlebars just before the front wheel hits the lowest point of the depression. Then ride out of it and finally pull up the rear, while shifting your weight to the front wheel of the bike to climb back out. This technique is particularly useful in cyclo-cross, but can also be applied on the road. In open terrain, select your route through the depression so as to avoid too abrupt a drop and subsequent climb, as illustrated in Fig. 9.6.

Fig. 9.6 Riding trough a depression

Paceline Riding

This technique, also referred to as drafting in the US or bunching in Britain, is merely a way of minimizing the air resistance by following very closely behind the preceding rider. It has been calculated that it allows a power saving of 15 percent for the following rider. Clearly, this technique must be mastered to make life in the saddle easier. On the other hand, don't forget that somebody still has to do the full work load, namely the person in front.

The last fact has seen many a paceline caught unawares, because the front rider was being taxed too much, while those following did not do their share of the work in turn. To ride an effective paceline, all riders have to take turns at the lead, and this is a skill that will be covered below. If there is either no significant wind, a head wind, or even a tail wind that's slower than the riding speed, stay exactly in one line, as though you were all on a rail. Keep the smallest possible distance between the rear wheel of the person in front and the front wheel of the one following, and cycle at an even pace.

Stay in the same gear, whether riding in lead position or not, so you can gauge the speed of the group. The person in front rides until he feels he can no longer keep the pace (that will be much longer for a strong rider than for a weaker one, but rarely is more than about 20 crank revolutions). When it's time for the lead change, he moves over to the side a little, while the other riders stay in line behind the new lead. The relieved lead rider drifts back to the end and picks up speed to fall in position just behind the last rider

Fig. 9.7 Course on curved road

The person who was in second position before has to take the lead now, but need not move over. When taking the lead, don't surge forward, but just keep going at the old speed. That same pace will be harder now than it was in second position, due to the increase in air resistance, to which only the rider in front is fully exposed.

If there is a significant cross wind, the paceline takes on the shape of a fan, each rider hiding from the wind, offset sideways behind the one in front. When there are more riders than the width of the road allows, there will be no point for the last riders to tag along in a straight line. Instead, they should start a second fan or echelon. Lead changes are done by the lead rider drifting back sideways with the wind, to finish up behind the last rider's wheel. At the same time everybody else moves over into the wind just enough to make room for him on the sheltered side.

Preventing Cycling Injuries

Bicycle racing is not an entirely risk-less undertaking. Neither are many other sports, but what scares off potential cyclists most is perhaps the risk of being involved in a collision with a motor vehicle. Yes, that risk exists in bicycle racing, as it does when crossing the street in front of your own house. Actually, this is but one of several kinds of possible injury causes in bicycle racing. You can learn to avoid most of the risks and minimize these and other injuries and health hazards. That is the subject of the present chapter.

Of course, collisions and falls are not the only forms of injury to the cyclist, even though they are the most obvious. When talking to experienced racers, you will soon find out that other forms of injury causes are often more prevalent in those circles. Saddle sores and torn tendons, inflamed knees and numb hands rank higher than broken collarbones and cracked skulls in their conversation about injuries, even though they get their share of broken bones too. We will take a look at both categories, starting out with those dreaded traffic accidents.

Falls and Collisions

Whether or not a motor vehicle is involved, any injury to the cyclist in all falls and collisions tends to be the result of the impact when the cyclist falls off the bike. He either hits the road surface, an obstacle on or along the road, or a part of the bike itself. There are a few cases in which the cyclist is literally run over by a colliding vehicle, but these are quite rare.

The results of an accident involving a motor vehicle are not necessarily more serious than simple falls and collisions with other cyclists, dogs, pedestrians or fixed objects. As a general rule, ride your bike as you would drive your car, always verifying whether the road ahead of you is clear, and taking particular care to select your path wisely at intersections. As a relatively slow vehicle, you must always look behind you to ascertain whether nobody is following closely before you move over into another traffic lane or away from the side of the road.

The same skills necessary to prevent traffic accidents involving cars will keep you from experiencing most of the other types of falls and collisions. Be watchful, consider the effects of your own actions, and use the technical skills described in the preceding chapters to divert when the situation becomes threatening. Four types of falls and collisions can be distinguished: stopping, diverting, skidding and loss of control. In the following sections I shall first describe these accidents, followed by a few hints about preventing and treating the typical injuries.

Stopping Accidents

In a stopping accident the bicycle runs into an obstacle which stops its progress. Depending on the cyclist's speed, the impact can be very serious. As the bicycle itself is stopped, inertia will keep the cyclist going forward, throwing him against or over the handlebars. The kinetic energy of the moving mass will be dissipated very suddenly, often in an unfortunate location. Your genitals may hit the handle-bar stem or your skull may crash onto either the road surface or the object with which the bike collided.

The way to guard yourself against these accidents is to look and think ahead, so you don't run into any obstacles. If necessary, control your speed to allow handling the unexpected when a potential danger may be looming up behind the next corner. Learn to apply the diverting technique described in the preceding chapters. The way to minimize the impact of the most serious form of stopping accident is by wearing an energy absorbing helmet.

Diverting Accidents

A diverting type accident occurs when the front wheel is pushed sideways by an external force, while the rider is not leaning in the same direction to regain balance. Railway tracks, cracks in the

The Soviet racer Oleg Logvin demonstrating primitive head protection methods during the 1985 Coors Classic. (Photo John Swanda)

road surface, the edge of the road, but also touching another rider's rear wheel with your front wheel, are typical causes. The effect is that you will fall sideways and hit the road or some obstacle by the side of the road. Depending how unexpectedly it happened, you may be able to break the fall by stretching out your arm, which seems to be an automatic reflex in this situation.

Typical injuries range from abrasions and lacerations of the hands and the sides of arms and legs to bruised hips and sprained or broken wrists. More serious cases at higher speeds may involve broken collar bones and injuries to the face or the side of the skull. The impact of the lesser injuries can be minimized by wearing padded gloves and double layers of clothing with long sleeves and legs. A helmet may prove worthwhile here too.

Diverting accidents can often be avoided if the cyclist is both careful and alert. Keep an eye out for the typical danger situations. Don't overlap

wheels, don't approach surface ridges under a shallow angle. A last second diversion can often be made along the lines of the diverting technique described in Chapter 9. In the case of a ridge in the road surface, use the technique of sideways jumping, also described there. When your front wheel touches the rear wheel of another rider, or if your handlebars are pushed over by an outside force, you may sometimes save the day if you react by immediately leaning in the direction into which you were diverted, and then steer to regain control.

Skidding Accidents

When the bicycle keeps going or goes in an unintended direction despite your efforts to steer or brake, it will be due to skidding between the tires and the road surface. This kind of thing happens more frequently when the road is slick due to moisture, frost, loose sand or fallen leaves on the road surface. Especially under these conditions, sudden movements, hard braking, and excessive lean when cornering may all cause skidding either forward or sideways.

These accidents often lead to a fall, resulting in abrasions, lacerations or more rarely fractures. Avoid them by checking the road surface ahead and avoiding sudden steering or braking maneuvers and excessive lean in curves. Cross slick patches, ranging from wet or greasy asphalt to railway tracks and sand or leaves on the road, with the bicycle upright. Achieve that by making steering and balancing reactions before you reach such danger spots.

Once you feel you are entering a skid, try to move your weight towards the back of the bike as much as possible, sliding to the back of the saddle and stretching the arms. Follow the bike, rather than trying to force it back. Finally, don't do what seems an obvi-

ous reaction to the less experienced, namely getting off the saddle to straddle the top tube with one leg dangling.

Loss of Control Accidents

At higher speeds, especially in a steep descent, loss-of-control accidents sometimes occur, meaning you just can't steer the bike the way you should be going. This happens when you find yourself having to steer in one direction at a time when you are leaning the other way, or when speed control braking initiates unexpected vibrations. Often this situation develops into a collision or a fall along the lines of either one of the two accident types described above. These accidents more frequently occur when the road is slippery due to moisture, loose sand or fallen leaves.

Prevention is only possible with experience: don't go faster than the speed at which you feel in control. The more you ride under various situations, the more you will develop a feel for what is a safe speed, when to brake and how to steer to maintain control over the bike. Once the situation sets in, try to keep cool and don't panic, following the bike rather than forcing it over. The worst thing you can do is to tense up and get off the saddle. Stay in touch with handlebars, seat and pedals, steer in the direction of your lean, and you may well get out of it without falling or colliding, though your nerves may have suffered.

Treating Abrasions

Abrasions, referred to in racing circles as road rash, are the most common cycling injury, resulting from any kind of fall. They usually heal relatively fast, though they can be quite painful. Wash out the wound with water and soap, and remove any particles of road dirt. There may be a risk of tetanus if the wound draws blood. If you have been immunized against tetanus, get a tetanus shot within 24 hours only if the last one was more than two years ago. If you have never been immunized before, get a full immunization, consisting of a shot within 24 hours, followed by two more after one and six months, respectively. Apply a dressing only if the location is covered by clothing, since the wound will heal faster when exposed to the air. Avoid the formation of a scab by treating with an antibiotic salve. See a doctor if any signs of infection occur, e.g. swelling, itching or fever.

Sprained Limbs

In case of a fall, your tendency to stick out an arm to break the impact may result in a sprained or even a fractured wrist. This can also happen to the knee or the ankle. Spraining is really nothing but damage to the ligaments that surround and hold the various parts of a joint together. Typical symptoms are a local sensation of heat, itching and swelling. Treat them by keeping the area cold with an ice bag. If you feel a stinging pain or if fever develops, get medical advice, because it may actually be a fracture that was at first incorrectly diagnosed as a sprain. This may be the case when the fracture takes the form of a simple 'clean' crack without superficially visible deformation of the bone.

Fractures

Typical cycling fractures are those of the wrist and the collarbone, both caused when falling: the one when extending the arm to brake the fall, the other when you don't have time to do that. You or medical personnel may not at first notice a clean fracture as described above. If there is a stinging pain when the part is moved or touched, I suggest you get an X-ray to make sure, even if a fracture is not immediately obvious. You'll need medical help to set and bandage the frac-

tured location and will have to give up cycling (except perhaps on the windload simulator or ergometer) until it is healed, which will take about five weeks. Some European sports physicians have been operatively treating collarbone fractures by means of bolts and pins, but I suggest you'd better let it heal the natural way, unless you are a highly paid professional racer.

Brain Injury

If you fall on your head, the impact may smash the brain against the inside of the skull, followed by the reverse action as it bounces back. The human brain can probably withstand this kind of treatment if the resulting deceleration does not exceed about 300 G or 3000 m/sec^2. Look at it this way: the head probably falls to the ground from a height of 1.5 m (5 ft). This results in a speed of 5 m/sec^2 at the time of impact. To keep the deceleration down below 3000 m/sec^2, this speed must be reduced to zero in no less than 0.002 sec.

Neither your skull, nor the object with which you collide is likely to deform gradually enough to achieve even that kind of deceleration. That's why energy absorbing helmets with thick crushable foam were developed. Neither flexible nor hard materials will do the trick by themselves. It's not a bad idea to have a hard outer shell cover to distribute the load of a point impact, and it is nice to get some comfort inside from a soft flexible liner, but the crushing of about ¾ in of seemingly brittle foam is essential to absorb the shock. The minimum requirement for a safe helmet is the American standard ANSI Z-90.4. Australian standards are tougher, but the British Standard is a farce, since it was written specifically so that (inadequate) British built helmets will meet it.

Other Health Problems

The remaining part of this chapter will be devoted to the health hazards of cycling that have nothing to do with falling off the bike. We will look at the most common complaints and discuss some methods of prevention, as well as possible cures. This brief description can not cover the entire field. Nor should most of the issues discussed here be generalized too lightly. The same symptoms may have different causes in different cases; conversely, the same cure may not work for two superficially similar problems. Yet in most cases the following remarks will apply.

Cycling injuries and sicknesses are probably best understood by physicians who are used to dealing with athletes. Yet even this does not necessary work out, since many of today's 'jock docs' are only familiar with their own sport (which in the majority of cases turns out to be running) and may not interpret some of the cycling problems correctly. At least they will know that a fit cyclist may have a low resting heart rate without being in a condition of shock, as has been assumed by doctors used to treating sedentary patients. So it may be wise to look around for a cycling doctor, which will be no problem if cycling is popular as a sport in the area where you live.

Saddle Sores

Though beginning bicycle racers may at first feel uncomfortable on the bike seat, they have no idea what kind of agony real seat problems can bring. Many famous and successful professional racers have literally sat on a fire through much of their racing career. What happens during the many hours in the saddle is that the combined effect of perspiration, pressure and chafing causes cracks in the skin which are entered by bacteria. The result can be anything from a mild inflammation to the most painful boils.

There is of course little chance of these things healing as long as you have to continue racing or training. As soon as any pressure is applied, when you sit on a bike seat or any other hard surface, things will get worse. Prevention and early relief are the methods to combat saddle sores. The clue to both is hygiene. Wash and dry both your crotch and your cycling shorts after every ride. Many riders also clean themselves with rubbing alcohol, which both disinfects and increases the skin's resistance to chafing.

You'll need at least two pairs of shorts (more if you go out on a prolonged ride several times a day), so you can always rely on a clean, dry pair when you go out on training rides or races. Wash them out, taking particular care to get the chamois clean, and hang them out to dry thoroughly, preferably outside, where the sun's ultraviolet rays may act to kill any bacteria remaining. Treat the chamois with either talcum powder or a special lubricant for that purpose. I prefer to use a water soluble cream, such as Noxema, since it is easier to wash out.

The quality of your saddle and your riding position may also affect the development of crotch problems. If early symptoms appear in the form of redness or soreness, consider getting a softer saddle, sitting further to the back of your saddle, or lowering the handlebars a little to reduce the pressure on the seat. If the problem gets out of hand, take a rest from cycling until the sores have fully healed. In the meantime keep in shape by means of other exercises (e.g. uphill running or even stair climbing, taking double steps, both of which approximate the typical movements and loads of cycling).

Knee Problems

Because the cycling movement does not apply the high impacting shock loads on the legs that are associated with running, it's surprising that knee problems are so prevalent. They are mainly concentrated with two groups of cyclists: beginners and very strong, muscular ones. In both cases, the cause seems to be riding in too high a gear. This places excessive forces on the knee joint, resulting in damage to the membranes that separate the moving portions of the joint and the ligaments holding the bits and pieces together. In cold weather the problems get aggravated, so it will be wise to wear long pants on training rides whenever the temperature is below 18 degrees C (65 degrees F), especially if fast descents are involved.

Going down together: the Italian tandem team Rossi and Finamove lose control of their machine during a track stand. (Photo H. A. Roth)

Prevent excessive forces on the knee joint by gearing so low that you can spin lightly under all conditions, avoiding especially climbing in the saddle with pedalling speeds below 60 RPM. Equip your bicycle with the kind of gear ratios that allow you to do that, and choose a lower gear whenever necessary. Once the problem has developed, either giving up cycling or riding loosely in low gears will aid the healing process. I suggest you continue cycling in very low gears, spinning freely. That probably prepares you to get back into shape and forces you to avoid the high gearing that caused the problem in the first place.

Achilles Tendon

The Achilles tendon attaches the big muscle of the lower leg, the gastrocnemius, to the heel bone. It is an important tendon in cycling, since force can not be applied to the foot in the pedalling motion without it. It some-

times gets damaged or torn under the same kind of conditions as described above for knee injuries: cycling with too much force in too high a gear. The problem is aggravated by cold, which explains why it generally develops in the early season.

To avoid it, wear long woollen socks whenever the temperature is below 18 degrees C (65 degrees F). It may also help to wear shoes that come up quite high, maximizing the support they provide. Get used to riding with a supple movement in a lowish gear, which seems to be the clue to preventing many cycling complaints. Healing requires rest, followed by a return to cycling with minimum pedal force in the low gear just mentioned.

Numbness

Especially beginning cyclists, not yet used to riding longer distances, sometimes develop a loss of feeling in certain areas of contact with the bike. The most typical location is the hands, but it also occurs in the feet and the crotch. This is caused by excessive and unvaried prolonged pressure on the nerves and blood vessels. The effects are usually relieved with rest, though they have at times been felt for several days.

Once the problem develops, get relief by changing your position frequently, moving the hands from one part of the handlebars to the other, or moving from one area of the seat to the other if the crotch is affected. To prevent the numbness in the various locations, use well padded gloves, foam handlebar covers, a soft saddle in a slightly higher position, or thick soled shoes with inner soles, worn over thick socks and laced loosely at the bottom but tightly higher up, depending on the location of the numbness.

Back Ache

Many riders complain of aches in the back, the lower neck and the shoulders, especially early in the season. These are probably attributable to insufficient training of the muscles in those locations. It is largely the result of unfamiliar isometric muscle work in keeping still in a bent forward position. This condition may also be partly caused or aggravated by low temperatures, so it is wise to wear warm cycling clothing in cool weather.

To avoid the early-season reconditioning complaints, the best remedy is not to interrupt cycling in winter. Even two longer rides a week at a moderate pace, or extended use of a home trainer with a proper low riding position, will do the trick. Alternately, you may start off in the new season with a slightly higher handlebar position and once more a low gear. Sleeping on a firm mattress and keeping warm also seems to either help alleviate or prevent the problem.

Sinus and Bronchial Complaints

Especially in the cooler periods, many cyclists develop breathing problems, originating either in the sinuses or the bronchi. The same may happen when a rider used to lowland cycling gets into the mountains, where the cold air in a fast descent can be very unsettling. It's generally attributable to undercooling, and the only solution is to dress more warmly.

After a demanding climb in cooler weather, do not strip off warm clothing, open your shirt or drink excessive quantities of cold liquids, even if you sweat profusely. All these things will cause more rapid cooling than your body may be able to handle. You will cool off gradually and without impairing your health, if you merely reduce your output and allow the sweat to evaporate naturally through the fibers of your cycling clothing. This works best if you wear clothing that contains a high percentage of wool.

Overtraining

This phenomenon, though not usually recognized as a cycling injury, should be treated as one. There are certain symptoms associated with overtraining and there are real hazards in ignoring these. It is simply a matter of having pushed your body beyond its limits in your efforts to extend those limits (which is largely what training is all about).

Two types of overtraining syndromes may be distinguished. Beginning racers are most likely to suffer from the sympathicotonous condition. It is due to inadequate preparation, i.e. too rapid an increase of workload in training or racing from one week to the next. The symptoms include excessive nervousness and tension, perspiration and a rapid pulse. The treatment is relatively easy: slow down for one week, and only increase training load very gradually.

More experienced racers sometimes suffer from the parasympathicotonous condition. This is caused by an excessive total work load, often exceeding the body's capacity to take in food for a prolonged period. Symptoms include listlessness and what seems like incurable tiredness. Here too, the answer lies in a reduction of the workload, though a doctor must definitely be consulted if the feeling of fatigue persists despite a drastic reduction in training effort.

Watch for the symptoms described above for the two types of overtraining and monitor your condition regularly to be conscious of any changes. This need not be as formally executed as is often recommended for top athletes. Of course, there is no harm in checking and recording pulse, blood pressure and temperature first thing in the morning, as well as before and after exercise. The morning pulse is a convenient indicator: if it increases more than it usually does between lying in bed and just after getting up, you'd better take it easy for a day. Perhaps equally useful is to ask yourself how you are feeling in general. If you have difficulty sleeping and tire earlier than usual, if you feel listless, have a poor appetite, perspire more than usual or feel unjustified anxiety, it will be time to suspect overtraining. Go and see a physician who is familiar with the problems of active athletes if two or three days of (relative) rest don't bring recovery.

If the diagnosis is overtraining, ease up for a few days to a few weeks. Whatever you do, don't participate in any races and don't try to force yourself by training harder. Relax your training regimen to the point of minimal fitness and technique exercises. This includes breathing, stretching and other gentle gymnastic exercises, as well as cycling in low gears. Excluded should be all anaerobic (i.e. high output) work, as well as any endurance training. As long as your exercise load does not get you out of breath or to the point where you are getting tired or bored, you are within the limits possible while recovering. Don't take up intensive training again until you feel well and your doctor agrees.

Part II
Increasing the Cyclist's Performance

11
What Makes the Bicycle Go?

It is easier to reach an optimal bicycling performance if one understands which factors affect the bicycle's speed. The things that make it go and those that limit it can and should be comprehended, if one wants to get the most out of the machine. That will be the subject of the present chapter.

Cycling versus Running

Bicycling is more efficient than walking and running. With the same physical output necessary to walk at 3 mph, the cyclist proceeds four times as fast. A comparison of athletic performance will demonstrate that at maximum output levels, the cyclist invariably goes at about twice the runner's speed. The difference lies in the energy required to lift the body several inches with every step the walker takes (see Fig. 11.1). This energy, which can be computed by multiplying the lifting height by the number of steps, is lost to forward motion in walking.

When cycling, the athlete's body remains at the same height, and in consequence essentially all energy used is recovered in forward motion. Even if the cyclist gets out of the saddle, his weight subsequently works via the bicycle's drive-train to bring him forward. It is as though the walker could roll down a little ramp from the high point of each step he took. But cycling is even more effective, since the speed remains more constant than it does when walking. The only cyclic acceleration and deceleration is that of the rider's legs, not the much greater mass of the entire body, as would be the case for the walker.

Just the same, cycling is no perpetuum mobile, because there are

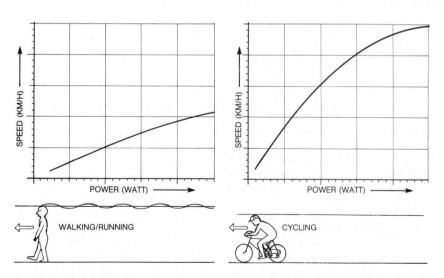

Fig. 11.1 Power comparison for cycling and walking

The work required to overcome gravity when riding
up a steep incline amounts
to the same as would be
needed to pull the weight of
bike and rider up over the
vertical distance equivalent
to the height of the hill.

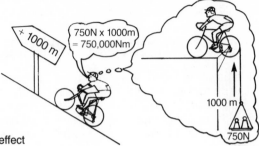

Fig. 11.2 Overcoming the gravity effect

certain resistances to overcome when riding the bicycle. On a level road these losses are attributable primarily to wheel rolling resistance, air resistance and friction. In addition, power will be required to get up to speed, and the gravitational effect must be overcome on inclines. Because the latter form is a useful device to illustrate the other losses, we'll treat it first.

The Effect of Gravity

Consider the situation depicted in Fig. 11.2. The cyclist must overcome gravity over a vertical distance of 1000 m (approx. 3500 ft), cycling up a steeply inclined road. Compared to the effect of gravity, all other resistances are of a minor nature under these circumstances (low speed, high output). So, in fact it amounts to the situation depicted as the cyclist's vision: pulling up a heavy weight over a given distance. The distance is the vertical difference that must be overcome, 1000 m in this case. The weight equals that of bike and rider. I have assumed a weight of 750 N (N stands for Newton, the scientific unit for force; in non-scientific units the equivalent would be approx. 170 lbs).

The total amount of work (or energy, which is another name for the same concept) required to overcome the effect of gravity can be calculated as the product of height and weight force:

$$W = S \times F$$

where:
W = work in Nm (Newton-meter) or J
    (Joule, which is equivalent to Nm)
S = vertical distance in m
F = weight force in N

In the illustrated situation that will be:

1000 m x 750 N = 750,000 Nm
                        (553,000 ft-lbs).

At whatever speed you climb that hill, the total amount of work required will always be the same. The difference between going faster or slower affects not the work, but the power, which can be considered the intensity of work in terms of time. Power is calculated as the quotient of work divided by time:

$$P_i = F : t$$

where:
P_i = power required to overcome
    gradient in Nm/sec or watt
    (which are equivalent units)
F = weight force (or weight) in N
t = time in sec

To do the given amount of work in 30 min (or 1800 sec) takes:

750,000 J : 1800 sec = 420 watt
                        (0.56 hp).

Done in half the time, the climb will require twice the power: 840 watt (about 1.12 hp) in the present example.

The foregoing calculations apply solely to the gravitational effect. In reality, more work and power will be required in each instance, since the overall efficiency is reduced by the other losses. Generally, climbing does not take place on such a steep incline as used here to illustrate the effect of gravity. When the incline is less steep, the gravity effect will become less dominant compared to the other resistances, as will be clarified below in the section *Total Losses and Total Power*.

It may be useful to look at the gravitational effect in terms of the required power as a function of the steepness of the incline (or the power bonus received on a decline, which will speed you up when going downhill). This may be done with the aid of the following formulas for power and resistance force respectively, and as illustrated in Fig. 11.3:

$P_i = R_i \times v$

$R_i = 100 \times i \times F$

where:

P_i = power required to overcome gravitational force on incline

R_i = effective gravitational resistance in N on given incline

v = riding speed in m/sec

i = gradient or incline in percent (negative value for decline)

F = total weight of bicycle and rider in N

Rolling Resistance

If the bicycle were to roll with undeformable, perfectly circular wheels on an equally undeformable, perfectly level surface, there would be no rolling resistance at the contact between tire and road. But since even the best roads and tracks have some unevennesses, such an undeformable wheel would cause serious shocks and vibrations, resulting in both discomfort to the rider and energy losses. To overcome these problems, the bicycle wheel is equipped with a flexible pneumatic tire which acts as a shock absorbing suspension.

Although the considerable losses caused by road shocks and vibrations are thus reduced, some energy is lost as the tire deforms at the contact with the road and around the irregularities in the road surface. The effect of these losses can be seen as the equivalent of a (slight) incline that must be overcome while cycling.

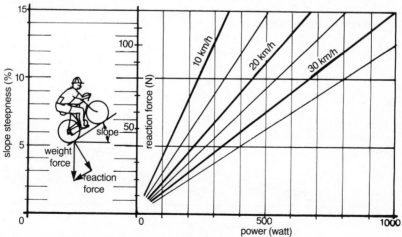

Fig. 11.3 The effect of steepness on force and power

Tire rolling resistance increases with the contact area between tire and road surface. Lower tire pressure or road surface roughness increases contact area and resistance. Additionally, the less flexible the tire at any pressure, the higher its rolling resistance.

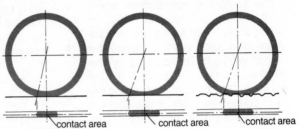

contact area   contact area   contact area

Fig. 11.4 Factors affecting tire rolling resistance

The 'steepness' of this equivalent gradient is called C_r or rolling resistance factor. For a well inflated tire on a smooth road C_r may have a value of about 0.002, being the equivalent of climbing 2 m for every 1000 m travelled. A poorer road surface, a lower quality tire or an improperly inflated one, all cause a higher rolling resistance factor, which may be up to four times as high (i.e. $C_r = 0.008$) under unfavorable conditions (see Fig. 11.4). The required output is determined by the following formula:

$P_r = v \times C_r \times F$

where:

P_r = power required to overcome rolling resistance
v = riding speed in m/sec
C_r = tire rolling resistance factor

F = weight force of bike and rider working on the tire (depending on the distribution of weight over the two wheels, that will be 60–70 % of the total weight on the rear and 30–40 % on the front)

As was the case with real hill climbing, the power loss is directly proportional to the (here imaginary) incline and to riding speed. Cycling faster or a greater rolling resistance factor amounts to the same as overcoming a greater difference in height during a given time period. The illustration Fig. 11.5 shows the power loss resulting from several rolling resistance factors at a range of speeds. It will be clear that these losses are of a minor nature as compared to the total power a racer has available. Just the same, every little

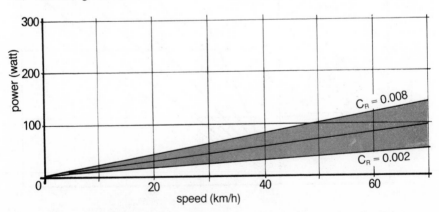

Fig. 11.5 Power loss due to rolling resistance

bit helps and the choice of tires may at times make the difference between winning and losing.

On smooth, level roads, the tire pressure is the most critical factor. Though regular wired-on tires are now available that are quite flexible and allow pressures as high as tubular tires, the latter still have the edge in racing. This is due to their greater flexibility, their lighter weight and the fact that they allow the use of lighter rims. Certainly on rougher roads, the tubular tire rolls easier and gives slightly less discomfort when inflated to the same pressure.

Air Drag

As the bicycle and its rider move forward, the air is disturbed, whichever way the wind is blowing. Though the most important effect is that of the rider, even such minor things as the effect of the wheel's spokes milling around at speed are of some consequence. Fig. 11.6 shows how the effective air velocity can be determined from speed and direction of the bicycle and of the wind relative to each other. Note that even a tail wind is felt as an effective head wind as long as you cycle faster than it blows. In its simplest form, the power loss due to air resistance is determined by the following formula:

$$P_d = F_d \times v$$

where:

P_d = power required to overcome air drag in watt

F_d = drag force in N

v = relative air velocity in m/sec

Unlike the resisting forces due to gravity and tire rolling, the drag force is itself highly speed dependent, namely with the square of speed. Thus, if we conjure up the parallel with the effect of hill climbing, it would seem like overcoming an increasingly steep incline as the speed is increased. A more accurate picture is gleaned from the detailed formula, where F_d is broken up in the factors that determine it:

$$F_d = 0.5 \times 9.81 \times \rho \times C_d \times A \times v^2$$

where:

F_d = drag force in N

ρ = air density in kg/m^3

C_d = drag coefficient

A = frontal area of bike and rider in m^2

v_r = relative air velocity in m/sec

When there is no significant wind, the relative air velocity is the same as the actual riding speed. In that case, the power required to overcome air drag,

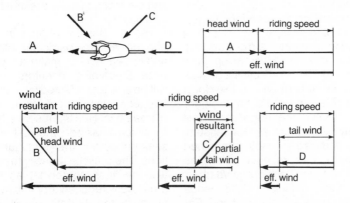

Fig. 11.6 Effective air velocity as a function of riding speed and wind

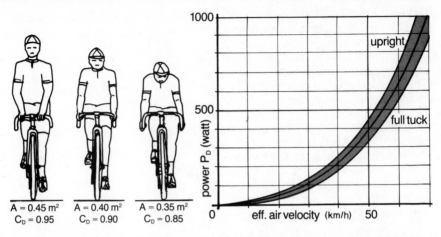

A = 0.45 m²   A = 0.40 m²   A = 0.35 m²
C_D = 0.95   C_D = 0.90   C_D = 0.85

Fig. 11.7 The effect of riding posture on frontal area and power to overcome air resistance

expressed in watt, may be calculated from either one of the following simplified formulas:

$$P_d = v \times F_d$$

$$P_d = 0.5 \times 9.81 \times \rho \times C_d \times A \times v^3$$

It will be obvious from the latter formula that the power required to overcome air drag is greatly influenced (namely with the third power) by the riding speed: at twice the speed the power required to overcome air drag is eight times as great, and a 50 % increase in output will suffice to overcome air drag at a speed that is only 14 % higher.

The frontal area A depends largely on your riding posture (Fig. 11.7). It is reduced as you reach a more perfectly tucked position, decreasing from 0.45 m² to 0.35 m² for a cyclist of average stature. It is of course less for a smaller rider and more for a bigger one, but since the larger rider will probably be stronger as well (assuming his body size is not determined primarily by the presence of excess fat), we can use the average values.

The drag coefficient C_d depends primarily on posture and clothing. For a racer in perfect tuck on an aerody-

namically designed bicycle the value may be about 0.8, increasing to 1.0 when sitting upright and wearing loose clothing. The reduction of air resistance is significant under all but the lowest cycling speeds. Since riding closely behind another rider reduces the air resistance by as much as 40 % at higher speeds, the rider can save significant power this way under most conditions. It has been calculated and confirmed experimentally, that this will allow a speed increase of 5 % for a two-man team and 10 % for four racers riding a paceline. The exception is climbing, when speeds are low and overcoming gravity is much more significant.

The air density ρ does not vary enough at any particular elevation above sea level to make a big difference. Since all competitors in a race will be similarly effected by (minor) differences due to air pressure, it is only of interest for time trial record attempts, for which it has become customary to seek out cycling tracks at high elevations. The cyclist's capacity to perform also declines somewhat as the air pressure is reduced. For this reason it appears the benefit of cycling at higher elevations is limited: above

2400 m (9000 ft) the benefit does not weigh up against the reduction in output for most racers.

Acceleration

In the preceding sections a given riding speed was assumed. However, in practice cycling is not done at a constant speed and the acceleration from standstill or a temporarily reduced speed to the ultimate speed requires significant power. This power depends on the mass that must be accelerated and the rate of acceleration. In fact, the situation becomes slightly more complicated, since the moving parts of the bicycle (and of the rider's body) must not only be accelerated forward, but also around their own axes. The basic formula for the force required to accelerate an object at a given rate is quite simple, namely:

$$F_a = m \times a$$

Minimum weight and air resistance with special rims, hubs and spokes from the French firm Roval.

where:
F_a = force in N required to accelerate the object
m = mass of the object in kg
a = acceleration in m/sec^2

The required power in watt is the product of this force and the speed in m/sec:

$$P_a = v \times F_a$$

where:
P_a = power in watt required to overcome acceleration
v = speed in m/sec
F_a = force in N required to accelerate

In addition to the linear acceleration of the bicycle, the rotational acceleration of moving parts (of bike and rider) should be considered to obtain the greatest accuracy in calculation. For the wheels the rotational acceleration is relatively straightforward, since their mass center of rotation is close to their circumference, and they rotate at a predictable speed. For other parts, like the cranks and the chain, this value depends also on the gear selected.

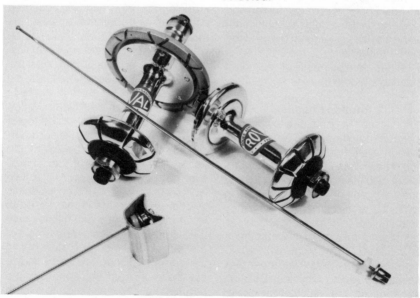

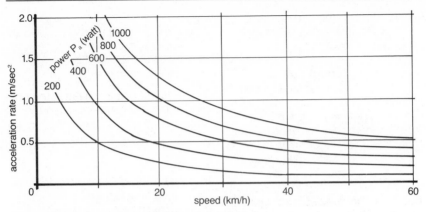

Fig. 11.8 Additional power needed for acceleration

In practice, the power required to accelerate the bicycle may be computed accurately enough by adding power to overcome the wheel's rotation to that for the total mass of bike and rider. It is by approximation correct to state that the effect of heavier tires and rims on acceleration losses is 2 times as great as the effect of the same weight for a non-moving part of the bicycle. Doubling the mass of the wheels gives reasonable accuracy for practical purposes. Fig. 11.8 shows the relationship between power and acceleration for a typical lightweight racing bicycle with rider in terms of the power required to accelerate at a given rate from standstill or any given speed to a higher speed.

Friction Losses

Minor losses are caused by friction between moving parts, i.e. the transmission system and the wheel bearings. These losses are generally proportional to the power output and may most conveniently be expressed in terms of a single compound efficiency factor η. For a hypothetical frictionless bicycle this factor η would have the value 1.0, while a value of 0.9–0.95 might be quite typical for most well maintained racing bicycles. Dividing the sum of the calculated power

losses by this factor η gives the total output that will be required to move the bicycle forward under the given conditions.

Mass and Weight

The two concepts of weight and mass are frequently confused in the minds of those not trained in the physical sciences. Mass is the total of all the material substance in an object: the sum of all the elementary particles. In the scientific system it is expressed in kg (kilogram) and can be measured accurately with balance scales. The mass of any object remains the same whatever happens and wherever it is: if your bike has a mass of 10 kg, it will have exactly that same mass on the moon as it does on earth or, more to the point, the same in Death Valley, 280 feet below sea level, as on top of Mt. Whitney, 14,500 ft above sea level.

Weight is the force by which the earth's (or the moon's if you should ever get out there) gravitational field works on an object. In the scientific system weight force is expressed in Newton and may be established with the aid of a spring scale. The weight of a given object, though it always has the same mass, varies according to the distance from the center of the earth's gravitational field: in Death

Valley you and your bike weigh more than in the High Sierras, even though the mass remains the same.

Both the mass and the weight corresponding to it in any given location affect the bicycle's performance. When climbing, every bit more weight must be dragged up to the top. The additional weight also increases the power required to overcome rolling resistance slightly. With respect to acceleration, it is the mass of rider and bicycle, and in particular of its wheels, which determines how much effort goes into reaching a higher speed quickly. It is probably true that the weight difference between one racing bicycle and the next is not significant enough to make a big difference in terms of the speed reached. Just the same, a lighter bike with lighter wheels is felt by most riders to improve their performance. That's worth exploiting – providing the weight reduction is not achieved at the cost of reliability.

Total Losses and Total Power

In the preceding sections we have looked at each of the various forms of resistance separately. Now it is time to add them together in order to determine just how much power is required to propel the bicycle at a certain speed, or conversely which speed will be reached with a given power output under various conditions.

It is possible to express the power required at a given speed, as well as the power to accelerate to or from that speed, as the power needed to overcome the sum of all resistances in the form of a compound formula. In its simplest form this formula would look like this:

$$P = v(F_i + F_r + F_d + m\,a) : \eta$$

where:
P = total power in watt required to propel the bicycle at a given speed
v = speed in m/sec
η = efficiency
F_i = resistance force in N due to incline
F_r = rolling resistance force in N
F_d = air drag resistance force in N
m = mass of bike and rider in kg (including a factor doubling the wheel mass if greater accuracy is required)
a = acceleration in m/sec^2

A typical well built racing frame made with the finest tubing, Reynolds 753. Though such very light frame tubes are less rigid than thicker walled tubes, the resulting flex neither reduces the speed nor does it increase power losses – it just makes the bike a little less precise to steer.

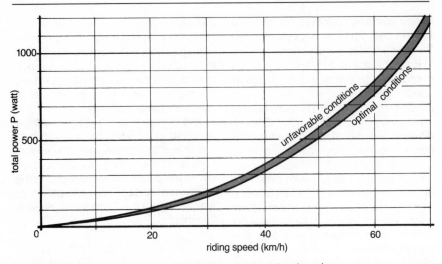

Fig. 11.9 Total power required as a function of speed on level road

The results of this formula at constant speeds (i.e. ignoring the factors m and a, which together represent the effect of acceleration) have been summarized for a range of speeds and gra- dients in the accompanying graphs, Fig. 11.9 and Fig. 11.10. For the (additional) effect of acceleration, refer to the earlier illustration 11.8.

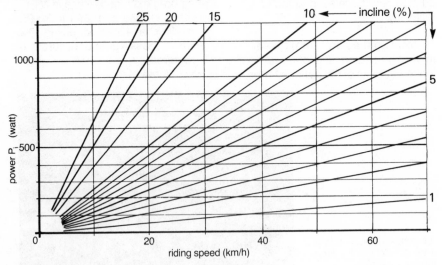

Fig. 11.10 Additional power needed for hill climbing

12
What Makes the Cyclist Go?

In the present chapter we shall take a close look at the cyclist as the motor that must produce the power to overcome the various resistances described in Chapter 11. First we shall concentrate on the total power trained and untrained cyclists have to offer under various circumstances. In the next section we'll compare available power with the power required to reach a particular speed, to establish which speeds can be attained under particular conditions. The detailed processes by which power is generated and work is performed by the athlete's muscles will be explained in Chapter 13.

Physical Efficiency

The human body takes in food and oxygen, converts it into energy and releases the waste products. The energy intake over a longer period can be established by counting the energy equivalency of the food intake. In the short run this figure is of little use, because the body doesn't burn off all the food it takes in right away. Instead, the oxygen intake can be used as a measure for the work done, since there is a known relationship between oxygen consumption and energy output.

Generally, about 75 % of all the energy is turned into heat, whereas about 25 % is converted into mechanical work. To put it another way, the human body's mechanical efficiency is 0.25. Actually, that is better than it may seem at first sight, since this is a ratio reached or exceeded only by the most modern industrial power plants, while your car engine and most steam turbines are quite a bit less efficient.

The efficiency is of some importance to our investigation of the cycling athlete's performance. It is customary in books covering this subject of research to refer to laboratory tests in which the cyclist's power output level has been measured on a bicycle ergometer. Older tests of this type have left much to be desired. Some such supposedly scientific work has been claimed to demonstrate clearly that cycling at any speed suitable for racing would be frankly impossible or at least very undesirable.

The problem with many older tests is that the researchers had concentrated too much on efficiency. They didn't understand the fact that the bicyclist isn't necessarily riding his bicycle in an attempt to conserve oxygen and calories. By concentrating solely on establishing the point of maximum efficiency, these researchers were ignoring the cyclist's desire to proceed and his ability to deliver more power, even if at the expense of a slight decrease in efficiency, which is nothing more than an increase in the ratio between heat energy and mechanical energy.

Measuring the body's efficiency has its uses in the field of bicycle physiology. But not for predicting what will be the best pedalling rate or what would be a good output level during a race. Instead, efficiency comparisons are suitable for determining such variables as the best posture and pedalling style. The recommendations for criteria like seat height, body angle and crank length in this book are based on such tests. For example, if at all output levels one seat height or crank length is associated with greater efficiency, that one should be used for that rider.

Measuring Power and Energy

Though in recent years researchers who are adequately familiar with bicycle racing have been conducting laboratory tests that go well beyond mere comparisons of physical efficiency, my approach is slightly different again. I refer to the large body of reliable data that is available from real-world racing. Combining the calculations in the preceding chapter with the results from actual time trials over various distances, provides data that are both reliable and supremely relevant to the subject of bicycle racing. Wherever I have based my discussion in this and the preceding chapter on published laboratory data, I have verified the data's practical validity by comparing it with the undeniable facts of the real racing world.

The total amount of energy delivered during a given period can be estimated by such a combination of theoretical and empirical work. This is done most accurately by comparing the total mileage travelled with the speed and other factors influencing the power for each section of the course. A simple substitute is to merely base the estimate on the total time and the average speed, either considering a multiplier factor for terrain conditions or adding the calculated energy required to overcome given climbs or head winds.

To establish just how much power a particular rider – you, for instance – can generate on a bicycle, one only has to compare the required time for a given distance with the graphs 11.9 and 11.10 from the preceding chapter. Two test situations seem most suitable: a prolonged time trial and a steep hill climb. A long time trial on a level road gives a good measure of the power that can be produced during the time required to complete it and can be repeated for various distances. The hill climbing situation requires the cyclist to ride up a short steep incline (10% or more) with a known elevation gain, to establish maximum power available during a short period by comparing the average speed achieved with graph 11.10. Repeating the same test from time to time, preferably riding a similar, but not the same, stretch of road, will give a good check on training progress.

Available Power

The power that an athlete has available to propel his bicycle eventually determines the speed at which he can ride or the rate at which he can accelerate to reach a higher speed. Different people of course have entirely different physiques, and consequently can produce entirely different power outputs. Some of this difference is genetically determined, but a significant portion is the direct result of training. Thus there is probably enough room for improvement, even if you should not be so genetically endowed as to be a predestined champion.

Fig. 12.1 shows two typical (though by no means universally representative) performance curves that relate the maximum power output to the time duration for which each power level can be maintained. These curves are for two types of cyclists: a highly trained racer and a reasonably fit recreational cyclist. Both are familiar enough with cycling to allow the use of these curves to determine their actual performance potential (a non-cyclist, tested the same way, would generally deliver less power due in large part to the fact that his cycling motion is not yet smooth and natural).

Note that these curves do not represent continuous power at the levels shown: each power output level on the curve can only be maintained dur-

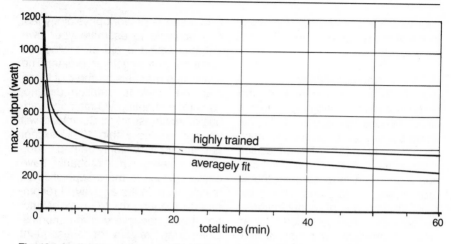

Fig. 12.1 Available power curves for highly trained and untrained cyclists

ing the corresponding time, followed by rest. In other words, if the 400 watt output is required of the trained racer for 30 min, this must be a pretty constant output from beginning to end, and followed by rest. If, on the other hand, one of the higher values in the LH portion of the curve is expended first, this same output cannot be delivered any more.

The most important things to observe on these curves are their relative position and their shape. Clearly the curve for the trained racing cyclist lies higher than for the less trained person. The racer can deliver more power for any time duration. This is the primary effect of training on the body's output potential. Although an inherently strong untrained individual may deliver more power than an inherently weaker person, the effect of proper training will be to raise the curve for any one athlete.

Long Term and Short Term Power
Let us now consider the shape of these curves. You will notice that power decreases with time, but by no means linearly: at first it drops off very steeply, and quite soon becomes much less steep. The most significant

aspect is the pronounced difference between very short duration and long duration power. For very short periods, an enormous power output can be delivered – well over 750 W (1 hp). As the time over which the effort must be maintained increases, the power drops off rapidly. At one or two minutes the curves bend quite abruptly and decline much less steeply from there on. In the next section we'll see why this is so.

The distinct difference between the short duration high power and long duration low power output portions of the curves can be attributed to the significance of anaerobic work where short duration high power output is delivered. The terms aerobic and anaerobic have become such buzzwords, that it may seem in order to clarify their meaning. Aerobic means in the presence of oxygen, anaerobic without oxygen, here referring to the mechanisms that produce the ATP (adenosinetriphosphate) in the mitochondria, which are the muscle's power cells. ATP is the substance that generates the muscle energy, as it is itself broken down. The available muscle energy is proportional to the number of ATP molecules formed, regardless whether the process by which that is done is the aerobic or the anaerobic pathway.

Aerobic Power

Aerobic power generation is the body's normal operating mode. In this case glucose molecules from the blood stream are broken down completely to form 38 ATP molecules each, as they are burned with the oxygen (hence the term aerobic) that is also carried in the blood. This is the most efficient way of producing energy; besides, it can be called a 'clean process', producing minimal waste to load the blood stream, which means less fatigue. However, it is relatively slow and limited by the body's capacity to carry oxygen to the muscle's mitochondria. The duration over which aerobic power may be given off relatively painlessly is limited by the amount of glucose stored in the blood.

Within the limits of strength of the muscles, the maximum aerobic power (i.e. the intensity of aerobic work performed in a certain time period) is limited by the cardio-respiratory capacity. That is the amount of oxygen lungs and heart can deliver via the blood stream to the muscles. The cardio-respiratory capacity is generally expressed in terms of the heart's stroke volume or in VO_2max. That is the maximum volume of oxygen related to total body weight that is absorbed with each heart beat. Typical values range from 30 ml/kg for an untrained healthy person to 80 ml/kg for world class road racers. Though training can increase it quite a bit, as the heart muscle is strengthened, some people just naturally have a bigger capacity than others, which makes them potentially more successful aerobic performers: stronger long distance cyclists.

An individual rider's current VO_2max may be established experimentally. Though it can be done most accurate-

ly in a sports or work physiology lab, it is possible to estimate your own VO_2max with the aid of a windload simulator or a bicycle ergometer. The instruction manuals for most of these machines include detailed descriptions for estimating VO_2max and various other fitness tests. Such tests will be accurate to within 10%, except perhaps for very highly trained endurance athletes (who probably have easier access to more sophisticated testing techniques anyway). I recommend repeating the VO_2max estimation test once every three months. Comparing results of subsequent tests allow you to establish whether your VO_2max is still increasing, as it will as long as you are training effectively and have not reached your absolute maximum yet.

Even amongst bicycle racers there are wide differences in VO_2max. Those in the higher categories of road racing almost all have high capacities, suggesting perhaps that there is little hope for more modestly endowed athletes. However even in road racing people with modest VO_2max but good sprinting power may keep up with the top in a close pack, eventually beating them in the sprint. Amongst track sprinters and other short-distance specialists, high VO_2max levels are the exception, rather than the rule, since their disciplines depend more on anaerobic power.

Anaerobic Power

The anaerobic mode is strongly activated when much higher output levels are required. Two metabolical systems constitute anaerobic power generation, referred to as ATP-CP and lactic acid systems, respectively. In the ATP-CP, or high energy phosphates mechanism, creatine phosphate (CP) is the source of ATP in a single enzyme reaction. The ATP-CP system operates extremely fast. It is limited by the amount of CP stored in the muscle tissue, and depends on the presence of favorable conditions for the enzyme reaction. It can provide short duration maximum energy bursts of up to about 15 seconds. In practice, this system is more important than meets the eye, since it is called upon just a little each time muscle forces exceed the low levels that can be permanently supported. That can be during the peak portion of every pedal stroke, e.g. while climbing or accelerating. The ATP and CP stores in the muscle, though depleted within 15 seconds of maximum output, are recovered relatively fast, namely within about three minutes.

The other form of anaerobic power is generated in what is referred to as the lactic acid system, and can supply energy for up to about two minutes at peak performance. It leads to a degree of depletion from which the body takes a long time to recover, and should therefore not be used, except in short duration events or near the end of a race. In this system a reaction called glycolysis takes place. In glycolysis sugars (both the glucose from the blood and the glycogen stored in the muscle and liver tissue) are broken down without oxygen (hence the term anaerobic) to form ATP. In this process an excess of lactic acid is formed. Lactic acid is also formed in other metabolic processes. However, whereas the small quantity resulting from aerobic work is immediately reconverted in aerobic work, the excess remains to be oxidized in the case of anaerobic work. This is the reason for the oxygen debt (heavy breathing, and sometimes dizziness after the work is done) that often results from anaerobic work.

The lactic acid process is fast and powerful, but wasteful in terms of energy efficiency. Each glucose molecule produces only two ATP

Beating the wind to go 50 MPH. Motor paced racing is especially popular on the European continent. (Photo H. A. Roth)

molecules, as compared to 38 ATP molecules in the aerobic process. If all your power were to be provided this way, a given food intake would only allow you to cycle perhaps 10 miles a day. However, so many more ATP molecules can be formed within a given (brief) time, that high output levels are possible. The power limitation – apart from the muscle's strength – lies in the conditions favorable to the enzyme reaction involved. These are largely influenced by specific training methods that stress the system and require correct food and favorable temperature conditions. The time during which this energy may be used is limited by the amount of stored sugars and the accumulation of lactic acid. It is assumed that training methods that frequently call on this metabolism may stimulate the removal of lactic acid, thus perhaps leading to an increase of time during which the powerful lactic acid system may be relied on in competition.

Unlike its aerobic counterpart, the level of anaerobic power cannot be easily established riding a bicycle by the amateur researcher, since too many other variables affect the time in a furious sprint. Instead, you may use a simple variant of the method employed in many laboratories to estimate this characteristic. Run up a flight of stairs as fast as you can, three steps at a time, while letting someone record the time, accurate to 0.1 sec, required to gain a certain height. Then calculate the maximum power for that time from the following formula:

$$P = h \times F : t$$

where:
P = power in watt
h = height in meters
F = weight in Newton (obtain by multiplying weight in lbs by 4.7 or by multiplying weight in kg by 9.8)
t = time in seconds

To put it all into some perspective, you may be interested to know what a really good sprinter can deliver anaerobically. A fast sprint of 200 m is ridden in approx. 10 sec, and that corresponds to a power output of more than 1000 watt or 1.4 hp.

Anaerobic Threshold

An athlete's anaerobic threshold is thought of as the level of power beyond which the anaerobic high energy phosphate and lactic acid systems are activated to a significant extent. This is the level at which the available oxygen is no longer adequate to break down and absorb the lactic acid resulting from anaerobic work. I find it dangerous to think of this point as a distinct output level. Even if it is, there remains the problem of establishing just where it lies. My experience, shared by at least some scientists, is that this supposed threshold is at one level today and at another tomorrow, even for the same rider. And as for establishing it, I am not satisfied with any conventional objective method.

Essentially, aerobic power is delivered whenever work is done. But so is anaerobic power: very little at low, very much at high output demand levels. The ATP-CP system is called upon for both short bursts of power

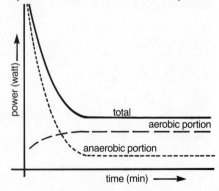

Fig. 12.2 Anaerobic power as percent of total power

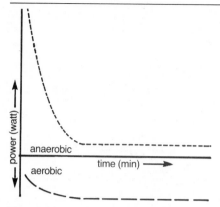

Fig. 12.3 Distribution of aerobic and anaerobic power

and for the brief peak muscle forces. When power demands increase beyond the maximum available anaerobic power level for periods exceeding short power peaks, the anaerobic lactic acid system is turned on fully. But even beyond this point the aerobic power output may continue to increase. The usual way of representing the phenomenon of simultaneous aerobic and anaerobic power development is by means of the illustration Fig. 12.2. Instead, I feel the situation may be shown by Fig. 12.3.

Especially if you want to develop your sprinting and climbing powers as well as an increased resistance to

pain, you will at times want to exceed the anaerobic threshold – i.e. the level where anaerobic power becomes a significant factor in power generation. One of the most effective ways to develop the capacity of your power plant is by pushing this level up higher as the result of frequently exceeding it. In addition, anaerobic capacity and muscle strength can be increased by exercising at such high output levels.

Power versus Speed

Finally in this chapter, here are some graphs and figures for the outputs that are possible and the speeds that may be attained in bicycle racing. This is done by comparing the available power with the findings from Chapter 11. First, consider the sprinter who rides the 200 m in a little more than 10 seconds: he's going at an average speed of 70 km/h (45 mph), requiring 1200 watt – impossible without the benefit of the downslope on the banked track.

For longer duration work, I have put together some of the graphs from the previous chapter with performance figures for various output levels. This will give you an idea of the speeds and accelerations that may be reached under various conditions by cyclists of

This bicycle shoe was especially designed to minimize air drag to reduce wind resistance to a minimum. Many track racers now show up this way. This one was first spotted at the world team time trial championships in Brno. (Photo H. A. Roth)

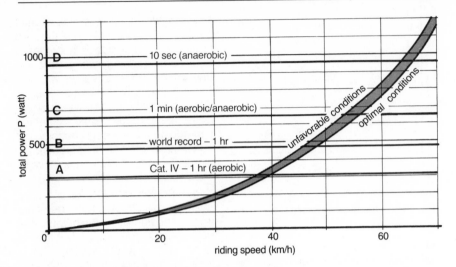

Fig. 12.4 Available and required power – on level road

different strength levels. I will not try to explain in words what can be gleaned from these graphs. If you are one who finds it hard to get information from such graphs, you may have an even harder time understanding the verbal discourse that would summarize the information contained in them.

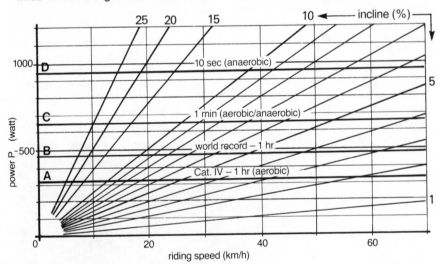

Fig. 12.5 Available and required power – hill climbing

13
Understanding Muscle Work

Equally important as is the body's overall capacity to do work at adequate intensity, is the ability of individual muscles to deliver power to the bicycle's drivetrain. In this chapter we shall take a close look at the muscles involved and at the way any muscle operates. Understanding the way muscles work, knowing which muscles are involved in cycling and what will increase the muscle's strength, allows the cyclist to gear his training program to maximize muscle power and efficiency.

The illustration Fig. 13.1 is not meant to portray the main attraction at a Russian circus, but rather to show the human body's muscles from a bicycling perspective. Identified are those muscles which play a major part while pedalling the bicycle, including those that are merely stressed while cycling, without necessarily being in motion. As will be apparent from the illustration, you don't cycle with your leg muscles only.

Muscles constitute about one third of an average trained cyclist's body weight; untrained individuals tend to have less muscle weight relative to their total weight. Like other parts of the body, so the muscles too consist of cells, which in this case contain about 70 % water. About half the dry muscle weight consists of protein, the rest is made up of approximately equal parts of fats and hydrocarbons.

There are two basic types of muscles: the rather flat and smooth autonomously operating ones, which contain the body's various organs, and the more cylindrically shaped voluntary muscles with a striped surface, which respond to the human will. The latter are referred to as skeletal muscles, since they attach to different bones of the skeleton and affect movement of the bones relative to one another. The heart can perhaps best be considered as an intermediate form, being of the striped type but operating involuntarily, i.e. not responding to the human will. Only the

Muscle man: the US track racer Nelson Vails, one of America's most successful track sprinters and short distance time trialists. (Photo Dave Nelson)

striped skeletal muscles are of interest in the present discussion.

The skeletal muscles terminate at both ends in one or more flexible but non-elastic tendons, which in turn connect to protrusions on the bones. There is at least one set of muscles around every one of the skeleton's joints: a flexor on the inside and a stretcher on the outside of the bent joint, shown in Fig. 13.2. We'll first take a close look at the way muscles produce work, followed by an analysis of the operation of the muscles most important to cycling, namely those that allow you to push the cranks around and around.

The Way Muscles Work

Looking close up (Fig. 13.3), each skeletal muscle consists of densely packed bundles of long fibers with a diameter of about 0.1 mm (0.004 in) each. These bundles are surrounded by a flexible mantle, called sarcomere to which the tendons are attached. There are two distinct types of muscle fibers in each bundle: white ones and red ones. The red ones have that color due to the presence of a high proportion of myoglobin, an oxygen storage protein, making them the main carriers of aerobic power. These red fibers are referred to as slow twitch (ST) fibers, since they take rather long to

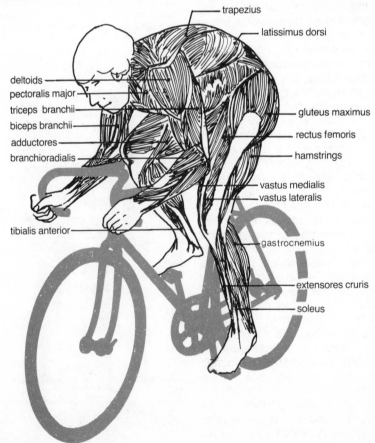

trapezius

latissimus dorsi

deltoids

pectoralis major

triceps branchii

biceps branchii

adductores

branchioradialis

gluteus maximus

rectus femoris

hamstrings

vastus medialis

vastus lateralis

tibialis anterior

gastrocnemius

extensores cruris

soleus

Fig. 13.1 The cyclist's muscles

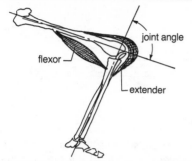

Fig. 13.2 Muscle configuration at typical joint

react to activation impulses (about 100 msec). The white fibers have much less myoglobin, and are thus less suitable for aerobic work. They are known as fast twitch (FT) fibers because they react to activation impulses within 20–30 msec. The latter are primarily the carriers of anaerobic power.

The proportions of the two types are probably genetically determined, though each can be developed through specific training. A muscle biopsy, removing and analyzing perhaps 20–40 mg of muscle fiber from a typical skeletal muscle, can show what the proportions in your muscles are. For do-it-yourselves, it may be enough to know that long, smooth and relatively slender muscles are those with a predominance of red slow twitch fibers. These are typical for athletes with good aerobic endurance but limited sprinting capacity. Sprinters tend to have the short and stubbily protruding muscles in which the white fast twitch fibers predominate, giving great anaerobic strength. Typical proportions of red to white (or ST to FT) fibers range from 25/75 for track sprinters to 75/25 for long distance time trialists, 40/60 being about average for non-cyclists.

Sleek muscles on a fast long distance racer: Jonathan Boyer, the first American to ride out a Tour de France. (Photo Dave Nelson)

Fig. 13.3 Typical skeletal muscle

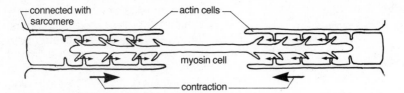

Fig. 13.4 Muscle contraction: actin and myosin cells

Just the same, each type of fiber is capable of some aerobic and some anaerobic work. Specific training probably does not develop only one type of fiber, since the proportions stay the same. And at least one sub-type of the white fast twitch fibers does not appear to respond to any training at all. A training program with a preponderance of short high-power impulses for particular muscles – both on and off the bike – will tend to develop the (anaerobic) strength within either type of muscle fibers. Emphasizing long duration aerobic work in training will tend to increase the aerobic strength potential of either type of fibers. Thus, it may for example be possible to increase aerobic capacity of your white fast twitch fibers beyond that of someone else's red slow twitch fibers.

What we have looked at as a single muscle fiber so far is in reality a complex structure, itself consisting of millions of minute fibers, called myofibrils. These are the actual carriers of muscle work. Each myofibril consists of bundles of long, parallel, mutually overlapping complex protein cells of two different types, called actin and myosin, respectively. Wherever the two types of fibers overlap we recognize the darker areas of the striped pattern, so characteristic of skeletal muscles.

As Fig. 13.4 shows, each of these myofilaments is a set of overlapping protein cell bundles, consisting of thick helically shaped myosin cells and thinner actin cells. In the relaxed

muscle state the actin cells protrude relatively far beyond the ends of the matching myosin cells. Projections on the myosin cells act as little hooks that allow the myosin cell to pull the projecting actin cells from both ends closer in towards its center. This results in a tendency to shorten each myofilament in the chains that make up the myofibrils. That happens when an electric impulse is sent through the nerve, which in turn releases enzymes to move the projection on the myosin towards the actin cell. As the protrusion moves over, ATP is disintegrated, releasing energy to move the protrusion back to its original position. Upon receiving an impulse, a number of protrusions tense up, pulling the actin cells from both ends further in towards the center of the corresponding myosin cell.

This movement can only take place in one direction, namely the direction that shortens or contracts the muscle. With this action each of the myofibrils tends to be shortened from both ends, contracting the overall muscle length. The muscle will only shorten if the muscle force exceeds the external resisting force. You will note that muscle work is done whenever the cell protrusions are tensing up, even if the external resistance is so great that the muscle cannot shorten. If the muscle is actually shortened we speak of concentric work, if it stays equally long of isometric work, and if it is actually lengthened by the extraneous force of eccentric work. Muscle work is done in each case, even though the mechanical effect is only positive in the case of concentric work, while it is zero for isometric, and actually negative in the case of eccentric work.

If a stronger muscle force is required, the nerve impulses must be strong, activating many of the myofibril mechanisms, and the muscle must be capable of quickly breaking up ATP. Each action is only brief, at the end of which each myofibril would relax with its actin and myosin cells in their original relative positions, resulting in an untensioned muscle. To achieve continuous muscle tension, a prolonged sequence of impulses must be given. Each myofibril action applies pressure to the blood vessels within the muscles. This results in a surge of blood upon relaxation, allowing the blood to quickly bring fresh stores of oxygen and fuel to the muscle.

Keep in mind that aerobic work is done primarily by the slow twitch fibers and their energy source is the ATP formed in the mitochondria during the oxygen process. The food for the anaerobic work performed mainly by the fast twitch fibers is exclusively the ATP formed via the lactic acid system. Doing lots of work to increase your aerobic muscle strength is not going to have much effect on your sprinting power. This ability depends primarily on your anaerobic power and the proportion and strength of the fast twitch muscle fibers. Conversely, even if you spend all your time doing weight training, resulting in enormously bulky sprinter's muscles, you may not have improved your endurance power, since that depends largely on the aerobic ability and the proportion and strength of your slow-twitch muscle fibers.

Muscle Strength

Though the composition of an individual athlete's muscles, i.e. the ratio of red and white fibers, is largely genetically determined, usage will tend to develop both the muscle's total size and its strength by increasing the number of fibers. Whereas the ratio cannot be changed, either type of fibers may be developed to work more effectively. In general, muscle training to increase muscle size must involve eccentric work, most effectively when at a level close to the maximum muscle force possible, and each training contraction being continued over the maximum range of movement.

It has become increasingly clear in recent years that a more specific type of muscle training, involving not the increase of muscle size, but rather of the muscle's efficiency, takes place when the typical movements of the sport are carried out frequently, again preferably close to maximum force level, but (in the case of cycling) at a high speed. The first type of training,

Few long distance athletes – whether bike racer or triathlete – have such a perfectly balanced muscular body as triathlon racer Dale Basescu. (Photo courtesy Bud Light)

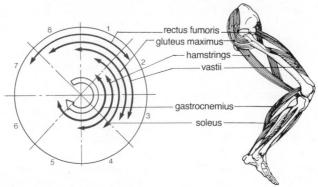

Fig. 13.5 Sequence of activation for major cycling muscles

which increases bulk and may increase short run strength, appears to lend itself well to weight training methods, while the latter form can only be achieved in actual cycling, even if it takes place on a windload simulator.

This works well for aerobic muscle strength. It is more difficult to develop anaerobic strength specifically for cycling, though obviously it too can be trained. This capacity is developed by frequently calling on just the kind of work that involves anaerobic output. It is a general observation that many strong anaerobic performers are lazy when it comes to training and do not seem to suffer for it: those blessed with great anaerobic muscle strength will probably get enough benefit from a few hard sprints, while riders who are less well endowed with fast twitch fibers may never get much better at sprinting, however much they work on it.

It has been found that muscles work most effectively when they operate cyclically with short contractions and relatively long relaxation periods. They also deliver more power when they are as it were pre-stressed. Both these points are considerations to keep in mind when determining the appropriate riding style. In cycling the former condition is satisfied when the legs go through such a motion that different muscle groups take turns in sequence, whereas the second condition is usefully applied when maximum force is required during sprinting, climbing or accelerating when the legs are restrained by getting out of the saddle or pulling on the arms.

Equally important for muscle effectiveness is their supply of fuel and impulse carrying enzymes. So is the fact that lactic acid and other by-products must be carried off and that small fissures, resulting from excessive use should not be allowed to inhibit the muscle's operation. For these reasons such factors as the muscle temperature, the enzyme household and the blood circulation must be attuned to the work at hand. Some of these factors are influenced by the food you eat, by warming up before exercise and by massage after strenuous work. In addition, your state of mind and your general state of health probably influence how effective your muscles are at a given time.

The Cycling Muscles
There are essentially six muscle groups that carry out most of the work involved in propelling the bicycle, as illustrated in Fig. 13.5. It is possible to analyze the nerve impulses in an EMG

(electromyograph), to establish which muscle is active at any point in the pedalling cycle. Though the EMG shows conclusively which muscles are active at any one time, it has not been possible to determine just how much work any particular muscle is performing at any one time. The illustration also shows which muscles were thus found to be active during particular sections of the pedalling cycle, which has for convenience been broken down into 8 octants.

Let us now take a look at the muscles around just one joint (refer back to Fig. 13.2). As we have seen in the preceding section, the only kind of work a muscle can perform is associated with the tendency to tension and become shorter. Clearly, in each kind of movement only one of the pair of muscles at the joint tightens up, while the other one must be relaxed, or at least it will be forced to become longer. It is of course possible – and wasteful of energy – to tighten both muscles simultaneously, the one restraining the other, as exemplified by the body builder's pose.

When contracted, the flexor tends to bend the joint, the stretcher to straighten it. Though many muscles attach directly to the two neighboring bones of a single joint, some reach beyond the next joint, such as for example the hamstrings at the back of the thigh. Fig. 13.6 shows the two cases simplified for some hypothetical joints, though our present discussion refers to a single joint situation. In fact, the illustrated example, bending the knee, is by no means one of the most demanding tasks in cycling and was selected only because it illustrates the principles involved most clearly.

Let us follow the movement of the knee joint and its associated muscles as it goes through the pedalling cycle (Fig. 13.7). As the stretcher muscle

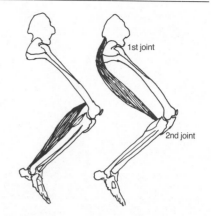

Fig. 13.6 Configuration of muscles covering one and two joints

shortens, tensing up, the bone of the lower leg to which it attaches at some distance from the joint is pulled closer to the upper leg. Thus the angle between the two bones at the joint becomes more acute. The effect of leverage depends on the relative locations of the point where the muscle's tendons attach to the bone. But it also depends on the momentary angle of the two bones relative to one another. Thus the effect of the same muscle force varies over the cycle of movement and is greatest when the joint forms an angle of about 105 degrees (in this case).

Simultaneously with this change in leverage, the muscle length also varies. This muscle is at its longest when the joint is fully extended, at its shortest when fully contracted. The difference in muscle length depends on the lengths of the overlaps of sets of actin and myosin cells within the muscle's myofibrils. When they overlap very little, only few protrusions on the myosin cells can operate to pull in the actin cells; when they overlap very far, the end of the range is soon reached. At either of these extremes the muscle force is therefore lower than in the middle range, which corresponds to a certain muscle length and joint angle.

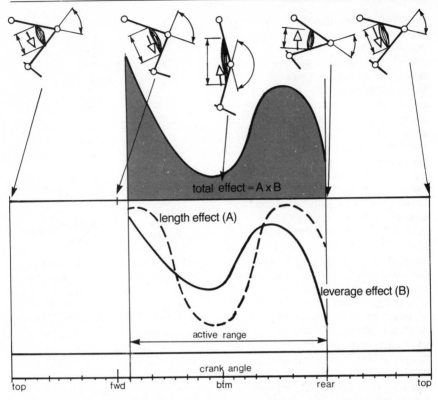

Fig. 13.7 Variation of significant factors over joint movement during one crank revolution

Finally, the speed of muscle contraction varies with the relative orientation of the joint in the cycle of movement, as dictated by the nature of the bicycle's drive system. The muscle contraction speed also influences its power and effectiveness. Though the conventional circular to linear motion of round chainwheel to chain provides certain constraints, the choices of crank length, gear, pedalling rate and saddle height influence all three factors that determine relative effective muscle force as it is transmitted to the bicycle.

In reality, it is all even more complex, since not one, but a whole series of different muscles operate during the pedalling cycle, some simultaneously, some overlapping, some at different times. This, in a nutshell, is the reason why so much research has been done to find the optimal position and the optimal pedalling rate. It is also the reason why so much controversy still exists, because it is obviously a very individual matter, which is impossible to capture in a simple rule of thumb that would be valid for all cyclists.

The complexity of the seemingly simple cycling movement can perhaps be appreciated by referring back to Fig. 13.5 and observing during which section of the pedal stroke the gastrocnemius is active. This muscle is actually the knee bender, and we've seen that the major work is done while extending the knee. When analyzing the movement of the leg in detail, it becomes apparent that during the third octant this muscle must be tensioned to offset other muscle forces that would tend to apply a forward force on the pedal during this part of the stroke.

It will not be necessary for the racing cyclist to know all the details of muscle movements. But if you are aware that all these things matter, you will be in a good position to know what kind of factors to influence when you find your performance is less than optimal. Experiment carefully and consciously with your posture, your riding style, your pedalling rate and your gearing. Vary the amount of pre-race warming up, the kind of clothing you wear, the food you eat; try rest, massage, calisthenics and stretching exercises. Experiment around until you have established how to get the most out of your muscles.

Increasing Muscle Strength

Muscles can be strengthened, and they can be made to work more effectively. That is one (but not the only) aspect of training. We've seen before that muscles will tend to grow and become stronger if they are frequently used concentrically at a level close enough to their maximum for longer periods, especially if they are forced to contract over as great a distance as possible. This implies that all muscle training must be dynamic and that no amount of isometric work, by which the muscles are merely held tensely, such as done in stretching exercises, will increase their strength. Muscle training, whether on or off the bike, should involve powerful muscle contractions.

Certain muscles are normally loaded isometrically in cycling, including those of the arms, shoulders and back. So these will not get strengthened by any amount of cycling, even though they can contribute significantly to your cycling strength – at least they will limit your pedalling force if they are not strong enough. To improve these muscles may require weight exercises, loading these particular muscles concentrically over an extended movement, either alone or in combination with other muscle groups.

That is really the only use for weight training in preparation for bicycle racing. Muscle work done in various cycling disciplines is very specific. Speed, duration and sequence of muscle operation while cycling, as well as the kind of nerve commands associated with these movements, are unique to cycling. In addition, the typical cycling motions are really combinations of several overlapping and simultaneous muscle activities, involving a sequence of commands and responses and a combination of muscle contractions that is impossible to duplicate any other way.

There are even significant differences between cycling at high and at low pedalling speeds, on the level and climbing. Consequently, it is unlikely that weight training and other forms of non-bicycle training will develop the various characteristics (of which absolute muscle strength is only one factor) needed for efficient and powerful cycling. This statement may disappoint anyone who has visions of scientific training as involving lots of machines and gadgets. The scientific approach is not reflected in the equipment you use, but in the conscious observation that helps determine which is the most effective way of training. So far, no better machine has been developed for bicycle training than the one you already have: your bicycle.

14
Gearing for an Optimal Pedalling Rate

Chapter 7, which was devoted to handling the bicycle's derailleur system, already indicated the importance of gear selection for an optimal performance when racing or training. In a nutshell, the message was that you should select a lower gear whenever your pedalling rate gets too low. In this chapter we'll take a closer look at the interrelated subjects of gear selection and pedalling rate.

That there must be an optimal pedalling rate – or at least an optimal range of pedalling rates – for a given power output, may be demonstrated by showing that neither an extremely high, nor an extremely low pedalling rate will allow cycling efficiently. First find a conveniently shaped 8-ton rock. Lie on your back with the knees bent and legs up. If you can not only hold it up during one minute, but also manage to straighten your legs, pushing the rock up slowly during that time, as shown in Fig. 14.1 you will be delivering 300 watt at the equivalent of 1 RPM. In that case you could select so high a gear that you will cycle 40 km/h (25 mph) at a pedalling rate of 1 RPM. If not, you will have to gear down for a higher pedalling rate at this same power output.

Next we'll try out whether a very high pedalling rate is possible, even if minimal output is required. You need no more than a bicycle and one of those electronic gadgets that measure the pedalling rate. Remove the chain and get on the bike, supporting yourself against a post or a wall with one hand. Start pedalling and increase the pedalling rate until you have reached say 1000 RPM. If you fail, you have just demonstrated that

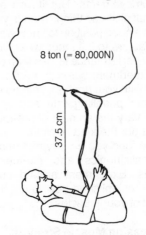

Fig. 14.1 Expending 300 watt at 1 RPM

there must be a physiological restraint that does not allow your body to do work at such a high pedalling rate. You will need to select a gear that allows a lower pedalling rate at any power output or riding speed.

These two examples show only that the extremes are not suitable. Similar, though slightly more sophisticated techniques, repeated thousands of times in different combinations would only serve to reinforce these findings and further narrow the range within the rather broad one just established. I'm not trying to teach you how to establish the optimal rate, but merely make you aware of the existence of such a rate. For racing it will suffice to follow the advice in this chapter to achieve the optimal combination of pedalling rate and gear selection.

A Complex Relationship
In fact, the subject goes beyond pedalling rate and gear selection alone. What we are trying to achieve

is the optimal muscle movement for maximum output. Factors that influence this muscle movement for any given power output level and duration are gear ratio, crank length and pedalling technique. Given the dimensional restraints on the design of the bicycle and the rider's position under international racing regulations, these are the only variables available to the regular racer. For non-sanctioned events, such as the International Human Powered Speed Championships, some other variables may crop up.

We've seen in chapters 11 and 12 that riding a given speed under particular conditions will require a certain amount of power, expressed in watt. To use the same convenient example as before, it will take 300 watt to propel an average size rider at a speed of 40 km/h on a level road. This power must be produced in the muscles of the rider's legs, each of which are extended once for every crank revolution. The first example above demonstrated that it can't be done at 1 RPM.

It really amounts to a kind of leverage effect: this much leg movement (consisting of a certain number of pushes over the length of the down stroke) to achieve that much bike movement. In order to achieve a given riding speed (corresponding to a particular power output), the total effective leverage results from the combination of rider physiognomy, crank length, gearing system and wheel size. This combination must have a particular value if the muscle extension speed and muscle force are to be kept within their most favorable range. Both the average extension speed and the average force can be easily calculated for any power output and riding speed.

The force required on the pedals to generate a given power can be simply stated as:

$$F_p = (P \times c) : (L \times RPM)$$

where:

F_p = average pedal force in N
P = power in watt
c = a constant
    (value approx. 10,000)
L = crank length in mm
RPM = pedalling rate in crank revolutions per minute

Humiliating: Beate Habetz suffering on the hilly Salanches course due to her coaches ignorance of proper gear selection. She had to give up. (Photo H. A. Roth)

Manipulating this formula will allow you to determine the power that can be developed at a given pedalling rate and a limited pedal force:

$P = (F_p \times L \times RPM) : c$

The latter formula shows that a higher power output may be achieved by increasing any one of the following factors:
☐ Pedal force
☐ Crank length
☐ Pedalling rate

To see what the effect is on the rider's ability to develop enough force, I shall now compare two examples based on the first formula. A power output of 300 watt shall be produced with a crank length of 170 mm at pedalling rates of 60 and 120 RPM, respectively. At 60 RPM the average force is:

$F_p = (300 \times 10000) : (170 \times 60) = 294$ N (65 lbf)

At 120 RPM the average force is:

$F_p = (300 \times 10000) : (170 \times 120) = 147$ N (33 lbf)

It will be clear that the latter situation is easier, even though the same power is produced and the same total amount of work is done in each case. Note that the gear ratio is not explicitly included in this relationship. That is because here we are not talking of riding speed, but of the power required to reach that speed under specific conditions. Going uphill, this same power output will be associated with a much lower riding speed (and consequently a lower gear) than on a level road. Let us now look at the available variables.

Changing the Variables
The possible pedal force is a function of your muscle strength and the maximum loading on your joints that will prevent injury. Strong, muscular

cyclists who try to increase power output by increasing this factor excessively may find themselves in hospital for knee surgery sooner or later. Five-time Tour de France winner Bernard Hinault is a case in point. Don't follow his example: he is not such a successful rider *because* of his high force pedalling, but *despite* of it – he would probably have been more successful and healthier if he had learned to develop his power a different way.

The crank length is limited to what is possible on the bike (both with regards to availability and ground clearance) and what is comfortable for the rider. Your physiognomy limits the crank length to something that does not force excessive joint angles. It is primarily a function of upper leg length: 50 % of the length as measured in Fig. 14.2 is generally recommended, although this variable is certainly worth experimenting with on an individual basis. Though most attention is paid to selecting longer cranks, you may need shorter cranks, which gives you less leverage, but may in certain cases be more than compensated through greater comfort.

Most adult bicycles are originally equipped with 170 mm long cranks, and that size corresponds exactly with 50 % of my own upper leg length. They are available from several manu-

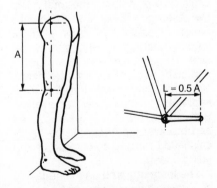

Fig. 14.2 Leg length and crank length

facturers in a range from 165 mm to 185 mm. Since the overall leverage is increased with a longer crank, and the affected factor is probably muscle contraction speed, a slightly higher gear ratio should be chosen whenever the crank length is increased. Conversely, a shorter crank calls for a somewhat lower gear.

Gearing and Pedalling Rate

At the limiting force, the pedalling rate can only be increased by choosing a lower gear. Early research into the optimal pedalling rate for bicycling had been done mainly by scientists who totally ignored the realities of bicycling for speed. They had concentrated all their efforts on finding the pedalling rate at which the human metabolism works most efficiently. Reasonable though this sounds, it ignored the cyclist's need to go fast, rather than to consume minimal quantities of food and oxygen, which is all that was established this way. It was found that there is a relationship between power and most efficient pedalling rate, corresponding to line A in Fig. 14.3.

If this relationship had indeed been valid for high performance as well as for minimal energy consumption, riders using such low pedalling rates

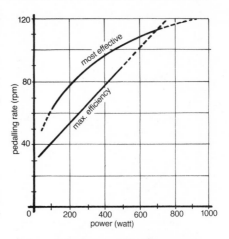

Fig. 14.3 Pedalling rate and efficiency

would have soon dominated the sport. In reality, top performers all use much higher pedalling rates, as the summary in Table 14–I demonstrates for holders of the World Hour record. In the RH column I have adjusted the pedalling rate for a standardized crank length of 170 mm: these are the pedalling rates the riders would have chosen to achieve the same muscle contraction speed if they had used standard 170 mm cranks.

The figures in Table 14–I apply to a very intensive one hour event. This is one case in which the riders take rela-

Table 14-I Pedalling rates and gearing used by World Hour Record holders

year	name	average speed (km/h)	gear developm. (m)	avge ped rate (RPM)	crank length (mm)	avge ped. rate corr. for crank length (RPM)
1942	Coppi	45.84	7.40	105.4	172.5	106.6
1956	Anquetil	46.16	7.40	105.9	171	106.5
1956	Baldini	46.39	7.40	106.6	175	109.7
1957	Rivière	46.92	7.40	107.9	175	111.1
1958	Rivière	47.35	7.55	106.8	175	110.0
1967	Bracke	48.09	7.69	104.2	175	107.3
1969	Ritter	48.63	7.69	105.4	175	108.5
1972	Merckx	49.43	7.93	103.9	177	107.8
1984	Moser	50.81	8.08	104.8	180	111.0
1984	Moser	51.15	8.11	105.1	180	111.3

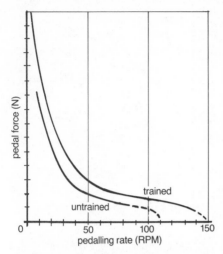

Fig. 14.4 Pedalling force and pedalling rate

the available power curve at its highest point.

Unfortunately, high pedalling rates don't come naturally. The beginning cyclist still has the cadence of walking in his system, and finds it hard to do anything much in excess of 60 RPM. Even on rollers without mechanical resistance the initially possible speed remains quite low, since your entire system – muscles, joints, nerves – have not learned to move this fast, and all your energy seems to get lost in internal friction. Practice pedalling fast on rollers, on the bike in a low gear, on a windload simulator. Gradually, you will raise your maximum pedalling rate to the point where you operate effectively at 120 RPM and higher.

To keep up with the pack, low pedalling rates will be useless in any gear, at least on a level road, as reference to the formula for riding speed from Chapter 7 will prove.

Even in the highest normally available gear of 110 in (development 8.70 m) obtained by combining a 53-tooth chainwheel with a 13-tooth sprocket, your riding speed at 60 RPM would be limited to 31 km/h.

tively little consideration for possible muscle or joint injury, as they must do during regular training and competition. Thus, if anything, the optimal pedalling rates for those more typical conditions must lie even higher. The situation may be explained graphically by means of the three related illustrations Fig. 14.4, 14.5 and 14.6.

Fig. 14.4 shows typical relationships between pedalling force and pedalling rate for trained and untrained cyclists. Force and riding speed have been multiplied to show power on the vertical axis in Fig. 14.5. Comparing the two illustrations shows that, even though lower pedalling rates result in reduced forces, the resulting gain in available power is significant. It also becomes clear that the combined increases in force and speed resulting from training result in significantly higher power.

Finally, Fig. 14.6 compounds the available power curve from Fig. 14.5 with a set of curves representing the power needed to maintain a range of pedalling rates in various gears. Optimizing the pedalling rate for maximum output is simply a matter of picking the required power curve that intersects

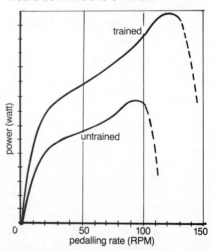

Fig. 14.5 Pedalling rate and power

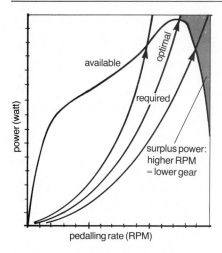

Fig. 14.6 Power, pedalling rate and speed

As for the gears that should be installed on the bike, I suggest aiming a little lower than what seems to have become standard practice in racing circles. Certainly in the first season of racing, there is no need for that 13-tooth sprocket in the back, let alone one with 12 teeth. Choose the entire range a little lower and you will sooner learn to develop a high pedalling rate, since you will not be tempted to ride in the excessively high gears that necessitate low pedalling rates.

Your guideline in all gear selection considerations should never be to copy what some other rider uses under the same conditions. Use your own pedalling rate as a guide. If you can't turn those pedals around at your presently achieved highest comfortable rate, preferably around 120 RPM, you should select a lower gear. If you can't maintain these rates under all but the most extreme conditions for lack of low gears on the bike, it will be in order to install bigger sprockets or smaller chainwheels.

Gears for Climbing
As a quick glance back at Fig. 11.10 (in Chapter 11) will reveal, dramatically

increased power outputs at any one riding speed are required to go uphill. Even on an incline of only 5 %, twice as much power is required to cycle at 20 km/h. To look at it another way, the same power output is associated with very much reduced riding speeds, as shown in Fig. 14.7. It should be no surprise that very much lower gears should be selected for going uphill. You need excess power in addition to that required to ride the same speed under easier conditions.

The situation remains similar to that shown in Fig. 14.6, with the difference that each power output level is now associated with a very much lower riding speed, as Fig. 14.7 demonstrates. Two problems may develop: you may not have gears that are low enough to maintain such a high pedalling rate, and your bicycle may become unstable at too low a riding speed, i.e. on very steep hills. However, as long as the limits of your gearing system are not reached, you will benefit by just staying in the saddle, gearing down and spinning your way up the hill, though macho competitors may sneer at you. In fact, it will be wise to select a freewheel and possibly chainwheels

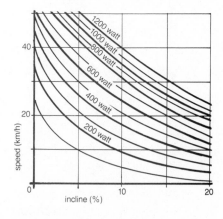

Fig. 14.7 Effect of hill on speed

that allow lower and more widely spread gears for racing or training in hilly terrain.

When the high pedalling rate cannot be maintained, because the lowest available gear just is not low enough, use the technique of honking as described in Chapter 9. Since you are then using an entirely different set of muscles in a different pattern (the muscle work is now performed when raising the body, rather then when pushing down the leg), a much lower pedalling rate is in order. This allows you to select quite a high gear. Though it is perhaps still best to maintain a pedalling rate in excess of 60 RPM if you can, this style of cycling allows the use of much higher gears than otherwise necessary to avoid joint and muscle injury.

Gears for Accelerating

During a race, as well as in many training situations, acceleration will be necessary, i.e. an increase in riding speed. Whenever the riding speed is increased, additional power is required, over and above what is needed to maintain the base speed. What do you do: increase pedalling force and pedalling rate in the same gear, change up or change down?

To accelerate, you have to achieve an excess of power, not required merely to maintain the current speed. The only way to do that is to make sure you are operating in the shaded area of Fig. 14.6, where available power exceeds required power. That shaded area increases in size as a lower gear is selected, and decreases for a higher gear. Clearly then, the message is to change down into a slightly lower gear in order to avail yourself of the surplus power needed to accelerate. On the other hand, you should not select too low a gear either, since that would reduce the maximum possible riding speed, as limited by your maximum pedalling rate. In that case, you'd very soon have to change up to a higher gear again in order to keep up the desired riding speed.

15
Stretching the Limits of Endurance

Bicycle racing in all its most popular forms is an endurance sport par excellence. Any typical major European bicycle race will be over a length well in excess of 100 miles in a single day. Next day there may be another bout like that, if not indeed the same race continues several days. Though American events tend to be somewhat shorter, three or more hours continuously in the saddle are nothing unusual. Even triathletes spend more time on their bikes than on the two other disciplines together.

What would be considered a monumental achievement in any other sport is taken for granted in cycling. At the competitive level cycling is about twice as fast as running. So, since the 26 mile marathon is the toughest and longest event in running, one might expect the toughest bike races to be perhaps 50 – 60 miles, and a typical race rather more like 10 miles. Not so: since over a century much longer distances and durations have dominated competitive cycling, even though short track events have their followers too.

The bicycle lends itself superbly to duration work. Whereas the runner must remain active all the time to continue moving at all, the momentum gained in cycling allows occasional coasting, and riding with significantly reduced power output does not im-

Susan Notorangelo, women's winner of the 1985 Race Across America. It takes enormous determination and endurance to merely complete – let alone win – the world's toughest duration event that takes the riders 3000 miles virtually non-stop from coast to coast. (Photo: Dave Nelson)

mediately result in an equally obvious drop in speed. Since cycling motions are gradual without severe impact or strain, if done correctly, even the longest races need not cause the kind of damage to muscles, joints and tendons that wipes out marathon runners for up to a week after competition.

Long duration events are of course overwhelmingly aerobic. At a low enough level, aerobic activity could be continued almost perpetually, allowing for little more than interruptions for feeding, sleep and some of nature's other demands. That is simply because at such a low level nothing very much more demanding takes place than keeping heart and lungs going to supply the muscles with oxygen and nutrients, while the skeletal muscles themselves are never strained to the point of serious exertion.

Even so, the beginning bicyclist on his first long trip, who probably maintains hardly more than a minimal output level, finds himself stopping for rest brakes at increasingly close intervals. After 30 or 40 miles he may be ready to hang his bike in the willows, if only he could figure out how to get home without it. And this person was not even doing any hard work, whereas in bicycle racing and training you will not only pedal, you will also be expected to put in some real effort. So there must be more to endurance on a bicycle than meets the eye.

Factors in Bicycle Endurance

There are a number of distinct factors that govern endurance while bicycling, which shall be covered in the following sections. Throughout your initial training and racing efforts the emphasis will shift from one factor to the next, as your training progress helps you overcome the restrictions formed by the more elementary ones,

and you start reaching the subsequent higher hurdles. Nobody, except some rarely talented and already fit athlete, achieves all this progress in a single season: be prepared to work on it for at least one year of preparation and one or two seasons of competition.

The very first factor that limits bicycling endurance, even at a minimal output level, is simply the motion of cycling. Three distinct characteristics of various types of motions are at work here. The beginning cyclist referred to in the example has probably overcome none of these yet, even if we assume he has mastered an even more elementary skill, namely that of finding the right posture on the bike, as was outlined in Chapter 6.

First there is simply the repeated movement of the legs, which must become virtually autonomous for really competent cycling. Slowly the beginner will have to build up his skill to progress from a conscious 'push, push' via an equally conscious 'round-and-round' to a smooth and automatic form of this same regular leg movement. Even so, at first it can only be maintained for a limited period of time: to keep it up for many hours demands having practiced it during even more hours at a stretch. It's a skill that can in part be mastered through many hours of riding a wind load simulator, but must also be trained on the road.

Then there is the complex of actions necessary to keep the bicycle balanced and following its intended course. It involves quick decisions and reactions on the road. Things like that occupy the mind of the beginning cyclist to the point of mental and physical overload. As time progresses and as you experience miles and hours in the saddle, many of the necessary thoughts, actions and reactions will leave pre-programmed paths in your nervous system.

Only when that point is reached will your cycling skills have developed to the point where purely physical factors determine your endurance. To achieve that, there is no substitute for riding the bike on the road under a wide range of conditions, ranging from fast and winding mountain roads to densely trafficked urban streets to precipitous trails. The final touch will be added in your first season of racing, closed in by a pack of largely unpredictable and unskilled Category IV riders, seemingly out to kill you.

The final stage of motion control is that associated with taking the right actions to adapt to varying conditions. That's not just a matter of physical environment, but includes your own condition. Once you have gained enough cycling experience, you will be able to almost subconsciously react the right way to signals from your own mind and body, as well as the outside factors demanding a change of gear, a change in the pace, the need for a drink or a bite. Sounds silly perhaps, but incompetent cyclists lose much of their endurance potential thinking about such simple actions, which the more experienced competitor makes correctly without either thought or loss of time. This is another skill that can only be developed with the bike on the road, and requires conscious attention until these things actually become automatic.

Endurance at Increased Output Levels

Even if long distance cycling is largely an aerobic exercise, it must be done at a certain elevated speed, both in competition and in training. To maintain a higher speed, the rider's aerobic capacity must be greater. One reason why beginning cyclists often fail to maintain a speed for any length of time is their inadequate aerobic capacity, which may be hidden by strong muscles and relatively high anaerobic capacity during shorter exercises. Thus many seemingly promising riders fail to maintain the set pace, even though they are remarkably powerful on shorter distances.

To avoid draining anaerobic energy in the early stages of a longer ride, the aerobic potential must be raised as high as possible. Not only would an early recourse to anaerobic systems soon deplete them, their lactic acid generation and oxygen debt problems would actually inhibit the remaining aerobic potential. The result would be a reduction both in speed and in endurance at any speed. Consequently, the cyclist must try to raise his aerobic power so high that there is minimal need to tap the anaerobic

Baronchelli and Hinault, suppressing pain during the 1981 World Championship in the French Alps. (Photo H. A. Roth)

sources. As explained in Chapters 12 and 13, this is achieved by consciously keeping a regular pace, avoiding the need for acceleration. In addition, training many miles at an output level close to the aerobic threshold will tend to raise that limit high enough to avoid passing it many times.

All high intensity work involves a certain amount of anaerobic work as well. This is the ATP-CP system, which is activated whenever higher muscle forces are required to provide the short muscle power peaks. No lactic acid is generated, but this system too is distinct from the regular aerobic one that runs on nothing but blood sugar and oxygen. Like the major anaerobic lactic acid system, it activates the fast-twitch muscle fibers. Training to maintain this work up for extended periods will probably also be a key to endurance work at high power output levels.

It cannot be claimed with absolute certainly, but it is probably possible to increase the effectiveness of this system, if not to actually increase the number of fast-twitch fibers. Requisites are both an optimally functioning enzyme household and frequent practice in using this system. Here are the factors that positively influence the enzyme household controlling the effectiveness of the system:

- ☐ a balanced diet with enough essential vitamins and minerals;
- ☐ pre-race warm-up and proper clothing for temperature control;
- ☐ sufficient liquid intake before as well as during the activity;
- ☐ a positive mental attitude.

Long Distance Cycling and Pain

Cycling far and fast may hurt. It is part of the macho image of bicycle racing, but it is also true that some people either do not suffer pain or have achieved, not (as some think) to ignore the pain, but to prevent it through training. Limiting the pain you feel will probably greatly increase your endurance at any higher output.

The pain threshold is the amount of exposure to pain where it is first noticed. It is probably at the same level for all people, man or woman, cyclists or not. But there are degrees of hurting: putting your hand in boiling water causes more pain than it does in 60 degrees C (140 degrees F), though the pain threshold is exceeded in either case. Somewhere beyond this threshold there must be a pain limit, beyond which one cannot endure pain, however much you grit your teeth.

That upper limit can be changed to a higher or lower level. When you're sick you are more sensitive, whereas either a positive outlook or fear may enable you to endure more. Then there is medication (or drugs, to call a spade a bloody shovel), primarily a group of alkaloids referred to as opiates. As it turns out, the human brain produces a form of proteins, known as neuropeptides, that – though different in chemical makeup – are identical in their spatial form and structure. At least one of these, beta-endorfine, has the same pain suppressing effect as e.g. morphine.

People with high levels of beta-endorfine are more resistant to pain. It seems many women have higher levels of this than most men (that makes reference to toughness as being a macho quality rather ironic), and there are significant differences between individuals of the same sex. But even within the same body the level is not constant, increasing with extended exercise, though it falls off again after a couple of hours. Though not definitely proven, it appears that a regular training regimen tends to increase the normal level of beta-endorfine in the blood. Thus, one way to attain greater endurance at a level which would at first hurt, is to train regularly for extended periods of time. This is additional to the direct training effect that increases the available power regardless of the pain level.

The Bonk as a Limit to Endurance
During extended rides at high output levels many riders experience a point where their body just lets them down. This experience is referred to as the bonk and feels at least as unsettling as it sounds: muscle and stomach cramps, feelings of heaviness in the legs and emptiness in the stomach, and a general giddy weakness. To endure on a long tough ride, you must avoid reaching this point, or at least to overcome it quickly once it does arrive.

Though popular belief amongst cyclists has it that this phenomenon is simply the result of the depletion of glucose in the blood, it is in fact much more complex. Besides, it is not merely a physical problem, since much of it must be attributed to loss of coordination in the brain and nervous system (this being indeed the result of glucose depletion, since that is the only form of energy the brain can use). The following causes may be involved, either alone or, more likely, in some combination:
☐ dehydration
☐ overheating
☐ low blood glucose
☐ depletion of muscle glycogen
☐ excessive lactic acid level
☐ loss of minerals or electrolytes

All these factors have something to do with nutrition. In addition to following the advice in Chapter 20 on nutrition, in particular taking enough liquids, especially in hot weather, your physical and mental fitness also has a great effect. Even the healthy, well trained athlete may at some point experience the bonk, but only after a much longer period of hard riding. Train at least once a week over the maximum distance of your longest race. That training ride must be absolved at a comparable level of exertion to prevent this humiliating experience from striking in a race.

Though prevention is the only true cure, there are a few things you can do when it hits you. When you do feel the bonk, don't try to push yourself harder, but choose a lower gear without speeding up the pedalling rate. Your riding speed and muscle force will fall back to a more comfortable level. Once you recover, you may be able to make up for lost time. Take isotonic liquid nourishment, containing adequate quantities of sugar and salt: 2–2.5% sugar and a teaspoonful of table salt per liter (about one quart). Half a bottle of this mixture every 15 minutes or so (or about half that quantity to prevent the problem in the first place) may do the trick. It won't give you magical endurance or strength, and is better to do before you reach this point, but it will relatively soon bring your nervous system under control, allowing you at least to use what physical strength you still have.

16
Basic Training Theory

The ultimate purpose of training is to improve performance. Training theory is the summary of the results of investigations into the various ways this goal may be reached. Eventually, these theoretical findings must be turned into practical training methods and adapted to what suits the individual athlete as it fits in with his or her other activities. Chapters 17 and 18 are devoted to the practical training methods for on-the-road and indoor training, respectively. The aspect of planning for individual needs will be covered in Chapter 19. The present chapter, on the other hand, provides the theoretical basis.

The overall concept of training is not limited to physical exercise alone. Correctly, it should include all methods that lend themselves to the improvement of athletic performance. Though most of the attention in this and the two following chapters is rightly focussed on various exercises, other aspects must be considered too. To give but one example, consider that the most universal measure of aerobic capacity, and indirectly of duration cycling performance, is VO_2max. As explained in Chapter 12, this measure relates oxygen capacity per unit of time to body weight. Consequently a change in body weight will affect VO_2max. You may well be able to increase VO_2max by e.g. 5 % if you can reduce your body weight by the same percentage, assuming you were carrying unneeded fat, as probably 90 % of all Americans are.

Fundamental to all training theory are the identification of trainability and the various specific training effects. The former will help you identify where

and when training will offer the greatest improvement. The latter allows you to establish which methods must be used to develop specific aspects of overall performance. Primarily, the overall training effect will be an improved performance due to exercise. This can be represented graphically as shown in Fig. 16.1: the improvement is quite dramatic at first, then tapers off as you get closer to your limits as they apply to the specific ability exercised and the method used. An important distinction would be between those effects that influence the athlete's overall condition and those that work on specific discipline-related abilities.

Training Effects
Perhaps the most essential factor to improve is the overall condition – certainly during the first period of training for bicycle racing or triathlon. This can be seen as the ability to perform any

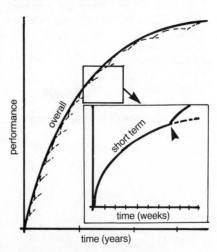

Fig. 16.1 General training effect

kind of work through the output of physiological power. That may be either aerobic or anaerobic or, more typically, a combination of the two that matches the demands of the sport discipline. In road racing and triathlon we are talking primarily, though not exclusively, of aerobic power. Anaerobic power is most needed for sprinting, both as a distinct track discipline and as the essential component that allows a road racer to get ahead of the pack, catch up with it or with an escaped competitor or storm up a steep hill.

Discipline-specific training effects have more to do with the particular movements peculiar to bicycling. Though most of these are common to all bicycle riding at speed, some can be distinguished according to the kind of racing for which they are important. In the following I shall keep the discussion as general as possible, merely

reminding the reader to consider each time which particular effects are the more important ones for his or her personal situation. In this connection it should be pointed out that it is established practice in bicycle training to train for all possible types of racing. Though it may be appropriate to emphasize certain skills, you will probably never be successful in cycling by training only for one specialty or the other.

Going from the general to the more specific, a list of desired training effects would include the following:

☐ increase cardiorespiratory capacity to maximize aerobic output
☐ raise the anaerobic threshold
☐ increase anaerobic power generation potential
☐ increase endurance potential
☐ increase efficiency of movement
☐ increase power and speed potential of essential muscles
☐ increase power of restraining muscles

Cyclo cross is an excellent way to diversify training. Taken at the 1985 Nationals in Santa Cruz. (Photo Darryl Skrabak)

Somewhere in the preceding chapters each of these points has cropped up. Here we shall look at them more specifically, with the purpose of establishing and systemizing the training techniques most suitable for each of these desired effects.

Consider, though, that the total is not necessarily the sum of the parts: it may be more or less. In some cases, increasing one aspect may have an immediate positive effect on total performance. In other cases it does not work out that simply. Developing muscle force, for example, may not have any effect on your cycling performance if that is not the limiting factor, but e.g. your capacity to perform aerobic work. Thus it should be obvious that you must work on all effects simultaneously, always emphasizing the factor that limits your performance most.

Specificity

One particularly important condition for effective training – and also one that is frequently ignored by those who are looking for shortcuts – is specificity of training. Simply put, it amounts to training just the kind of thing you will be doing in a race. To be a bicycle racer, train on a bicycle. To train for long distances, ride long distances in training, to race in the mountains, train in the mountains. I realize that racing conditions cannot always be duplicated in training. In that case, use some imagination to come up with good simulations of the conditions sought.

Overload, Compensation, Rest and Recovery

Before continuing to the individual effects to be trained, I should mention these very important factors. Overload is the basis of many effective training techniques: to improve your time in a race over a specific distance,

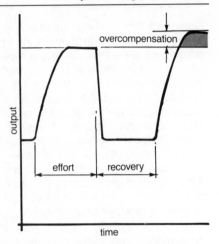

Fig. 16.2 Overcompensation effect

aim at training both at a higher pace than you can presently handle (over the given distance) and over a higher distance (at the given speed). This may seem to contradict the specificity requirement emphasized in the preceding section, and it does if you train over distances that are a lot longer or shorter, under conditions that are very different. You may have to experiment around a little, but it is probably safe to say that distances that are up to 10 % longer and speeds that are up to 5 % higher are reasonable.

The compensation effect is the ability of the body's systems to recover from an elevated load by overcompensating to the point that it allows a subsequent higher output level. This same effect is at work in mechanisms ranging from short term interval training to peaking programs during weeks preceding a major event. It is also the same principle that plays a role in e.g. blood doping and the more harmless practice of carbohydrate loading.

In each of these methods, the body is first depleted in a particularly strenuous regimen, followed by a period of recovery. Before the system reaches its normal condition, a period of increased capacity is reached, and the principle of all these methods is to exploit this period. The principle is shown in Fig. 16.2. The benefit lies in the ability to accept a higher workload during that time, allowing e.g. increased training intensity (in the short run) or a superior competitive performance (in the long run), the ability to accept more oxygen (in the case of blood doping or altitude training), or the ability to store greater quantities of glucose (in the case of carbohydrate loading).

The recovery period between the last peak and the subsequent increased performance is quite individual and must be established by experiment for each rider. Somewhere a balance must be established, where the overcompensation resulting from the preceding exertion is still significant, while at the same time the body is rested enough to work efficiently, as suggested by Fig. 16.3.

It has been found that recovery is also necessary between very extensive training or racing days. Avoid training very hard or long on consecutive days, unless it is specifically geared towards depletion in connection with the long-term compensation effect. To achieve optimal performance, the entire training and racing program must be periodized to achieve

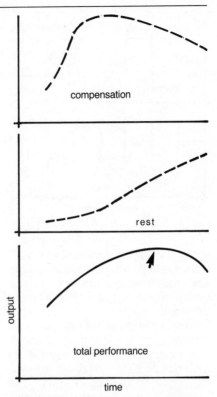

Fig. 16.3 Rest and compensation effects compounded

something as shown in Fig. 16.4 and Fig. 16.5, representing the long term (macro) and short term (micro) cycles, respectively. This system should also consider the phenomenon shown

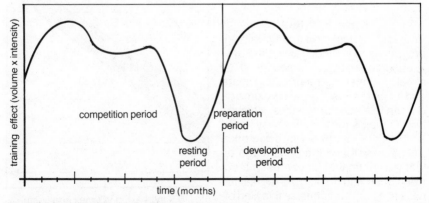

Fig. 16.4 Periodization: the macro cycle

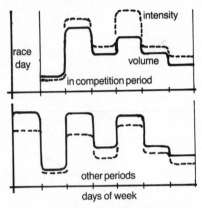

Fig. 16.5 Periodization: the micro cycle

in the short cycle curves of Fig. 16.1: when the improvement due to training one system reaches the limit, the next period should set in with a different emphasis.

Rest is also a form of recovery, and it plays a role in training and preparation. Actually, a sleepless night is not much less effective in providing physical recovery than deep sleep. The problem is more a psychological one, which may be minimized now that you know that it is not as physiologically devastating to have a lousy night's sleep. It may also be a consolation to know that it is not the last night, but rather the one preceding that one, which has the greatest effect on your fitness on race day.

Aerobic Output
Probably the first step in any training program is to work on raising the athlete's aerobic output potential. It is simply a matter of strengthening heart and lungs to allow a greater volume of oxygen to reach the muscles. Increasing $\dot{V}O_2$max is the technical way to describe it, and Fig. 16.6 shows how both $\dot{V}O_2$max itself and the percentage of that maximum that can be used tend to increase with training. All regular fitness programs emphasize this kind of work, since it is perhaps the best indi-cator of general health and fitness. If you are a runner or have regularly participated in another sport, chances are this is not your limiting factor. If, on the other hand, you tend to get out of breath before your muscles begin to ache and strain, or your normal resting pulse is high and increases rapidly with exercise, you probably need to work most on your aerobic output.

Regularly measure your pulse, either at the wrist or just to the side of the Adam's apple (count for 15 seconds and multiply by four to get BPM or beats per minute) and keep a record of it. Take one daily reading before getting up and one shortly after getting up before doing any strenuous work each morning. If the latter reading is regularly over 70, or exceeds the first reading just as regularly by more than 7, you almost certainly need a lot of aerobic training to lower it. If, on the other hand, the difference between the two varies greatly from one day to the next you may be suffering from overtraining – see Chapter 10.

As you become more accomplished as a bicycle racer, the resting pulse should gradually go down quite a bit. A full first season of training should decrease it to something like 50–60.

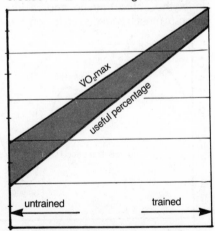

Fig. 16.6 Increasing $\dot{V}O_2$max and useful percentage due to training

Values of 35–45 beats per minute are nothing unusual amongst top cyclists. But don't feel you must get down to that same point, since different people may reach their optimum performance at widely different heart rates.

Aerobic power is increased by doing work at a relatively high aerobic level for continuous periods of at least 20 minutes at least 4 times a week. If it's merely a matter of increasing basic aerobic fitness, training need not necessarily be done by cycling, although that will additionally improve your bicycle performance through other effects as well. This relatively low level in terms of duration and frequency may be adequate to reach basic fitness, but doing more work more frequently will prepare you for real training a lot faster. When you start bicycle training seriously, much longer training periods and distances will be required to have any substantial effect at the elevated performance level.

Either way, the aerobic training program will gradually allow the system to bring more oxygen to the muscles at a slower heart rate. Your resting pulse will decrease and you will feel better, because any exertion has less of an impact on your heart rate. The effect of endurance training is most evident on what may be called respi-

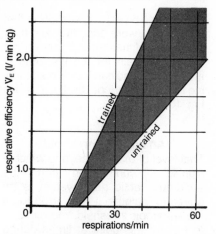

Fig. 16.7 The effect of training on respirative efficiency

ration efficiency, as shown in Fig. 16.7: it lowers the number of respirations required to achieve any given volume of air taken in by the lungs. How to go about it in detail will be discussed under the heading *Aerobic Training Methods* below, and in chapters 17 and 18.

It may be interesting to note that the effect of this kind of elementary training (as well as that of several other forms of training), is not lost as easily as it is gained. Once you have reached such a level of physical fitness, very little work may be adequate to maintain it. Besides, after an interrup-

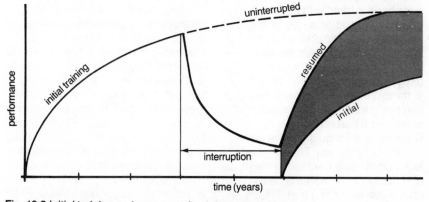

Fig. 16.8 Initial training and recovery after interrupted training

tion of up to 5 years, it was found that people who were once fit reach their old level of fitness much faster than those who train for the first time in their lives or who had interrupted training for longer periods, as illustrated in Fig. 16.8.

Anaerobic Threshold

That level of exertion beyond which a significant contribution from the anaerobic lactic acid system is required to maintain it is referred to as the anaerobic threshold. You will want to exceed this point at times during your training regimen, because one of the most effective ways to train is pushing this level up higher by exceeding it frequently. In addition, it is assumed that anaerobic capacity itself can also be increased by exercising at such high output levels. Fig. 16.9 shows the effect of anaerobic training on the anaerobic threshold: the outward shift of the curve representing lactic acid concentration in the blood will bring increasingly higher output levels (here represented by % VO_2max) within the range of physical comfort.

There are several objective (though perhaps not conclusive) methods to establish whether the threshold has been exceeded. Since anaerobic work goes hand in hand with the generation of surplus lactic acid, an analysis of the blood for lactic acid concentration will tell whether anaerobic work has been performed. Alternatively, the oxygen consumption can be used as a measure, the underlying assumption being that anaerobic work sets in whenever a certain oxygen consumption rate (itself a guide to the work intensity) is exceeded. The simplest objective method is measuring the pulse and comparing it with the base pulse rate, again assuming that this is a reliable measure of the work load.

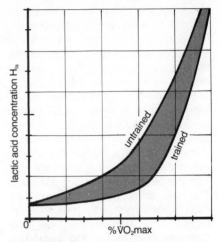

Fig. 16.9 Anaerobic training and anaerobic threshold

To complicate things, the anaerobic threshold is not fixed at a given power output level or its corresponding oxygen consumption rate or heart rate. And as for the other method, lactic acid is not the thing you can easily measure anywhere but in a fancy laboratory. Consequently, I favor a seemingly less objective, but ultimately sensitive and conclusive technique of establishing whether you have reached the anaerobic range: it's all in the way you feel.

Learn to listen to your body. Ride frequent intervals at speeds close to your absolute maximum and establish how it feels. If it doesn't hurt and you recover quickly after an increase in the pace, you probably haven't reached your momentary anaerobic threshold. Eventually, you'll be able to feel when you are there and when you are not. I do suggest you reinforce these subjective findings by taking your pulse occasionally. Beyond a certain pulse rate you are probably doing anaerobic work, though this figure is also affected by other variables, and changes in the long run as you become more thoroughly trained. Even though this is not the ultimate foolproof indicator, as many people seem to think, it is convenient to establish and reliable enough as long as you correlate the readings to the way you feel from time to time.

Your momentary threshold is neither a certain riding speed, nor a certain pulse rate or oxygen intake, nor a certain lactate concentration in the blood. Much less is it the speed that was reached with any of those values some other day. Instead, it is the level where you feel your breathing apparatus can't keep up with the demand for energy and you're hurting. People who concentrate too much on watching their speedometer or measuring their pulse are basing today's assumption on yesterday's performance, which may not be right; they may be either too low or too high. Once you are attuned to your body, you'll always be close to right when you use that as a basis.

Anaerobic Training
Anaerobic training takes place when workouts regularly exceed the anaerobic threshold. Since it overloads the body's systems and raises the lactic acid level in the blood, anaerobic work hurts. After every such workout you will require a recuperation period. As was explained in Chapter 15, regular high-intensity and duration training of any kind will tend to reduce your sensitivity to pain, and consequently anaerobic workouts gradually become less painful, allowing you to use this method of work more and more frequently. Generally, anaerobic workouts constitute shortish intervals of very high intensity work during an otherwise aerobic ride. The intervals may constitute either faster pedalling at the same resistance, or a higher resistance at the same pedalling rate. The former may be referred to as speed intervals, the latter as force intervals.

It cannot be said with certainty whether anaerobic training actually increases your anaerobic capacity, whether it just shifts the anaerobic threshold, or does both. Fact is that virtually all riders make faster progress when their training includes anaerobic work than when it doesn't. Anaerobic training sessions also tax the muscles very much more than aerobic work does. This has the added benefit that the muscle strength is trained more effectively than with most aerobic methods.

Anaerobic training is not for everybody at all times. It is neither suitable for the beginning cyclist in his first season, nor is it wise to take too much of it at any time. It is hard work and should never be done on consecutive days. After avoiding it altogether during the first year, it will be wise to take a brake from anaerobic training during the two—three months period of relative rest, and only get back into doing this kind of work after you have trained aerobically for at least four weeks.

Endurance Training
In Chapter 15 the factors that possibly limit a bicyclist's ability to handle long duration work were outlined. Obviously, training to increase endurance must include actual long duration rides, but probably not as many as used to be assumed. If your training schedule includes enough other kinds of workouts, one really long ride a week will be adequate. This ride should be at least as long as the toughest race you intend to compete in, and should approximate racing conditions by including more intensive periods of differing duration, ranging from 10 second sprints to 10 minute high speed or high force periods. This is one kind of workout that cannot be done anywhere but on a bicycle on the road:

you'd go insane trying to absolve the equivalent of 90 miles on a windload simulator.

Technique Training

Technique training improves the fluency of movement. One of the most significant effects of initial training is to make the required repetitive movement more fluent and seemingly automatic. When this point is reached, much less energy is wasted than when the legs have to be consciously turned. Technique training is especially required in the initial phase of any training program, and also during the first six weeks of any season if there has been a resting period preceding.

Your pedalling work must become unconscious, yet it will require a lot of very conscious attention to a smooth pedalling style to achieve that. One excellent way is riding a bicycle with a fixed gear (i.e. without a freewheel), using a gear so low that a pedalling rate of at least 100 RPM can be maintained on virtually all terrain encountered. Just the same, training to improve the fluency of movement must not be limited to just pedalling a bicycle, since there are other factors that may hinder your pedalling fluency, but are not easily affected while riding. Stretching and calisthenic exercises, as well as rest, adequate warm-up and post-ride massage all tend to positively influence this factor.

Leg Muscle Training

Since most of the work you will do as a cyclist comes out of the various leg muscles that were described in some detail in Chapter 13, these are the muscles to develop. This involves more than merely making the muscles bigger and stronger. It is not bulk that counts in cycling – otherwise every accomplished body-builder should be a better cyclist than most top racers. Leg muscle training must mainly be specific, i.e. it must duplicate the speed and the form of movement of actual cycling. Only this will train the muscles to be good at doing exactly that kind of work that will be demanded from them in cycling.

The amount of muscle fiber is the elementary measure of a muscle's potential strength. This can be developed by doing enough cycles of concentric muscle work at a high enough force level. But it is only one of several factors of importance in this respect. The sequence of activity of the various muscles, the contraction speed and the typical range of contraction are all at least as important. Unlike basic strength, these aspects cannot be trained anywhere but on a bicycle – be that on the road or on a windload simulator.

All muscle training exercises should duplicate as closely as possible each of the specific kinds of work that will be demanded in competition. In order to increase sprinting strength, only very fast anaerobic work will do the trick, while aerobic work at a high enough resistance level will improve the kind of muscle strength that is mainly associated with the red slow twitch fibers that are used primarily during aerobic power generation. Do not expect miracles though: if your genetic makeup includes a low proportion of fast twitch fibers, no amount of high intensity work will turn you into an excellent sprinter. You may be flogging a dead horse, so monitor your progress and taper off if you are not improving.

Training of Restraining Muscles

These are the muscles that are not used concentrically during cycling very much, but help by countering forces created with the leg muscles. The arms, shoulders, back and stomach muscles fall in this category. Since they are not used concentrically, they will not get strengthened during cycling, even though they may limit your performance. These muscles can only be strengthened through weight training and calisthenics or other gymnastic exercises. In addition to exercising the muscles for greater strength, stretching and calisthenics may be useful to achieve greater suppleness in these and other muscles.

A basic understanding of which muscle does what and how certain exercises affect a specific muscle will be necessary. Reference to the explanation in Chapter 13 and the specific instructions in Chapter 18 will take care of that. Remember, only the muscles that are contracted will be strengthened: to strengthen the stomach muscles, no amount of body bending will help, unless you pull up forcefully. Triathletes probably do not need as much of various gymnastic exercises if their training schedule involves enough swimming, since the muscles used concentrically in swimming are largely the same ones that are loaded isometrically in cycling.

Basic Training Methods

In the following sections you will be shown the basic training methods used to achieve the various training effects described above. Each section will summarize the groups of training techniques – both on and off the bike – that are based on the same training principle. The specific training techniques or exercises will be covered in more detail in chapters 17 and 18, followed by Chapter 19, which is devoted to selecting an overall schedule that meets your specific personal needs.

Aerobic Training Methods

Aerobic exercises are all those forms of training in which the body is not forced to operate beyond the anaero-

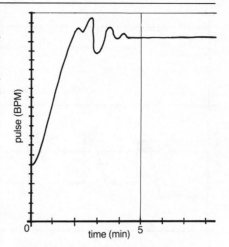

Fig. 16.10 Pulse variation after start of exercise

bic threshold and hence no surplus lactic acid is generated. This group of exercises can include both short and long duration work, both on and off the bike. They are most suitable to increase general aerobic power (if performed close to the anaerobic threshold, even if not for very long periods) and endurance (if continued for a long period of time). The rule of thumb to establish whether an aerobic exercise is effective is the pulse rate. If anaerobic work is not desired, the pulse, measured in beats per minute, should not exceed the maximum level determined by the following formula:

$$BPM_{max} = 0.85 \times (220 - \text{age in years})$$

For a maximum increase in $\dot{V}O_2max$ and aerobic power, the pulse rate, though remaining below the value calculated above, must exceed the level determined by the following formula:

$$BPM_{min} = 0.75 \times (220 - \text{age in years})$$

During the early stages of exercise the pulse rate tends to increase more or less as shown in Fig. 16.10. Consequently, it should be clear that the pulse must be measured after at least five minutes of exercise.

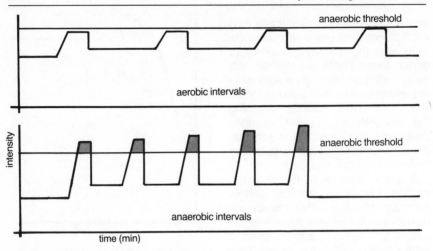

Fig. 16.11 Interval training

Anaerobic Training Methods

These include all exercises – again both on and off the bike – in which the surplus lactic acid generating anaerobic system is activated. Their benefit lies in an increase of overall anaerobic capacity and probably in an increased immunity to the pain that causes the lesser athlete to give up. In addition, muscle strength may be increased with this form of work whenever it is more geared towards high muscle force than toward high speed work. This kind of training should not be attempted until after a satisfactory basic level of fitness and a smooth riding style have been reached: don't do it in your first season.

Anaerobic work can not be maintained for a long time. As mentioned before, it may be most reliable to learn to judge by the way you feel whether the anaerobic level has been reached. Since all anaerobic work is of a very short duration, and the heart doesn't respond consistently to this kind of load variation, there is no point in trying to monitor your pulse in an attempt to establish whether you are working anaerobically. Paying attention to the way your body reacts, you should be able to determine subjectively whether you are doing something not just harder, but quite differently than you are doing when working aerobically.

Interval Training Methods

These methods are based on the overcompensation effect discussed earlier in this chapter. They include any forms of exercise that include a repeated increase and subsequent reduction of workload from a lower aerobic base rate of power. Each interval training session consists of a number of repeated exercises. One high output period with one recovery period is referred to as a repetition, while a sequence of perhaps five or more of these repetitions is referred to as one set. A full interval training session may consist of several of these sets, separated by longish continuous aerobic rides.

Interval training may be either aerobic or anaerobic, even though the recovery periods are always aerobic. In anaerobic interval training the high power surges are largely anaerobic, whereas in aerobic interval training the higher load periods are still aerobic and of a longer duration (several minutes, as opposed to less than thirty seconds each). Both techniques lend themselves equally well to cycling on the open road and to work on the windload simulator or ergometer. The very intensive anaerobic intervals should not be attempted by a beginning racer who has not yet developed a mature riding style and adequate aerobic strength.

Any kind of interval training exploits the body's tendency to overcompensate after intensive work, thus allowing an even higher level of performance in the next period of increased output. Fig. 16.11 illustrates the effect as it applies to interval training. In other words, these methods simply enable you to train at a higher level of intensity, be that only for short periods. This is also the reason beginning racers should be careful to avoid overtraining, which may result if too much high intensity work, is included before the racer is ready for it.

The training effect on muscle condition, staying power, aerobic power, as well as probably anaerobic threshold and anaerobic power (in the case of anaerobic interval work) are quite dramatic. This should make this form of training the mainstay of any program for people whose time is limited. This is certainly so once they have reached a basically adequate level of aerobic fitness, staying power and cycling technique through a more varied training program during the first few years.

Force Training Methods

That's a term not used much elsewhere, but I consider it essential to distinguish this general category of training from weight training, which is but one particular form of it. It is nothing but specific muscle training. The muscles are strengthened by being used concentrically at a high force level, whether that is on the bike in sprinting or climbing, or by means of weights or an exercising machine. The underlying principle is that a muscle increases in size and strength when repeatedly used concentrically for a protracted time at a level close to its maximum force.

Since the muscles should not be merely strengthened, but must also be developed as specifically as possible for the particular movements and speeds of bicycling, I feel weight training should only be done if it is supervised by a very competent coach. Fine for athletes selected to train at a famous training center, but you and I had better refrain from experimenting with weights and exercisers. Use your bike instead, though always only for relatively brief periods, separated by longer periods of cycling at lower workloads and in lower gears. Muscles are strengthened on the bike by pushing very hard in a relatively high gear for pure strength, selecting a lower gear and spinning faster at maximum workload for a more bicycle-specific muscle speed training effect.

As discussed in the section *Training of Restraining Muscles*, above, the non-active (i.e. restraining) muscles must be treated differently. Training restraining muscles, such as those of the arms, shoulders, back and stomach, cannot be done on the bike. It must be done in the form of weight training, although various kinds of calisthenic exercises may be equally effective, and the latter or stretching will improve the general condition of these muscles.

Technique Training Methods

These include any kind of work to improve the fluency and efficiency of movement, both on the road and on the windload simulator. The latter has the advantage of allowing close observation (use a mirror if you can't round up a competent live observer). Pedalling unconsciously fast and smoothly is what you are trying to achieve, and doing the same very consciously is what will get you there. This form of training is much neglected, especially by those who work without a competent coach. It should be practiced as much as possible during the first year and always in the early preparation period of each subsequent year.

Other Exercises

This category includes any exercises that can be done in places ranging from your living room to a gym without either a bike or any other mechanical aids. These exercises must also be done with some knowledge of what can be achieved and how to do it, for which reason there are detailed instructions in Chapter 18. Much overrated in the US are stretching exercises. Though these can be used effectively, they don't do anything that can't be achieved doing e.g. calisthenics with less chance of doing something wrong. Breathing exercises achieve both an increase of the effective lung capacity through repeated use when inhaling and exhaling more fully than is usually done, and an improved general feeling of wellbeing. Yoga exercises can also be of benefit for this same purpose, for which you are referred to any book on that subject.

Personalized Training

Before we shall go on to specific training methods in the next two chapters, let me give you some basic advice. You are the one to do the training and you are the one to decide how to go about it. Perhaps the most serious mistake to make is blindly copying someone else's training schedule or methods. Don't think that any kind of training will equally benefit all cyclists. Train to strengthen your own weaknesses, but also learn to emphasize the development of those aspects that best exploit your natural inclinations. If you seem to be a good sprinter, there will be no point in wasting hundreds of hours trying to become equally good at long distance work. In that case it will be better to merely develop your endurance ability to reach the level where you can keep up with the pack, then make the most of your sprinting ability by training that to the utmost.

The other very individual aspect is the total intensity of training you are able to handle. Don't try to train like a professional, or even like a top national amateur, if you are not. To compete successfully at the level of Category II or III Senior, you can probably get by admirably with a training schedule that includes less than half the number of hours that are often recommended. You will probably need one long ride each week, but an intelligent use of more intensive training techniques and a prudent division of your available time will allow you to minimize the hours spent training to something manageable for a person with a normal professional and social life.

17
On-the-Bike Training Methods

In this chapter we shall finally get down to brass tacks with some practical training procedures. Presented here are those techniques that must be carried out on the road, followed in the next chapter by advice for indoor training. In Chapter 19 we'll put it all together, showing you how to make up your own individual training schedule. If you have absorbed the preceding chapters, you have most of the information needed to understand the effects each of the techniques here described has on specific aspects of your performance potential.

Any training methods that can be done on the bike have the potential advantage of allowing greater specificity than most other forms of exercises. As explained in Chapter 16, specificity – i.e. the quality of training in approaching the actual kind of movements and other characteristics to be developed most closely – is essential for effective progress. It will be worthwhile to always keep this requirement in mind when selecting the specific training exercises, whether with regards to speed, pedalling force, terrain type or distance. Emphasizing a particular element in each training ride will also be important: to give an example, pay attention to technique to improve technique.

On-the bike training methods include several broad categories. These can each be divided into a number of distinct exercises, that are each based on the same training principle. In the following sections the various specific exercises within their respective training methods shall each be explained. Five broad categories of training methods can be distinguished:

☐ LSD or aerobic training
☐ Aerobic interval training
☐ Anaerobic interval training
☐ Technique training
☐ Control method training

None of these methods alone, nor even all of them together, make a satisfactory comprehensive training program. Even if all your bike training is done on the road, in which case you may be tempted to ignore the advice on off-the-bike training in the next chapter, you should not forget to include several essential supplementary activities that fall outside the preceding list.

In the first place, every strenuous ride for training or competition should be preceded by a low intensity warm-up period of at least 5 minutes, considerably longer in colder weather. This will condition your joints and muscles and activate the enzyme systems that are essential for muscle effectiveness. In addition, some breathing and gymnastic or stretching exercises should be included in any daily training program, as well as massage after hard long distance riding. Refer to Chapter 18 for details of these techniques.

LSD or Aerobic Training

LSD stands for long slow (or steady) distances. Don't take that S for slow too literally: your speed should at least suffice to work up a sweat, even in cold weather. This used to be the staple diet of bicycle racers and fitness seekers alike. It consists of nothing more than riding a considerable distance at a relatively high but aerobic output level. Its effect is an increase in aerobic capacity and endurance, mainly through a training induced increase of the cardiorespiratory capacity and its efficiency.

Done over relatively short distances (20–40 minutes duration), this is basic fitness work. Carried out over longer distances, it is still the aerobic mainstay of most training programs and is particularly useful during the early part of any season. Although the way you feel can be a reliable indicator of the power expended, the heart rate in BPM can be used to determine whether you are working hard enough. Use the following familiar formulas from Chapter 16 as upper and lower limits. The pulse should be measured after at least five minutes of intensive work (i.e. after at least ten minutes of riding, including five minutes of warm-up):

$$BPM_{min} = 0.75 \times (220 - \text{age in years})$$

$$BPM_{max} = 0.85 \times (220 - \text{age in years})$$

In an elementary fitness training program the beginning athlete should absolve a twenty minute session of this at least 4 or 5 times a week until the rest of his training program has reached the point of including a much greater amount of work. This won't be anything like enough to qualify as endurance training, and is only a fraction of the distances covered later in the training program. It is merely the simplest way to reach an aerobic basis from which to prepare for bicycle training for the person who is not adequately fit to start out seriously. Triathletes are often tempted to do most of their bike training this way. So they should in the early stages; but once they have developed riding style and stamina, they too should include some of the other bicycle training methods in their schedule.

To increase aerobic power once this elementary level of cardiorespiratory fitness has been reached, maintain LSD rides on your schedule at least twice a week. The distance should be increased gradually until at least once a week your training ride slightly exceeds the longest distance you expect to ride in competition. Preferably such an ostensible LSD ride should be spiced with small doses of some of the other elements of your training program. Pay close attention to riding style and pedalling rate during these rides. Initially maintain a relatively low gear and gradually raise your pedalling rate until you can spin for hours on end at 120 RPM. Only after you have reached that, should you very gradually start choosing slightly higher gears to increase speed, maintaining the same high pedalling rate.

Aerobic Interval Training

This method may also be referred to as extensive interval training, as opposed to the intensive form of interval training that includes brief high power anaerobic efforts. It consists of a relatively long aerobic ride, interrupted repeatedly by periods of increased intensity. During most of the ride your pulse should remain below the lower limit of the formula above, while you should approach the maximum aerobic rate during the intervals. If all is well, the body's tendency to overcompensate after periods of hard work will have an effect similar to the one illustrated in Fig. 16.2 in Chapter 16. In each subsequent interval you may be able to work more intensively, leading to a more rapid increase of aerobic power, muscle strength and endurance. Ideal training for time trialists and triathletes, but also very valuable for all other road racers.

Aerobic interval training methods include any form of aerobic riding characterized by differentiated speed or intensity. This may range from structured rides, planned out in advance, to occasional speeding in higher gears or faster spins in the same gear, to the accidental changes forced by riding in hilly terrain or in heavy traffic. The latter technique is only recommended for those who have enough traffic sense and experience to be safe in traffic and who have enough self discipline to stay within the aerobic range, even if the next traffic light will turn red on you if you don't speed like the devil. Fartlek is a fancy Scandinavian term for the unstructured form of aerobic interval training.

Aerobic interval training is the next stage once you have mastered the LSD technique. After the first season it should form the aerobic backbone of your training program. A 20–30 mile ride like this, consisting of perhaps five faster or tougher repetitions of 1–1.5 miles each, separated by easier periods of 2–3 miles each, will

Anaerobic workout: Claudia Lommatzsch and Annemarie van Vierstrate in a finishing sprint. (Photo H. A. Roth)

probably be more effective aerobic training than an LSD ride over twice the distance. Since it is harder to care for proper technique while doing this work, it is not recommended for your first season or the early part of any subsequent season. Later in your racing career, aerobic intervals may gradually replace essentially all LSD work after the first month of each season, except the weekly long ride.

Anaerobic Interval Training
That's aerobic rides, repeatedly interrupted by very fast or hard intervals. They help increase anaerobic strength, improve sprinting and climbing performance, and raise the anaerobic threshold. To the casual observer this may seem like the same thing as the type described above, but there are some significant differences: the work intervals are shorter and much more intensive, requiring anaerobic output, and the recovery intervals are ridden at a considerably lower intensity. Dur-

ing the work intervals the pulse will rise above the maximum figure suggested by the formula above, and it may be somewhat higher for each subsequent interval.

The first set of intervals must be preceded by a relatively light warm-up ride during at least 10 minutes. Then a number of sets, each consisting of several repetitions is ridden. Each repetition consists of a high intensity effort over a relatively short distance, followed by a recovery period over two to three times that same distance. The repetitions should have increasing and declining lengths, and between sets the heart rate is allowed to return to about 100–110 BPM. Once you are familiar with the process, there will be no need to check your pulse each time, since you will have developed a feel for your condition. Between consecutive sets the power output level may be reduced by gearing down, so that a high pedalling rate is retained without requiring excessive force. A typical set may consist of 5–7 repetitions with varying length efforts; each session may consist of anywhere from 5–10 such sets, separated by periods of moderate aerobic riding.

The length of the efforts is commonly expressed in terms of either time or distance. However, I consider it most conveniently expressed in crank revolutions, since they are easiest to count. Remember that in a reasonably high racing gear each crank revolution corresponds to about 7–8 m (say an average of 25 feet). The intervals must be relatively short, since the anaerobic power would be soon depleted otherwise. Typical effort distances may vary to reflect the kind of riding they are to prepare for, and it is wisest to use both long and short effort sets within your training program. A typical criterium training program would comprise a number of

sets, each consisting of repetitions with efforts of 15, 25, 35, 25, 15 crank revolutions. A typical program for road racing and time trialing might include longer repetitions, such as 20, 40, 60, 40, 20 crank revolutions. In either case, do not attempt to ride more sets than you can handle feeling fit, because the training effect does not depend on how fatigued you feel, but on how high the output was, and the output invariably falls off as you become too tired.

Anaerobic interval work is a wonderful training technique to strengthen sprinting and climbing power, though it doesn't hurt to include some of it in every training schedule, whether for road racing, cyclo-cross, track racing, time trialing or triathlon. Whatever your goal, it is recommended not to do hard interval work (or any other form of anaerobic training involving high muscle forces) the day before or after a race. In fact, it will be safest never to do it on consecutive days: alternate days with and days without anaerobic training.

Commonly, distinction is made between speed intervals and power intervals. The latter is a misnomer for what should correctly be referred to as force intervals. In speed intervals, mainly suited to develop muscle speed and staying power, choose a slightly lower gear and increase the pedalling rate until a distinctly higher speed is reached, at which point a higher gear may again be in order. Force intervals are good for increasing muscle strength, in addition to general anaerobic power. To do this, choose a slightly higher gear and try to increase the pedalling rate at the same time. With either type of work, drop back to aerobic levels before you are thoroughly exhausted, since you will not recover if you allow your body to do too much anaerobic work at one time.

Neither of these exercises should be attempted by newcomers. Wait until you have developed a flawless riding style and have absolved at least one racing season. Otherwise, the potential for injury is significant and your riding style may suffer. During the first few months of this kind of work, I'd use speed intervals only, not introducing force intervals until later. If signs of overtraining develop (as outlined in Chapter 10), force intervals should be the first thing to drop from your schedule; if signs persist, refrain from all anaerobic work, including racing.

Technique Training

If any form of training is frequently neglected, this is it. Few riders and coaches seem to be aware that an improved technique – including both strict pedalling style and bike handling – can do more for a rider's overall performance than any kind of training for strength, once a basic level of fitness has been reached. Triathletes who do not have a cycling background are well advised to emphasize this form of training. I suggest setting aside at least a fifteen minute portion of each training ride, or two longer sessions each week, in which you pay close attention to pedalling, gearing and handling techniques. This is particularly necessary during your first year as a racer, but should not be neglected in subsequent years either.

Refer to chapters 6–9 for the kind of exercises and the things to watch out for in technique training. Certainly in the early preparation stage of each new training year the pedalling style should receive close scrutiny. This is best done on a bike with a fixed gear in a lowish gear, selecting light and level terrain for this purpose. For your other technique rides, find different kinds of terrain occasionally, to be-

Greg Demjen breaks away from the pack, leaving the sprinters behind, during the 1985 Redlands Bicycle Classic in Redlands, California. It takes a strong solo rider to pull this off. (Photo Dave Nelson)

come familiar with the bike's behavior under widely varied circumstances. If at all possible, group rides should also be included, in which you can practice techniques of drafting or pacing, as well as skills needed for riding close together without accidents.

Control Method Training

This is my term for those procedures that allow you to evaluate your performance and progress. It can make your training more specific and scientific. The principle is that repeating identical exercises at different times during your training year will give some conclusive answers about the effectiveness of your training procedure, and may suggest on which techniques to concentrate. At the same time, this method may make it clear where your natural abilities and your weaknesses lie. I recommend it to bike racers and triathletes alike, since it is an effective way of monitoring your condition, as well as allowing you to establish whether you would not be more successful participating in other forms or racing.

To carry out the control training, identify several different stretches of road with which you are adequately familiar, that have particular characteristics: some longer and shorter smooth level stretches, some climbs of different gradients. Determine some simple landmarks, such as milestones. Try to find several very similar stretches that under neutral conditions take the same time to cover. If at all possible, include at least three of the items on the following list in the trial stretches you select:

☐ 200 m or 0.1 mile on level roads
☐ 1 km or 0.7 mile on level roads
☐ 5 km or 3 miles on mainly level roads (to be ridden both ways) or a loop of twice that distance

☐ 20 km or 12,5 miles on mainly level roads (to be ridden both ways) or a loop of twice that distance
☐ a number of short climbs of similar steepness with identical differences in elevation (e.g. 10 m or 30 ft)
☐ one or more long climbs of similar steepness with identical differences in elevation (e.g. 50–200 m or 150 to 600 ft)

About once a month, instead of your regular training program for that day, and after some light warm-up work, ride two or three of these at your maximum output for the appropriate distance, measuring your time accurately. Keep a systematic record of your times and any peculiarities you noticed during the ride, as well as the way you felt afterwards and your pulse rate during recovery. Summarize this information in the form of a table, which allows you to easily compare results for any one discipline over time.

After four months it will be time to evaluate the changes between the results. Whenever significant continuous trends of improvement show up, you may conclude that further improvement is possible by continuing the same or similar training methods. When, on the other hand, little or no improvement is apparent, you are either flogging a dead horse or not training effectively to develop the particular skills needed for that discipline. Referring back to Fig. 16.1 in Chapter 16, you have probably reached one of the dips in the set of short-cycle curves shown there, indicating it is time to change horses.

Decide on the basis of the preceding chapters whether you should modify your training in one or more points to become more effective. However, it is just possible you have reached a genetically determined limit in a particular discipline. In that case, no type or amount of training will bring much progress. No need to neglect that discipline altogether, but time to concentrate on some other aspect.

If your anaerobic performance in sprinting and climbing is not improving, even after you have tried more intensive training techniques, you may decide that your strengths lie elsewhere. In a race, try not to get yourself in the situation where a final sprint will be decisive. If, on the other hand, your sprints are fine but long time trial performance does not improve, even with longer and more intensive training techniques, you may perhaps decide to either stay behind others in a road race to sprint for a better placing, or you may try track racing if there happens to be a velodrome in your part of the world. Intelligently used, control method training will help you gear your training and racing techniques to establish the most suitable disciplines and achieve the best performances possible.

Motor Pacing

One effective training method that should probably be practiced more in the English speaking world is motor paced training. In Europe light motorcycles are used quite extensively to allow the cyclist a very high wind shelter effect, which helps to develop speed and endurance without doing much damage to muscles. Motor pacing is possible with the help of a car as well, providing the cyclist does not ride right behind it, so he can pass it on the side if necessary. The greater width of cars makes this a less practical proposition, since the car must keep its speed down to something the cyclist can handle, and that may hold up other traffic. For that reason, I recommend using a motor cycle for motor pacing.

Just about any training method on the bike can be combined with motor paced riding. LSD rides can take place at high speed over considerable distances. Aerobic and anaerobic interval training rides might comprise efforts ahead of the motorcycle and recovery periods behind it. Team time trial training lends itself in particular to motor pacing, since it corresponds so closely to the kind of work done in that form of racing. It can be done either with the entire team, with individual riders or with two-man teams. In any training program, occasional motor pacing provides a nice change from the usual routine. Consequently, there will be no need to do it very often. A session like this once or twice a month will probably be enough to make the training program more varied and provide adequate benefit.

18
Indoor Training Methods

In this chapter we shall consider the various methods of training that can be carried out without the use of a bicycle on the road. Included are both exercises that are useful but impossible to do on the bike, and methods in which other techniques are used to substitute for riding the bicycle on the road. The former ones are needed to supplement the training regimen wherever pure bicycle training is not suitable or adequate to develop certain skills, the latter are mainly used when unfavorable factors inhibit bicycle training out of doors or when close observation and analysis during the exercise is required.

Calisthenics and Stretching

These forms of exercises in bicycle training comprise a complex of simple movements to loosen joints and increase the flexibility of muscles. Some of these exercises may also help to develop muscles that are not adequately used concentrically in cycling to be trainable by riding the bike. In addition, light exercises of this kind can be useful to loosen and warm up before hard training or competition. This may achieve an optimal enzyme activity, necessary for maximum muscle performance, as well as minimizing fatigue. Finally, this kind of work may ease recovery after long duration hard riding.

The difference between calisthenics (or gymnastics) and stretching lies in the continuity of movement. In stretching the movement is slow and an extreme position is held statically for at least 30 seconds. In calisthenics the movement is quite rapid and repeated, without any static hold-

ing. Each type has its adherents, and my opinion is that a combination of the two forms is best. Certainly when the weather is cold, stretching will do more harm than good. For that reason I recommend refraining from that kind of exercise outside when the temperatures are low: do calisthenics instead. Even if the air is not cold, your muscles and joints are probably not warm enough when you first start out. For that reason, stretching exercises should always be preceded by some form of warming-up, either cycling, jogging or doing calisthenics. The basic principles to keep in mind when doing any of these exercises are summarized in the following list:

☐ Both calisthenics and stretching exercises are not a substitute for bicycling. They merely complement cycling by achieving the following:
a. increase joint movement angles of the same joints used in cycling;
b. strengthen muscles that are used isometrically in cycling;
c. condition the muscles to use a larger range of movement between maximum contraction and maximum reach;
d. prevent aches or cramps resulting from tenseness while cycling.
☐ Especially stretching, but also vigorous calisthenics must be carried out when the body is warmed up somewhat, e.g. after running or riding the bike on rollers at a low power level.
☐ In calisthenics joints are loosened and muscles are conditioned as the body is bent and subsequently stretched in a swinging motion over the greatest joint angle possible

(this angle will usually increase significantly with repeated practice).

☐ Of the muscle pairs at any joint, the single muscles that are stretched in calisthenics may be strengthened; however, not as a result of the stretching itself, but of the subsequent contraction when the joint is straightened forcefully again.

☐ In stretching the joints and muscles are conditioned to extend fully by forcing them statically in an extremely extended or contracted position, which is reached gradually and then held for at least 30 seconds.

On the following pages are depicted some useful exercises of both types in Fig 18.1 and Fig. 18.2. These are selected in part specifically for bicycle training, in part for their general effect on the athlete's overall physical well-being. The descriptions have been kept to an absolute minimum, since what you are expected to do should be obvious enough from the pictures, while their purpose, as well as the details of their execution can be figured out on the basis of the preceding remarks. One 10–20 minute session each day will be adequate for most cyclists. Triathletes may also include some of the specific exercises recommended for their other activities, for which they are referred to any general triathlon manual or books dealing with each of the other disciplines.

Breathing Exercises

Efficient breathing technique can have a significant impact on an athlete's performance. In addition to the effect of breathing depth, influencing the amount of oxygen that can be absorbed, there is also an effect on the nervous system: deep and regular breathing allows the brains to better control movements, reactions, thoughts and emotions, both during

exercise and when at rest. The latter effect may well allow the racer to divide his powers more effectively, to make more intelligent decisions during a race, and to train more consciously.

Perhaps the simplest and most effective breathing exercise is probably not recommended in any other sports training manual, but works wonders. It consists of a 20 minute walk at a brisk but regular and unhurried pace, consciously breathing in and out during the same number of steps each time. Start off with cycles consisting of inha-

Mark Gorski and Curt Hornett in a close sprint at the Dominguez Olympic Velodrome. (Photo Dave Nelson)

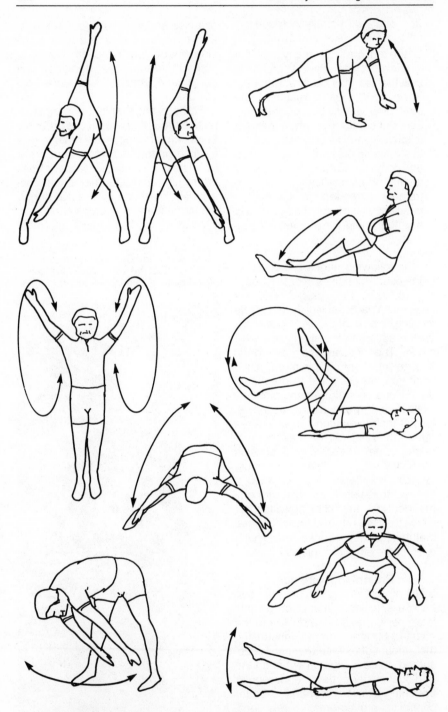

Fig. 18.1 Calisthenic exercises

Fig. 18.2 Stretching exercises

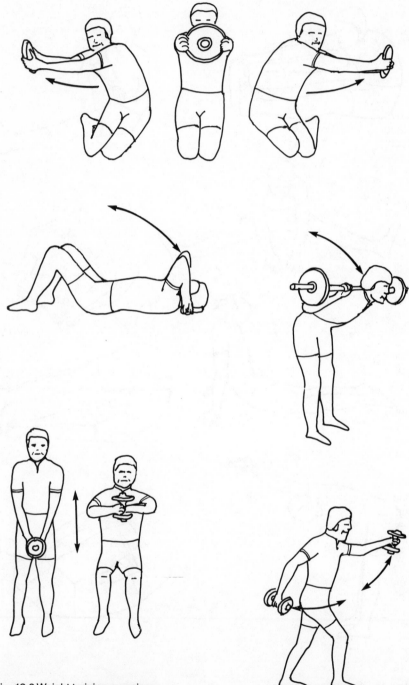

Fig. 18.3 Weight training exercises

lation during 6 steps and exhalation during the next 6 steps. Over the course of several weeks, gradually increase the length of these cycles until you are regularly breathing in and out over periods of 9 or 10 steps each. Carried out daily, this exercise is by no means a waste of time that could otherwise be used for more intensive physical training, but builds the foundation for an excellent breathing technique and an unperturbable state of nervous control.

The other essential breathing exercise is equally simple. Breathe in and out several times as deeply as possible. When exhaling, try to push the last puff of air out of the farthest corner of the lungs; when inhaling try to take in as much air as your lungs will allow. First do this standing up, bending forward when pushing the air out, raising the upper body fully when breathing in. Follow this by a set of these when lying on the back, keeping the body relatively still. Two sessions daily, comprising perhaps ten respiration cycles each, are adequate to maximize your effective lung capacity. A good time to do breathing work is in between sets of calisthenic exercises or after a moderate-power bout of work on rollers or windload simulator.

Weight Training

As you may have noticed, I am no advocate of weight or force training methods. They are used by some successful bicycle racers – but also by lots of unsuccessful ones. Many others have had great successes without ever lifting a weight or strapping themselves to any exercising machine. This kind of work is intended to strengthen muscles. But, as we've seen before, muscle strength alone is no indicator of bicycle performance. In fact, the muscles must be conditioned to perform just the kind of work, at the same speed and in the same sequence, as required when cycling. No weight training technique will do that even remotely as effectively. And if you really think you need this kind of work to develop your leg muscles, climbing stairs, taking two or three steps at a time, will be equally effective.

The only muscles for which I consider this technique to be of any use at all, though even that is not certain, are those that are used isometrically when cycling. These are the muscles of the arms, shoulders, stomach and back, as well as to some extent those of the calves. These are the essential restraining muscle groups that are not strengthened during cycling, since isometric work does not develop muscles, and may perhaps be trained by means of selective weight work.

Depending on the desired effect (fast high-power work for sprints or sustained strength for regular riding and climbing), choose more or less explosive methods of movements. Pure force training, which develops bulky short muscles, is done repeating at least five times with a weight or force of 80% of the maximum that can be lifted once. For more moderate training, weights or forces more like 50–60% of that maximum may be used and lifted more frequently. Do your weight training in the form of several brief periods preceded and separated by light exercises, such as low-intensity aerobic work on the windload simulator.

Obviously, my skeptical approach leads to an entirely different set of exercises than what is usually recommended for cycling. But I am convinced that this is the only right approach, unless the object is not bicycle training but body building. Fig. 18.3 shows some of the useful weight exercises that correspond to this principle. You will probably get by fine without weight training, just the same. What really counts should be concentric force training, and that is quite possible without any fancy gadgets: simple calisthenic exercises such as push-ups, sit-ups, rowing and torso raising will probably work just as well and can be done anywhere without any gadgetry. Either way, three or four sessions a week, depending in length on your available time will be adequate.

Roller Training

The old fashioned way of indoor training for bicycle racing is with the bicycle placed on a set of rollers. It's hard to balance the bike at first, but it has its charm once you get used to it. Whether it does you any good remains to be seen. The rollers provide virtually no resistance, which allows you to pedal without much effort at the maximum pedalling rate your body will be able to handle. That is probably the only use for this form of exercise: it allows you to work on increasing your maximum pedalling rate, which is essential for beginners and useful for any cyclist after a longer layoff.

On the rollers you will still perspire and you'll have the feeling of doing quite a lot of work. Virtually all the power you develop, 75 % of which is heat lost through the skin anyway, is wasted on overcoming the resistances within your own leg joints and muscles, as you pedal at your maximum rate. You're working like mad without doing any external mechanical work. The absence of cooling air, normally present when cycling outside, makes this work quite unpleasant, and probably not very healthy. I'd say 15 minute sessions are all that can be handled without risk or discomfort, though some maniacs work with rollers for hours, convinced they are achieving something worthwhile. If you don't already own a set of rollers, it will be wiser to buy a windload simulator instead.

Fig. 18.4 Bicycle ergometer training

Ergometer Training

An ergometer is a kind of stationary pedalling device with a big flywheel and a variable resistance, as shown in Fig. 18.4. Changing the resistance and adjusting your pedalling rate allows variations in power and apparent speed, comparable to differences during actual cycling. That's a big improvement over the roller training described above. Yet it's not the last word in stationary bicycle training either. In the first place, all bicycle ergometers are hopelessly uncomfortable, having been designed for (and by) those sedentary types who are more familiar with armchairs than with bicycles. More importantly, the kind of resistance offered does not allow you to simulate actual riding situations, where the required power increases exponentially with the speed, due to air resistance. Finally, it is impossible to cool the rider on a conventional ergometer.

Everything that can be done on an ergometer can be done at least as well on a windload simulator. But most things can be done better on the latter, while other things are impossible to do properly on the ergometer. That's why the practical training methods for stationary equipment given here will all be based on the use of a windload simulator.

Windload Simulator Training

This equipment is the answer to a maiden's prayer. It overcomes the inadequacies of ergometers on the one hand and of rollers on the other hand. Here the bike can be attached to a structure on top of a set of rollers that drive a set of wind turbine wheels, as shown in Fig. 18.5. As the speed of the rear wheel increases, either due to faster pedalling in the same gear or to the selection of a higher gear at the same pedalling rate, the air resistance increases exponentially, resulting in the drastic increase in required power typical of cycling at higher speeds under real-world conditions.

Several of these devices can be equipped with a system of air ducts to guide the air that is scooped up by the turbines to discharge a stream of cooling air blowing at the rider's face and chest, which is surprisingly effective. The windload simulator, especially when equipped with such a cooling system, combines the best possible simulation of real world cycling conditions, with the advantage of being stationary, allowing close monitoring and use under conditions unfavorable to riding the bike. Mounting an electronic speedometer with additional functions for pedalling speed and pulse rate monitoring provides you with the ultimate in stationary training and monitoring equipment: an exercise physiology lab of your own. Referring to the preceding chapters will allow you to make sensible training decisions, to be implemented both on the windload simulator itself, on the road or in other training practices.

Virtually every one of the training techniques described in Chapter 17

Fig. 18.5 Windload simulator

for cycling on the road can also be carried out quite satisfactorily on the windload simulator. Excepted are only those technique elements that relate to the bicycle's handling. You can ride a moderate gear and speed for a protracted aerobic exercise. You can spin frantically in a low gear to improve your pedalling rate, or you may carefully observe your pedalling style at different speeds and power levels. You can simulate sprints and climbs and you can carry out various types of interval training for more effective high intensity aerobic and anaerobic workouts.

Perhaps more than for any other of the training methods described in Chapter 17, the windload simulator is the ideal tool for control method training. The situation is not so strongly affected by extraneous influences and it is easier to monitor and record the results in terms of minutes and seconds. The effects of the work on your body can also be observed and recorded more easily.

Set up a schedule of windload simulator exercises that correspond more or less to the items on the list from Chapter 17. Carry these (or at least the ones that seem relevant to your training goals) out once a month, keeping close track of progress. But don't forget to do the most important part: evaluate the changes and developments over time as a function of your training methods, modifying your techniques as dictated by that evaluation. Train your weak spots only as much as seems justified by a continuing improvement of the results. Maximize the benefits offered by your natural strengths, which you can easily identify by comparing your performance in races with those of others.

Just as recommended for regular on-the-road training, you should select a personal training program with a purpose in mind. Chapter 19 will deal with that subject. The various warnings given in Chapter 17 for regular bicycle training largely apply to indoor training as well. Don't start out hard without warm-up and don't break off training immediately after an anaerobic or otherwise high intensity exercise, but continue work at a reduced output level for several minutes before stopping. Also observe the rule that both intensive anaerobic workouts involving high muscle forces and extremely long training periods should be avoided on consecutive days, as they should be on days immediately preceding or following a race.

Massage

Though it may not appear to be a training practice, massage has long been recognized as a suitable way of improving both performance and training progress, as well as preventing cramps and injuries. In the context of this book, the most useful remarks on massage will be some guidelines for self-administration. It's nice if you have a specialist to do it for you, but you can do it yourself quite effectively. Since only you can tell how you really feel, this may well be the most effective method anyway.

The most probable justification for massage is the encouragement it provides for the enzyme and blood circulation systems local to the muscles. Another theory holds that in hard repeated muscle exercise, such as cycling, though even more so in running, small fissures are formed and wastes (mainly lactates) accumulate in these fissures within the muscle. Massage is then presumed to encourage the removal of blood and wastes and to reinstitute a complete flow of blood that can take care of full recovery.

Whatever the merit of either theory, in practice massage works well and is recommended especially after particularly long or hard rides. It prevents the 'day after' muscle aches and allows more effective training, even if it is not administered immediately after a race or heavy training session. Proceed as follows:

1. Take a shower or merely wash the legs in warm (but not hot) water, and dry them thoroughly. There is no real need to use massage oil. Having shaven legs – hallmark of the bicycle racer – probably makes it easier to do the subsequent massage.

2. Lie comfortably on your back, at such a distance from the wall that you can stretch your legs above you as shown in Fig. 18.6.

3. Grab the middle of one of the thighs firmly with both hands, surrounding the muscle bundles; rub forcefully with long even strokes down from that point towards the hip. Continue this for about one minute.

4. Now do the same for the section of the thigh from the knee down to the location just beyond where you started under point 3. Work down in

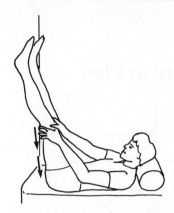

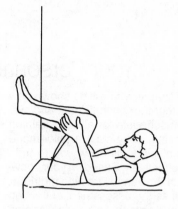

Fig. 18.6 Upper leg massage

Fig. 18.7 Lower leg massage

similar regular strokes, continuing for about one minute.

5. Repeat the work covered in points 3 and 4 for the other thigh.

6. Move back from the wall to take the position shown in Fig. 18.7, with the knees bent and the lower leg horizontally.

7. Carry out a similar massage of the lower legs, working towards the knees, as described in points 3–5 for the thighs.

8. Briefly massage the muscles of lower and upper legs with about ten long strokes over their entire length.

9. Rest a few minutes, lying down on your back with the legs higher than the rest of the body.

10. Should you have used massage oil, wash it off to prevent it from clogging up the pores of the skin, then wipe the legs dry and dress to keep warm.

19
Your Personal Training Plan

In this chapter you will be shown how to put together an individual and systematic schedule for all your training and racing. Only such a tailor-made personal plan will allow you to train really effectively. Based on your knowledge of the various training methods, as well as the assessment of training goals and personal strength, keeping in mind the time you have available, you should be able to decide which methods and techniques to employ and how much time to devote to each.

This training plan should be broken down into four stages, corresponding to different time horizons. You will need an overall or long range plan for your active cycling life, an annual one for the current or next year, an intermediate range plan for any one of the periods of 2–5 months into which the year is divided, and finally a short range or weekly schedule that summarizes your daily training routines in detail. Each of these plans must be constantly under consideration for review at time intervals appropriate to their particular time horizons. Revision intervals thus range from once a week for the daily schedule to once a year for the long range plan.

No book can give you a ready made plan like this. Copying the plan structured by famous coach A for successful racer B is probably the worst thing you can ever do. Coach A has determined that plan on the basis of the strengths, needs and potentials offered by that particular racer, whom he knows intimately. Had he known you as well, he might have made up an equally suitable plan for you, but it would look quite different, since your strengths, your needs and potentials

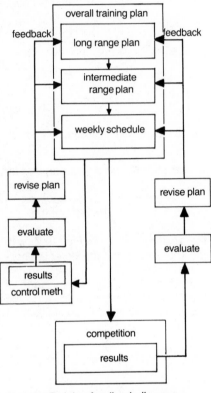

Fig. 19.1 Training feedback diagram

are not the same. The best I can do is show you how such a schedule may be structured and how to go about designing one that suits you personally.

Even so, it will take time. Don't expect to sit down one evening with pen and paper and draw up your training plan, let alone do that before you start racing. And whatever you may have been led to believe elsewhere, a computer won't do this any faster or more reliably. Instead, you must see the structure of your training plan as a growing organism that slowly incubates, develops and matures. Above all, it should be constantly adapted and revised, as you evaluate the results of your training methods to date, reflected by both racing performance and the control methods described in chapters 17 and 18. See Fig. 19.1 for a schematic representation of the relationships between plan and practice.

Though the training plan will vary from one individual to the next, I do not recommend emphasizing just one discipline or the other during the year. Try to be an all-round cyclist – one who can handle time trials as well as sprints, criteriums and road races, cyclo-cross and, if possible, track events. You may be better at the one than at the other, and developing your specific skills to maximum advantage will be useful. Yet you must master all skills adequately if you want to be a good racer. Though this may not apply quite so directly to triathletes, their bicycle training schedule should look very similar. Finally, at the end of this chapter, you will be shown how to prepare for particularly important events in certain disciplines during the final weeks before they are to take place by means of a regimen referred to as peaking.

The Long Range Plan

Your overall or long range plan should be the most informal one of the four. Perhaps it consists of no more than a handwritten list, stating for each year what you consider significant. It will cover a period of at least several years – your bicycle racing career as you expect it to develop over time. This plan should be re-evaluated about once a year, as you consider your progress and expectations at the end of the racing season.

It should not go into any great details about the training techniques you intend to apply at any one time during your active cycling life. Instead, it should generalize your goals and give a rough outline of the ways you feel they may be reached. Break up the plan by years, indicating for each year what you intend to achieve, in what kind of competition you intend to participate, and how intensively you will occupy yourself with particular training disciplines during that year. Before drawing up or revising this plan, consider especially the following questions:

☐ How important will the sport be in your life – both in the next few years and in the remote future?
☐ How much time will you have available during the various stages of your active cycling life for training and racing?
☐ What are your particular strong points and weaknesses, and how can they best be exploited in your overall plan?
☐ What is the risk involved to your lifestyle and career plans if you have perhaps decided upon a plan that cannot be carried through?

All aspects of this plan will be subject to change once you are getting more and more involved in the sport. Just the same, for most people the initial aims can be maintained if chosen realistically. Decide on your primary goals in simple terms, which may be anything from 'stay fit until old age' or 'race in the pack for many years' to 'become a Category I racer in three years time' or 'be selected for the Olympic team'. Needless to say, those with the latter goals will be more likely to revise their plan downward sooner or later. At this stage also determine on which type of racing you will want to concentrate: though the bulk of racing takes place on the road in the form of criteriums, you may well prefer to concentrate more on track racing or cyclo-cross. Someone else may decide to move from triathlon to bicycle racing or vice versa.

Next, determine what it will take to reach your goals. That may be anything from a modest weekly pensum of riding to many years' cruel training, or moving to a part of the country where your chosen discipline can be developed more effectively. Before proceeding, consider once more whether it's worth the trouble and what will happen if you're not quite as successful as you had expected. After all, if you are very ambitious, chances are that you soon discover your goals were unrealistic. If you make drastic changes to your life pattern to accommodate those goals, these can not easily be corrected. It may be better to revise your goals to match the possibilities than it is to try it the other way round. If you should turn out to be that one in a million who can rise to the top quickly, it will soon enough show, at which time it will be early enough to take such drastic steps.

The Annual Plan

Your annual training plan covers the next or present year, divided up over preparation, training, competition and rest or recovery periods. It can be revised at any time during the year, but might best be kept intact as much as possible. If you find it doesn't work as well as you had hoped, it may still not be wise to change horses in mid stream. Instead, adjust next year's schedule to reflect your experiences. Though you can revise a program that is clearly counterproductive at any time, you should generally give the year's plan an honest chance first. Try to get a clear understanding of the way this schedule affects your condition, your lifestyle and your racing performance, so you will be able to determine what to do differently next year.

It is customary to build up the yearly training plan in the form of four distinct periods, varying in length from two to five months. Neither the terms used for the various stages, nor the exact time periods allotted to each are sacrosanct. However, in most cases the values given here will be appropriate. For road racing anywhere in the Northern hemisphere, the year may perhaps best be divided up roughly as follows, keeping in mind that some of these periods may overlap the given dates by several weeks and that the participation in wintertime competition (e.g. cyclo-cross) may force a shift in these periods.

Preparation Period
(December–January)
Before the start of the next training season, this is the period to work on general aerobic condition, basic

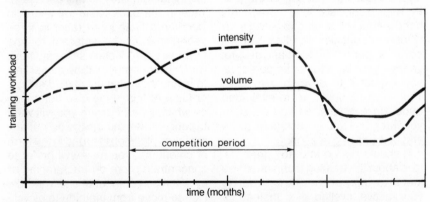

Fig. 19.2 Graphic representation of workload variation during the year

pedalling technique and perhaps muscle strength. If you take up racing for the first time, it is the kind of training to start with and to keep up much longer, even if the time of year is a different one. The emphasis should be on aerobic rides in lowish gears, paying attention to pedalling rate and style as well as breathing technique. Riding should preferably be done on the road, though the windload simulator or ergometer may be substituted if conditions don't allow riding outside. In addition, you will need to do light calisthenics, stretching and breathing exercises.

Development period (February–March)

This is the main training period as far as developing strength, speed and endurance is concerned. Gradually, you should introduce more aerobic and (in later years) anaerobic interval training. Start control method training at

Another kind of racing: mountain bike racing at Santa Rosa, California. (Photo James Cassimus)

this time, to monitor your progress. More and more, you should introduce distances and exercises that are similar in speed and variation to the kind of racing you intend to do later in the year.

Competition Period (April–September)

Though in many parts of the world you may not be able to race as frequently, you will probably do best to adhere to a schedule that simulates the work done by somebody who rides two races a week. If you can't participate in real races, at least do something that simulates racing conditions on those days which might otherwise have been devoted to racing. The rest of the program can perhaps be relaxed a little, but concentrate more and more on the particular discipline in which your chances are best. Work towards a climax to gradually peak around the time of the most important races, which are probably your category's district championships at the end of the season.

Resting Period
(October–November)
No need to take the word 'resting' too literally, but this is a time to ease off on the amount of training work. Though I feel it is best to continue cycling, many people purposely change to other physical activities. Whatever sport you do, keep it relatively light, avoiding really exhausting work, whether in terms of duration or speed and power. It may also be the time to start working on dietary weight control, if you found you were carrying too much body fat during the season. It is an excellent period to evaluate your performance and the effect of your training schedule so far, talking to others and comparing notes. At the same time, you may read up on the physiological findings related to the sport, as published in many sports publications throughout the year. This allows you to get more familiar with training and racing methods in general and with your chosen sport in particular.

The Intermediate Range Plan

This is the schedule for shorter time spans within the various periods just described. These sub-periods may range in length from three weeks to two months. With the exception of the resting period, divide each of the main periods into three parts of unequal lengths. The short first part is used to introduce and gradually increase the kind of exercises characteristic for that main period. The middle and longest part should emphasize clearly the kind of work to which this period is mainly devoted. In the final part you may intensify your efforts to come to a distinct peak in performance (in the case of the competition period) or gradually start a transition to the next period by introducing features characteristic for it.

The Weekly Schedule

Each of the intermediate range periods may be broken up into minor periods of one week each. Within any one of the intermediate range periods the schedule for each week may generally be quite similar, though they will fluctuate in terms of intensity from one week to the next. Obviously, the longest sub-period (the middle part of the competition period) will be most similar over the greatest number of weeks. Yet you should also consider whether any shift of emphasis may be desirable within such a period of perhaps two months.

Divide each week up into the seven days, and the days according to your available time. You may not often

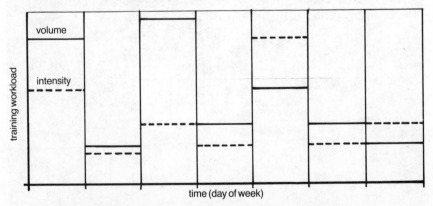

Fig. 19.3 Graphic representation of workload variation during the week

have uninterrupted blocks of time available for four-hour training rides. This will force you to divide up your time, and intensify the exercises you do in each of the available time blocks. Allocate your time wisely: for example, don't waste valuable winter daylight hours grinding away on a windload simulator or doing weight training, when you could be out riding the bike, which is so much harder when it is dark and cold.

No need to be guided by the number of hours spent working out by some of the top racers, who have little else to do. Actually, these athletes might perhaps do well to reduce their training workload too. Especially in the competition season, the training intensity per training ride is more important than the number of hours spent in the saddle. The same goes for other forms of training. Train consciously and intensively, rather than in drudgery. Of course, you must still try to get some rides in that are quite similar in length and terrain type to the hardest races you will be participating in, in order to satisfy the need for training specificity.

Generally, the schedule during any one sub-period will stay similar from one week to the next. On the other hand, there will be significant differences between weeks in one period and weeks in a different main training period. Consult the preceding guidelines to determine what to emphasize during each of the main periods of your training season, and keep your own preferences and limitations in mind.

It will obviously be impossible for me to lay out detailed weekly schedules for every week of the year, if only because I don't know you or your personal needs. It will again be up to you to decide – all I can do is tell you what to consider and give you an illustrative example, not meant to be copied, but to be used for inspiration. In the following, I shall give one usable schedule for the main sub-period within the competition season of a typical senior racer as an example, to show how he divides his time over the various basic forms of exercises during the week.

Day 1 – racing day: Ride a real race or a simulated one in the form of repetition and interval rides, including some control work; in addition, do only light aerobic warm-up, stretching, breathing and massage.

Day 2 – rest day: Calisthenics or stretching, breathing and either no cycling at all or some light aerobic work.

Day 3 – duration training day: An LSD ride of at least the length of your longest race, as well as some of the other elements of your training program.

Day 4 – light training day: Light aerobic rides with aerobic interval work, in addition to smaller volumes of the various other elements.

Day 5 – hard training day: Fast aerobic and anaerobic interval work over a long distance, including some of the other elements.

Day 6 – intermediate training day: Combine some elements of days 3 and 5, but not all, and done less intensively and of shorter duration.

Day 7 – light training day: Similar to day 4.

Some riders respond more positively to a program in which the intermediate training day precedes the racing day. This is the case when the compensation effect outweighs the recovery effect for a particular athlete after a particular workload. Experiment a little by comparing both your results and the way you feel when following the above schedule with those when you have reversed the programs for days 6 and 7.

Remember that this is really merely an example, valid at best only for one period for some riders. It's a reasonable way to show how such a schedule may be built up, but it is not intended to be strictly adhered to. Perhaps it's a good starting point, but you must actively experiment and think about ways to modify the schedule that suits your possibilities and needs, leading to maximum improvement of your performance. That may take several months, but if you work on it consciously and intelligently, you will be able to devise your own optimal training schedule along these lines.

Peaking

Though for most competitive events you will have to rely on your general condition as an adequate basis, you may want to do particularly well in certain important events. Examples are district and national championships in various disciplines. Not only will you want to maximize your general condition and overall cycling strength for such events, you will also want to specialize for the kind of discipline involved. It does make a difference whether you will be riding a time trial, a criterium, road race, track sprint or cyclo-cross. Such specialization for certain disciplines is a luxury you can't afford the rest of the year: you merely have to work on being as good as possible at all aspects of cycling. However, for such important championships you may decide to prepare specific skills. This process of thorough preparation for a particular event and discipline is referred to as peaking.

The process of peaking is in part based on the overcompensation effect described in Chapter 16. It follows a similar pattern for each discipline, though variations for particular types of racing will be outlined in the appropriate chapters. After a period in which very intensive riding is practiced to essentially deplete the body, the recovery phase is used to arrive at a level of maximum performance just at the time of the important event. The actual peaking period is usually three weeks, though the one or two weeks preceding may also become involved if you need to improve certain skills which are important for the specific discipline.

About four weeks before the event, analyze just what to emphasize by way of skills, strength and techniques. Decide whether you have to do any compensatory work to improve certain skills in that week, and draw up the plan with a detailed schedule for the three week period of actual peaking. That includes such mundane things as making travel arrangements and equipment decisions for the actual race, but it also requires a particular training schedule for the three week period preceding the race.

Three weeks before the race (which itself will probably be at a weekend), intensify your training regimen in terms of time, work and speed. Also start including some exercises that are particularly relevant to the specific event. Which exercises these will be for any particular discipline will be outlined in the relevant chapters of Part III. Two weeks before the event you should include about four days of very intensive work – preferably a stage race or a very hard training and racing regimen that simulates it. This will provide the depletion base, after which the recovery phase will set in, leading to the best possible condition at the time of the critical race.

During the next week, after a brief rest, continue the regimen with emphasis on the relevant discipline with more attention to speed and intensity than distance. This will be followed at the next weekend by participation in

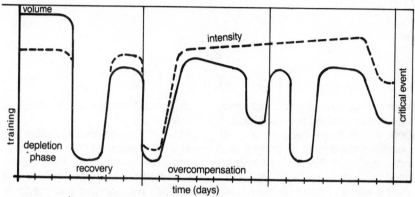

Fig. 19.4 Graphic representation of peaking

minor competition. The final week is again devoted to your regular training routine, but with reduced total mileage: 75–80 % of normal total weekly distance. That is achieved mainly by cutting out the LSD rides, or at least reducing them in length to the same length as the critical race. The last hard training day should be three days before the actual race, followed by two days of relatively light but fast training and a warm-up session leading right up to a few minutes before the start of the big race.

As with all training methods, you will have to experiment a little to find the system that is optimal for your individual needs. You may find that you need more or less rest just before the important event. Or you may fare better with a longer or a shorter peaking period. However, I should warn you to avoid doing too much peaking, since it will detract from your overall yearly training plan. In fact, the benefits gained in the one event may not offset the loss to your overall performance in the long run. In general, I think many athletes spend far too much time peaking and too little time building up long term strength. It will be best to train hard and systematically all year, peaking only for those few events that really justify it – which may be none at all in many cases.

20
The Cyclist's Diet

There is hardly a subject about which more nonsense has been written and about which more people hold preconceived notions than that of food and diet. So, at the risk of being accused of adding more of the same, here's a whole chapter devoted to the subject of food and drink. In cycling circles you will encounter staunch vegetarians and veritable carnivores, carrot munchers and pill poppers, all claiming the key to success lies in the way they fill their belly. Though the subject is not without interest, I would suggest considering it more soberly: forget about fad diets and concentrate on selecting your food consciously.

In America cyclists and triathletes seem to largely come from the same ranks as health food freaks and other diet conscious people. Nothing wrong with that, but many of the theories propounded in those circles are only relevant for people with a sedentary lifestyle. However, it makes a great difference whether you spend your day lounging about in an office, a car and at home, or spend four hours or so each day burning up calories on a bicycle. What the cyclist or the triathlete needs is not a diet but a clear understanding of the function of food as it applies to his performance and overall health. Most of all, athletes must realize the following facts:

☐ Endurance sports require much more in the way of calories and allow the kinds of food that would be fattening or otherwise undesirable to the non active person.
☐ As for the supposedly superior nutrients, such as proteins and vitamins, an active athlete does not necessarily need more than an inactive person of the same weight.
☐ More is not necessarily better: if X grams of protein or Y milligrams of some vitamin or mineral are required, then it does not follow that twice these quantities will improve your performance even one bit.

The Tasks of Food
Your body, including every organ, muscle and bone, needs food to function properly. The tasks that must be fulfilled by the things you eat and drink boil down to providing the following:

☐ Energy to keep the body's temperature at the necessary level for the various systems to operate.
☐ Liquids to conduct heat, control body temperature and to allow various physiological processes to function.
☐ Energy needed to perform mechanical work by means of muscle action.
☐ Building materials needed to grow and replace cell structures.
☐ Enzymes that allow the other processes to operate efficiently.

The most important substances to ingest that are necessary or useful to carry out these functions are listed as follows:

☐ Water
☐ Carbohydrates
☐ Fats
☐ Proteins
☐ Vitamins
☐ Mineral trace elements
☐ Fiber bran

The following sections will first describe each of these major substances, followed by an analysis of the tasks for which the body needs food and drink. I'll show how the various food substances fit into the complex of functions that must be fulfilled for the human body to operate effectively, especially under such physically demanding conditions as presented by bicycle training and competition. Finally, some special cases concerning nutrition that are often discussed in cycling circles will be presented.

Water

About 70 % of your body weight is water, which serves several different functions. It is the major carrier for other substances in the body and is essential for the process of temperature control. Water must be replenished as it evaporates or is excreted. It needn't always be taken in

Ute Enzenauer winning a close sprint finish at the 1981 women's road racing World Championship in Prague (Photo H. A. Roth)

the form of plain water, since it is contained in most foods, especially in fruits, vegetables and meat. And of course almost any beverage will provide it quickly.

Within the body many substances, such as sugars and minerals, are passed from the water into the cells by means of osmosis. That is the process of filtering through a thin membrane, whereby the transfer is always from the side with the higher concentration to the side with the lower concentration. Consequently, the concentrations of essential substances (e.g. sugar and in some cases table salt) in the water you drink should be just a little higher in the liquid than it is in the body cells. Thus, the way to introduce sugars into the body is to bind them in what is referred to as an isotonic solution, meaning it has at least the same concentration of dissolved materials as the liquid in the body cells. For sugar that means about 2–2.5 % sugar, which is less than half the concentration that is provided (and largely wasted) in most commercial sports drinks.

Carbohydrates

This predominant energy source, comprising both sugars and starch, is present in virtually all foodstuffs. The difference between sugar and starch is that the latter takes about two hours longer to provide energy, as it must be turned into usable sugar in the digestive system first, while most sugars (especially dextrose) can be taken up in the blood stream very shortly after they are consumed. However nice it may seem to get something that works quickly, starch-rich foods are to be preferred over sugars, since they also provide other nutrients and keep the body's digestive system in better trim. They should be the staple of the active duration athlete's diet.

Particularly rich sources of starch are all grain products and potatoes. Yet starches are also contained in virtually all other vegetable foods and in meat. Natural sugars are contained in most fruits and honey, while refined sugars are provided only too generously by just about all ready made foods and drinks. Whether natural or refined, they provide energy equally efficiently (ordinary refined sugar at the lowest cost). Though you may want to take a sugared drink for quick energy on the road, try to avoid sugars in your everyday diet, except in the form of fruits and natural juices, which also contain other valuable nutrients and digestive aids.

Fats

Although appropriately derided as a no-good in the inactive person's diet, fat is the most energy-efficient nutrient. However, fats as consumed are slowly digested and converted. Fat is used in the body as a store of energy and an insulator. It's present in meats and dairy products, but also in many nuts and various vegetable sources. The distinction between polysaturated and unsaturated fats is probably not as significant to the active sportsman as it is to the sedentary type.

It is probably true that the majority of people in the western world have accumulated too much fat. But it is very hard to avoid eating it altogether, since it is tied up with proteins in so many products that we have grown fond of. The tender American steak contains twice as much fat as the tougher stuff consumed in the rest of the world, and it will be hard to convince most people they don't need to eat as much meat as they do, or that less tender meat would be better for them.

In the body, fat is used as an energy source in the form of free fatty acids (FFA). These are carried in the blood stream and are used much like sugar for energy. As consumed, the fat first builds up as padding in various places, to be released in the form of FFA as needed to supply energy when work must be done at a certain level. This will be covered in more detail under *Food for Energy* below.

Proteins

Proteins are various combinations of a group of aminoacids contained in meats and dairy products, as well as – though in lesser concentrations – in legumes and grains. For the body to use proteins for cell building, the aminoacids must be present during any one meal in a certain ratio, which is most closely approximated by egg white, fish and meat. Other forms of protein foods are only adequately efficient if eaten in some combination of various types, e.g. legumes with potatoes, bread with milk, or beans with rice.

Contrary to popular belief, athletes don't need more protein than other people of the same age and body weight. For each kg body weight only about 1 g of protein is required per day. Slightly more may be needed by growing youngsters and during the initial building-up phase of training, when the muscles are developing. Most American adults get at least three times as much protein as they need.

Excess proteins, i.e. those not used for cell building, are simply burned up to provide energy, much like carbohydrates. A crying shame, since proteins are on average 5 times as expensive and considerably harder to digest. For the latter reason, protein-rich meals should not be eaten during or shortly before racing or hard training rides. Breakfast and lunch should be heavy on starches and low on fats and protein, while the best time to eat meals containing more protein is perhaps about 6–7 PM: Late enough not to interfere with demanding physical activity, yet early enough to be largely digested before the night.

Vitamins
Primarily a group of acids that is required in small quantities to provide the enzymes necessary for operation of various functions. Vitamins are distinguished into water soluble and fat soluble ones. The water soluble vitamins (B and C) leave the body fast, so they must be taken in daily, while the fat soluble ones (A, D, E and K) can be stored in the body over longer periods. Various vitamins are contained mainly in fresh fruits and vegetables, organ meats and whole grain products. A well balanced and varied diet will provide all the essential vitamins you ever need.

Consequently, there is probably no need for vitamin supplements if you include these foods in your diet, and there is no need to take vitamin tablets during races or training rides. Especially the fat soluble vitamins should be taken in moderation to avoid large build-ups with questionable effects on your health. The water soluble vitamins B and C, being necessary for energy production in the body, may have to be supplemented if performance falls off and no other cause is evident. Since any excess of these is excreted, there's no risk of getting too much. In some cases you may benefit by taking modest doses of multi-vitamin tablets on a regular basis, certainly if you are for some reason not able to adhere to a well balanced food intake.

Minerals
Also referred to as electrolytes, some minerals are required in small quantities for enzyme functions. Those only required in the minutest quantities are referred to as trace elements. Most are present mainly in vegetables, some fruits and grains. The most familiar of these elements is the sodium which becomes free when ordinary table salt dissolves in water. Others, such as potassium, calcium, and iron (the latter needed as a carrier of oxygen in blood and slow twitch muscle fiber cells) are equally needed. Since these electrolytes are water soluble, their excess is excreted with urine and perspiration. Consequently, after a very long and hard ride in hot weather, a case may be made for their replacement if heavy perspiration depletes their level below their required minimum concentration in the body.

Back in the early seventies a smart businessman decided to analyze perspiration and offer a drink containing all the elements lost that way. No medical evidence has ever been presented to support the need for this, but that has not stopped dozens of manufacturers from introducing expensive and awful tasting liquids containing too much sugar and useless electrolytes. Nor has it discouraged millions of cyclists from buying and – what is worse

– drinking this junk. Totally unnecessary of course: the water and sugar can be provided in a more appetizing form and better balanced proportions, while the only electrolytes that matter can be replenished by adding some table salt and eating a banana. Beyond that, eating a reasonably balanced diet will take care of all your electrolyte needs.

Fiber Bran

Fibrous materials, which are contained largely in unprocessed vegetable and grain products, are necessary to stimulate the operation of the digestive cycle. With the exercise of your training program, you will not need it as much as most sedentary folks, but you may not get enough to feel well. Cycling with clogged intestines is not very efficient and enjoyable. Again, the famous balanced diet, with whole grain bread instead of the white pulp usually dished up in most households, cooked and raw vegetables and various fruits, will keep you well supplied. If not, use bran cereals or add bran flakes to other foods.

Food for Energy

The overwhelming majority of the food you eat will be used to provide energy – both the heat energy to keep your body warm and the mechanical energy that allows you to do muscle work. Carbohydrates, fat and proteins all lend themselves to that purpose.

They can all be converted into the glucose that is transported in the blood or the glycogen that may be stored in the liver and muscle tissue. Thus, they can ultimately all be burned to form the ATP that constitutes the raw material for muscle work. However, these three foods are not all equally efficient, and they require different proportions of oxygen to perform their task. Furthermore, different kinds of foods – even with similar constituents – require longer or shorter digestion periods before they can be used effectively. Table 20–I summarizes the major differences between the three basic energy sources, while Table 20–II may help you get some feel for the time it takes the body to digest certain foodstuffs.

The amount of work expended and the food energy consumed can best be measured in kJ, which stands for kiloJoules. To relate this to more familiar units, 4.2 kJ = 1 kcal, which is what's really meant when calories are referred to in older works about nutrition. An average person leading a quiet life needs about 7000 kJ of energy a day. A hard day's cycling will add anything up to 4500 kJ of mechanical energy.

Considering the human engine's efficiency of approx. 0.25, that means an additional 18000 kJ must be provided, adding up to a total daily energy requirement of about 25000 kJ. That is also just about the maximum your

Table 20-I
Characteristics of carbohydrates, fats and protein as energy sources

food type	energy content		respiration quotient RQ	typical time to digest hours
	(kJ/g)	(kcal/g)		
carbohydrate	17.2	4.1	1.0	
sugars				0.1–2
starch				2–3
fat	38.9	9.3	0.7	6–8
protein	17.2	4.1		6–8

Table 20-II Digestion times in hours for various food types

time in stomach	food types
1–2 hours	water, coffee, tea, boiled rice, soft boiled egg, fresh water fish
2–3 hours	milk, coffee with cream, boiled or baked potatoes, low-fiber cooked vegetables, fruit, white bread, hard boiled egg, omelette or fried egg, salt water fish, veal
3–4 hours	whole grain bread, fried or French fried potatoes, fried rice, fibrous vegetables (e.g. spinach), salads (without dressing), beef, ham, boiled tender chicken
4–5 hours	beans, high-fiber vegetables, boiled or fried meat, poultry and game
6–8 hours	mushrooms, bacon, sardines in oil

body can take up in a day. Any energy expended in excess of this (that happens in heavy mountain stages of the Tour de France and similar races) will go at the expense of your body weight. On the other hand, eating more than enough to supply that food will not even make you fatter: it goes straight through your system.

As you can tell from table 20–I, fats are easily the most energy efficient nutrient, offering twice as much energy per gram as either carbohydrates or protein. The fat you burn passes into the system as free fatty acids (FFA). That's not the fat you have just eaten, but derives from the stuff that has accumulated in various places on the body. These fat stores are formed by all excess foods not needed for immediate energy supply, which is always converted into fat, except if it exceeds the maximum digestive limit mentioned above. At most levels of output the body uses a combination of free fatty acids and glucose for aerobic energy production: mainly fat at low levels, mainly glucose at higher levels, as represented in Fig. 20.1. Note that the range is rather wide, individuals differing somewhat. The typical female body tends to favor fat metabolism, a further shift towards fat metabolism occurs as an effect of aerobic training.

The respiratory quotient RQ is used as an indicator to establish to what extent energy is generated by burning carbohydrate and free fatty acids (FFA), respectively. Up to about 75 % of VO_2max the low value for RQ indicates that most energy is provided by the fat metabolism. To maximize endurance, try to stay within that range as long as possible during a long race.

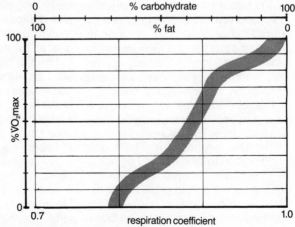

Fig. 20.1 RQ: fat versus carbohydrate for energy

It is possible to determine which proportions of the energy come from fat and carbohydrate metabolisms, respectively, at any time. This is done by comparing the volumes of exhaled carbon dioxide and inhaled oxygen, called the respiratory quotient RQ. If RQ is 1.0 all energy comes from carbohydrates, if it is 0.7 from fat. Any intermediate ratio allows the physiologist to determine how much fat and how much carbohydrates are being burned. On really long exhausting rides, such as mountainous stage races or the very toughest triathlons, the supply of carbohydrates is in danger two ways. At high output levels it is used up first and fastest, and its supply is limited to what can be taken up by the body in a day. You may run out before the end of the race.

No such problems at low output levels, such as touring and conventional LSD rides, where free fatty acids are preferably burned. The supply of fat on even the leanest body will probably suffice to cycle half way around the world at a modest speed. But to the road racer who has to keep up a murderous pace all day and still have enough power left for a dash or a climb, the supply problem may become evident. Anywhere beyond 75 % of VO_2max he'll be burning virtually only carbohydrates, as evidenced by an RQ close to 1.0. The glycogen in liver and muscles, the glucose in the blood and the food in the belly are the only energy supplies available, and once these are gone, it's all over.

The obvious way to prolong the energy supply is by reducing the pace to a level below 75 % VO_2max as much of the time as possible. That's one good reason to take it easier by riding in an echelon. This reduces the wind resistance enough to make all the difference on a long fast ride. Another technique to maximize the fat burning, as evidenced by a low RQ, is simply to do more training at continuously high output levels. This tends to shift the balance more towards the fat metabolism. Finally, some researchers (and many cyclists) feel the fat metabolism can be stimulated by taking caffeine.

Everything in moderation though: probably not more than 4 mg per kg of body weight (2 mg per lb). That is the equivalent of about two small cups of strong coffee at the beginning of a race for the average body. Anybody who drinks more at any time or who takes strong caffeinated drinks just before the end of a race is fooling himself, since it can have no positive effect. Even when used as suggested here there is a problem with caffeine, since it works as a diuretic, i.e. it encourages liquids to leave the body in the form of urine. Consequently, in hot weather, particularly for a race involving a lot of climbing, the use of caffeine may be dangerous: you will need all the water you can drink to act as a cooling medium.

Carbohydrate Loading

That's a technique used by some athletes who have to perform well in 2–3 hour duration activity only once in a blue moon. It's no use for short or really long rides, nor for stage races, and dubious at best even for its intended purpose. The idea is to exercise to exhaustion several days well before the big event, after which you start eating carbohydrates in generous supplies, without doing very much in the way of hard work. The assumption is that the muscles will absorb lots of fuel reserves in the form of energy carrying glycogen.

For bicycle racing it is a highly questionable technique, especially if one considers that muscle glycogen stores never satisfy the bulk of your long duration energy requirements anyway. If it works at all, then only for competitive events over time periods of about 2 hours – neither much longer, nor much shorter. In addition, chances are that the benefit of continued training in the days leading up to the event would have been greater to your performance, as they certainly are to your overall long term condition. You can try it, but you may find the results to be negative.

The Role of Water

Water is quite essential to the body's proper operation. This contrary to at least one European cycling myth which claims that drier is faster. That statement may apply to the English time trialists who ride 25 miles in 50–60 minutes on a cold day, after which they may indulge in all the beer they can down before the pubs close. But it is nonsense when we are considering

Fast action on the track. These are the juniors at work during a points race. (Photo H. A. Roth)

any intensive activity of several hours duration, especially in hot weather.

Water is tied up in the body with several other substances, for which it acts as a carrier. It is particularly important for regulating the body's temperature. During vigorous cycling in hot weather the cyclist may lose water faster than he can possibly drink it. Half a liter, or about one pint, an hour is all the body will absorb, while it may evaporate at twice that rate. To keep the body at the optimal temperature for muscular and mental work, water is used. Whenever the temperature threatens to get too high, the pores and sweat glands are opened and sweat is excreted, the natural evaporation of which will cool the body.

Especially in warm weather and on long exhausting rides, you will therefore need more water than you can carry in bottles on the bike. Start drinking well before the start, and drink frequently in moderate quantities during the ride. Allow perspiration to evapo-

rate, rather than wiping it off. Since water is also an excellent medium to tie up sugars and electrolytes isotonically, it is frequently suggested to carry two bottles on a hot and exhausting ride: one with plain water for cooling, the other with a water based mixture containing 2–2.5 % sugar and up to a teaspoonful of table salt per pint. Personally, I prefer natural fruit juice over this man-made mix. It serves the same purpose but tastes a lot better.

Weight Reduction

The quickest, easiest, healthiest and cheapest way to improve your performance may well be by reducing your weight. That's assuming you are like most people, who carry unnecessary ballast in the form of excess fat. Good road racers are lean, as are good long distance triathletes. They have body fat percentages not exceeding 8 % and 12 % respectively for men and women. The higher optimal fat percentage for women corresponds nicely with the previously observed phenomenon of their more active fat metabolism.

The body fat percentage can be determined by means of several techniques, most simply by measuring certain skin folds, which any sports physician or paramedic can do. If you are determined to lose weight, don't try to force it in the racing season, and don't try to do it only by eating less. Use a combination of various techniques. Eat less and differently, taking more fibrous matter and less fats and sugars; do more physical work in addition to your training – walk or use your bike instead of the car, the stairs instead of the elevator.

A Bicycle Racer's Meal Planner

It is possible to eat adequately without any other advice than that contained in the preceding paragraphs, and perform admirably in competitive cycling.

However, for those who prefer some additional guidance, here are some specific hints on how one might divide the required food intake over a cycling day.

Breakfast:
Aim for a high starch intake, combined with vitamins, fibers and minerals and modest amounts of proteins, avoiding sugars and fat. Fruit or fruit juice; whole grain cereal with e.g. banana or dried fruit and low fat milk or natural plain yoghurt, whole grain bread. Try to eat breakfast at least two hours before a race and at least one hour before heavy training rides.

Lunch:
If your day is an active one, including racing or training in the afternoon, aim for a relatively light lunch after a big breakfast, again containing more starch than proteins and avoiding fats and sugars. Eat salad with bread or other starch foods, combined with small quantities of e.g. meat or cheese. A sandwich should not be lots of meat or cheese with a little bread, but rather lots of bread with little meat or cheese – breadwiches is what my colleagues disparagingly called the food that kept me going while they were stuffing themselves with fat and proteins. Drink low fat milk and have a desert of plain yoghurt or fruit.

Supper:
This is rightly your heaviest meal and the one time to include more protein foods, though it will still be preferable to go easy on tender (read: high-fat) meats. In addition to meat or other protein foods, eat generous quantities of starches and fresh or cooked vegetables and fruit. Drink natural fruit juice or low fat milk. Hold off on salad dressings, gravies and sauces. Try to have dinner relatively early in the evening.

Get some light exercise, even if it is only a 20 minute walk, after dinner to help digestion.

Snacks:
If the urge strikes during the day, the active athlete can indulge in snacks between meals. In fact, it will be even wiser to eat six small meals than three big ones, if one does a lot of racing or training. When eating in between meals, avoid junk food, though. Instead of sugared and fatty stuff, choose any of the relatively light foods that give you something to munch on, contain starch, fibers and minerals or vitamins. You can eat fruit, crackers, raw or cooked vegetables and plain yoghurt; drink water, tea, low fat milk or unsweetened natural fruit juices.

21
Shortcuts to Success?
From Doping to Motivation

Probably even stronger than man's delight in competition is his desire to vanquish. By whatever means. That has led him on an endless search for shortcuts, ranging from illusive magic potions to the more realistic practice of outright cheating. In competitive cycling the use of doping in an attempt to influence the outcome of races has long been widespread. In the present chapter we'll take a look at the means employed and their effects, followed by a discussion of what appears to be a far more potent, and less harmful, booster: motivation.

It would be unreasonable to object to every means of improving the athlete's performance. Practice and training, technique and tactics, diet and care – all have similar effects, and not only would nobody suggests outlawing these, they are largely considered the very essence of the sport. Yet, somewhere there must be a thin wavy line that separates legitimate from odious practices. Just where that line runs may be subject to the same kind of bickering as applies to any border dispute. The various national and international sports associations have their own views, differing from one to the other in detail, but agreeing in principle: forbidden is any supposedly performance-boosting substance that is alien to the own body if it lies outside the sphere of normal foods, especially if it may have negative side effects.

All very vague and of questionable validity, especially when considering the difficulty of testing. Some relatively harmless or ineffective substances are outlawed simply because they can be easily identified in the athlete's urine or saliva, while others can be taken with impunity because there's no practical way of establishing their use. Then consider the circumstance that most of the forbidden substances are also used in legitimate medicine. This has led to the disqualification and punishment of athletes who have taken simple prescription medication, some of them outlawed in cycling, even though ineffective as a means of improving performance. Most absurd indeed is the fact that the majority of substances used in doping have been demonstrated to be ineffective for their intended purpose: what is the point in forbidding a supposed magic potion that isn't one?

Perhaps the most reasonable definition of doping is taking any substance that improves performance while endangering the athlete's health in the long run. Most popular doping substances, at least in the quantities taken for that purpose, have the latter effect – even if the sought after effect is often absent. Even if a doping substance should improve your performance in one competition, it seems absurd to take it. After all, you're not involved in the sport for just that one race, but for the sum total of all the training and racing you'll ever do. No form of doping will increase either your long term performance or the joy you get during your active sports life.

Let's take a look at some of the substances used in bicycle racing, without encouraging their use. The smartest way to classify the various doping substances is probably according to the desired specific effect. The following groups may thus be distinguished:

☐ vegetative stimulants
☐ psychostimulants
☐ sedatives
☐ pain killers
☐ hallucinogens
☐ hormones

In addition, I shall say a few words about fringe phenomena, ranging from blood doping to tonica. The chapter will be concluded with some remarks about a less harmful and more effective way to maximize performance, when we talk about the athlete's motivation.

Vegetative Stimulants

These are meant to stimulate the cardiorespiratory complex via the metabolism. They can work either directly or indirectly. Typical examples from the former group are nitrides, such as nitroglycerine, used in medicine to widen the heart's coronary artery. This effect presumably allows a greater stroke volume, i.e. increases the volume of blood pumped with each heartbeat. It only works that way at submaximum levels, since at maximum performance the heart already receives the greatest possible stimulation. The athlete's heart performance is limited, not by insufficient stimulation, but by its maximum strength and volume, neither of which are increased by widening the arteries. Similar arguments can be used to prove the ineffectiveness of other cardiotonica, which may or may not improve the performance of the sick heart, but don't do a thing to increase the performance of the healthy organ.

No, this is not a four-man tandem. It is the Soviet four-man team riding in perfect synchronization during the team time trial World Championships on the track. (Photo H. A Roth)

Indirectly operating substances work via the central nervous system. These products range from relatively harmless caffeine (which is forbidden only in excessive doses) to universally forbidden substances like nicethamine to legal sympathicomimetica such as adrenaline and noradrenaline. The latter substances are identical to those produced in the body, where they are effective in quickly mobilizing energy. No beneficial effect has ever been demonstrated to be associated with taking these substances. They stimulate the brain, but that effect lasts only about 30 minutes, after which you may be left emotionally disturbed – not a good condition for any kind of maximum performance.

Psychostimulants
This group of stimulants, which works on the mind, includes all amphetamines, as well as efedrine and cocaine. All these substances affect the psyche by encouraging the release of adrenaline and noradrenaline. Efedrine, a substance often found in medication to relieve sinus conditions, opens the nasal passages and allows more air to be taken in. That doesn't help the healthy cycling athlete, however much he fears running out of breath without. Though it may help raise a limited performance to the maximum, it will never raise a maximum one any higher.

Amphetamines, once hailed in medical circles as cure-alls for disturbances ranging from depression to excess appetite to insomnia, have been widely used in sports doping for their stimulative effect on the central nervous system and the alleged decrease of fatigue. Their documented effects include a much higher maximum pulse and a slower recovery. However, even at the faster pulse, no increased power output has ever been established. It seems they decrease the metabolism's efficiency, hardly a desired feature. As for their usefulness in avoiding fatigue, this only works at low output levels, which are totally irrelevant in competitive sports. The negative side effects are very real though: inadequate appetite, sleeplessness and headaches, not to mention addiction.

Cocaine, rarely used outside the American continent, has roughly the same effect as amphetamines. This substance is less direct as a stimulant of the central nervous system, leading to less pronounced side effects. A positive effect has never been convincingly demonstrated either, and it is known to be adictive.

Sedatives and Tranquilizers
Whereas the alleged benefits of most other substances used for doping purposes are attributed to stimulating the athlete, sedatives and tranquilizers do the opposite. If a case can be made for any kind of doping, this group is the one. The Belgian experimental psychologist Hueting lists the following four advantages:

☐ Tranquilizers relieve the athlete of the performance-limiting nervous tension and worries about the race, known as pre-start state.
☐ They can help him get a good night's sleep when either tension or mainly physical causes (e.g. the problem of having to sleep in a noisy motel in unfamiliar surroundings) might otherwise keep him awake much of the night.
☐ They can provide an escape from the vicious cycle of inadequate nightly rest, combined with fatigue and listlessness during the day, which interferes both with effective training and racing, extending all the way to early stages of overtraining.

☐ They can help the athlete concentrate, particularly in disciplines requiring delicate motoric skills, such as the track sprint.

Alcoholic beverages are perhaps the simplest and oldest (and the most legal ones – for those over the age). Amongst the modern synthetic tranquilizers used, barbiturates and benzodiazepines represent the group of common medicines with which insomnia can be treated. These need more time to act and keep their effect longer than alcohol. They usually work and are not particularly harmful if taken in moderation. However, the effects can just as easily turn out to be negative, e.g. when the tranquil state turns into one of indifference, or when addiction becomes evident. There is a sound case to be made for psychotherapy as a much more effective solution to any problems that have been treated with tranquilizers.

Pain Killers
Pain plays a major role in the limitation of endurance, and it is tempting to suggest suppressing pain may prolong your high-output endurance. Opiates, cortison and aspirin are all used as pain killers in an attempt to increase staying power. No scientific tests have ever demonstrated their effectiveness for that purpose. These products may all have their place in medicine. As such they may have been used successfully to treat one ailment or the other, thus indirectly improving the sub-maximal performance of the sick athlete. Yet it seems unwise to take them in the hope of improving the maximum performance of a healthy racer.

Hallucinogens
The whole spectrum of natural and synthetic hallucinogens – from marihuana to LSD – has been used as doping, particularly on the American continent. Their sought-after effect is on the mind: feel good to ride well, notice no pain and push the body beyond its limitations. Yes, these products all affect the athlete's mood and expectations, but they can't do a thing for his performance. Despite the stories told by those who attribute miraculous successes to their use, I suggest you steer clear of them. They are likely to disturb your mental and physical equilibrium, leading in the long run to poorer results.

Hormones
These substances are often considered the most modern form of doping. The nature of the product seems to have attracted disturbingly many respected physicians to their administration. Four groups of hormones have found their way into the doping lists: epinephrine, corticosteroids, anabolic steroids and sex hormones. Unlike the other doping substances, hormones are natural to the body, being produced in certain quantities in various glands. This makes it harder to test for their doping use. They have their legitimate place in medicine, and it is not their use as such, but their excess that is objectionable.

Epinephrine is nothing but an other name for adrenaline. It is naturally produced in adequate volume in the adrenaline gland of the kidneys. It has the function of increasing blood pressure and stimulating heart activity for short power bursts by closing peripheral blood vessels. No help at all in a duration sport like road racing or triathlon, and at best of questionable benefit in sprints or short time trials.

Steroids constitute a group of structurally similar hormones that are produced in several different glands. Of these the group of corticosteroids, and in particular the glucocorticoids (generally simply referred to as cortison), produced in the adrenaline gland, have been much debated as potential agents to improve performance. Often used in combination with amphetamines, they are supposed to suppress certain forms of pain. In addition, they accelerate the protein metabolism, turning proteins into carbohydrates for faster energy, while also allowing greater use of fat metabolism. That's indeed what happens once you are literally on your last legs, nearing exhaustion. Thus these substances might be one answer to the dreaded bonk.

Corticosteroids will probably not make you any stronger, nor will you get greater reserves, and there are some side effects that may even decrease your performance. They capture water and sodium, both of which are sorely needed during longer races, and so tend to increase the blood pressure. They help suppress pain at the joints, which is less desirable than it seems, since serious infections may well be overlooked this way. Not recommended, but probably not as harmful as many of the older doping tricks.

Anabolic steroids, also produced in the adrenaline gland, help in the building of protein cells, specifically those of the muscles. In addition, they tend to harden the skeletal bones. The same effects are found in the synthesized anabolica, which have the advantage of avoiding some of the negative side effects. Since anabolic steroids are closely related to the male sex hormones, their use by women seems more than just questionable. The bone hardening effect is particularly dangerous to young people, whose growth may be inhibited.

Apart from the question of their legality, the benefit derived from the use of anabolic steroids and anabolica is uncertain. Your maximum performance depends on much more than the size and strength of your muscles. Body-builders should dominate the sport if muscles mattered, yet many of the strongest cyclists are outright skinny. Besides, the increase in muscle size derived from these hormones is probably no greater than the effect of training, which does much more than increase muscle size alone.

Natural sex hormones are also used in doping, in particular the male hormone testesteron, which has effects that are similar to those described above for anabolic steroids. However, the female sex hormones are also used, and indeed seem to represent one of the few medically justifiable uses, namely in the guidance of a female athlete's menstrual cycle. A woman's performance potential is generally reduced in the period between menstruation and ovulation. Once she has reached an adequate physical condition through training, there seems to be some justification, and probably little harm in medically controlled shifts in the cycle. This way it is possible to avoid having major competitions coincide with the lows during the wrong time of the month.

Blood Doping and Oxygen
In recent years blood doping has received some publicity. It amounts to a particular form of what might be described as oxygen doping. The idea is to maximize the blood's capacity to capture oxygen in order to supply it to the muscles for energy production. The oldest and simplest form is training at great altitude, where thinner air and lower air pressure deliver less oxygen, before a competition. This will condition the blood to temporarily pick up the oxygen more greedily when one returns to sea level. Then there is the possibility of administering oxygen directly during recovery to

prepare an athlete for a subsequent performance, which has been widely practiced in (American) football but was never demonstrated to help one bit.

The particular form of oxygen encouragement called blood doping was first publicized during the 1976 Olympics in Montreal, when the 5 and 10 km races were won by athletes who had received it. Since then, it has been used in many sports, especially for Olympic and world championship competitions. After a blood transfusion, the athlete continues training. During this time the body madly starts to generate replacement red blood cells to take up oxygen, until shortly before the race the 'old blood' is reinfused. This will quite literally thicken the blood, since the excess liquid is soon lost, increasing the proportion of oxygen carrying red blood cells per volume unit. A positive effect has never been proven, least of all for long distance races, and the whole operation is of course well outside the realm of the average racing cyclist.

Tonics

Not on the doping lists, but often used for the same questionable purposes, are a number of products widely advertised as being beneficial. They may be distinguished into short term agents, i.e. those that are thought to improve performance immediately after they are taken, and those that are taken regularly in the hope of increasing strength gradually. An ineffective, though generally harmless, example of the former is what some coaches and racers refer to as an 'atom bottle': a tiny bottle containing a caffeinated beverage with a lot of sugar and whatever other silly things the rider has faith in. It is amusing, though rather pathetic, to watch how nervously a pack of racers starts taking these little bottles shortly before reaching the finish. An excellent time for a surprise attack is of course just when the opponents are most concerned with these ineffective tonics.

Many of the commercial long-term tonics turn out to contain products that range from ATP to potassium, from vitamins to calcium and from magnesium to ginseng. They are reputed to achieve such minor miracles as reducing fatigue, avoiding the bonk and accelerating recuperation. Some of these products have their legitimate, though limited, uses either in your regular diet or in case of sickness. For a healthy athlete, none is any use to increase performance, improve appetite, lessen fatigue or work any of the many other miracles for which they are recommended. And if you're not healthy, the self-prescribed administration of any of these or other substances will not make the difference between barely hanging in and performing well.

In fact, there is a distinct danger, though most of these things will not negatively effect your performance any more than they can improve it. The danger is that if you perform poorly despite taking such a potion, you will either lose confidence in your own abilities or revert to even more (or more potent) tonics, and eventually to forbidden products with acknowledged negative health effects. Let training be your way to the top, and if you don't reach the top in your chosen sport, consider it adequate to reach your own personal high. Only one person can win a race, and a hundred 'losers' needn't all be heartbroken after each race. Though it may be nice to dream of winning, participation and training should be the real essence of the sport.

Motivation and Performance

Despite all my skepticism, there is no denying that many athletes have performed well under doping and attribute their success to this habit. In the European cycling press one particular story drew attention to the supposed benefit of anabolica recently. Two Belgian sports journalists – themselves accomplished cyclists – reported how they rode an uphill time trial twice: first without, then with amphetamine. Their times improved by 2 and 8 percent, respectively.

That proved it for many uninformed readers (and unfortunately for some who should have known better). To see just how inadequate and irrelevant this demonstration was, you may try to conduct a similar experiment. Ride a time trial over about 10 km (6 miles) and repeat it after four hours of rest. Instead of using any known drug before the second ride, you may e.g. wear pink socks. Chances are that your performance has improved significantly wearing pink socks.

Of course, the pink socks had just as little effect on your performance as taking amphetamine. You were merely benefitting from the repeat effect, attributable both to the same compensation effect, referred to when I described the benefits of interval training, and to increased familiarity of the terrain and the distance. That doesn't prove or disprove the ineffectiveness of doping: all it says for sure is that such tests are not reliable. But it also suggests that there may be other ways to improve your performance.

The realization of testing inadequacies and speculation about other methods have triggered some interesting work during the last ten years or so. Not only has it thus been established that the repeat effect can be used to advantage, e.g. by riding through a course at least once before competing, it has also lead to the development of more useful testing methods. Without boring you with further details about the more reliable testing methods that make some findings more credible, I shall briefly cover some of the most important of these findings in the following sections.

In addition to doping, several factors have been investigated. One of these is the effect of cheering or encouragement. It is a familiar sight that a local athlete often stands a good chance of doing well. In bicycle stage races, relatively obscure competitors have often won stages that end in their home towns, carried, it seems, on the enthused cheers of their local supporters. Well, it turns out cheering is not what does the trick. No amount of cheering and encouragement were found to make an athlete stronger or smarter.

Nor does the local winner usually give more than he has: though he may return to obscurity, the peak performance appears to be generally within his natural capacity, which he just once taps for 100 %, instead of the usual 95 %. The secret lies not in the cheering of the crowd, but in the determination of the athlete's own mind. If you can give yourself the kind of internal pep-talk that makes the local win his home town race before every competition, you will be well on your way to performing 100 % all the time.

A much more promising factor than either doping or cheering is referred to as KOR, which stands for knowledge of results. The athlete who is kept abreast of his own performance right from the start of the competition in terms of distance and time, especially if these are also compared to the performance of other competitors, will consistently perform better than when kept in the dark. This principle is particularly important in time trialing, where the competitors as references are lacking. This largely explains recent time trial successes by individuals and teams who were kept informed by their coach via radio. But such benefits are not restricted to highest echelon competition. The same system can also be applied to make training more meaningful by checking and keeping close records of times and distances.

Very significant is still the presence of other racers. Some riders are considered natural time trial talents, and they are often able to work at their peak for long periods on end without slacking. But for virtually all racers, including some of these natural time trialists, it has been repeatedly observed that they can catch up with another rider who is in sight much more easily than maintain the same speed without such a visual reference. The same applies to riders who have been overtaken: suddenly they may manage to muster enough strength to keep up. As a racer, you may be able to use this principle by establishing your own references along the way.

Especially triathletes are often in a situation where they are chasing the wrong competitors: just because the person ahead of you got out of the water first, that doesn't mean he's a formidable cycling opponent. Though less common, the same may apply in bicycle racing. Thus the chances are that you pace yourself to someone who is too slow as a reference for your potential performance. For this situation, and whenever there isn't another racer in sight, you may be able to establish artificial references along the course. To do that, constantly pick objects in view some distance ahead of you and chase one after the other until you reach the last reference point, the finish line.

One final method of optimizing your performance is what I call KYE: know your enemy. Become familiar with other competitors, both those who are your direct opponents and others in the field who can tell you something about the former. Talk both about the particular race, the sport in general, the others in the field and about personal matters. Round off your knowledge by reading the reports in cycling and other sports journals with an emphasis on your fellow athletes as individuals. Get to know their characteristics, their strengths and weaknesses, as well as more personal points. This knowledge will almost certainly allow you to catch the right wheel in an escape, to avoid wasting energy on useless attacks. In short, it will make you more effective in competition.

Part III
The Practice of Bicycle Racing

22
Competitive Cycling

The chapters of this final part of the book are devoted to the practice of bicycle racing, both in terms of participation in and preparation for various distinct types of bicycle races. Also included is a brief chapter dealing with cycling in triathlon competitions. The final chapter is devoted to the record keeping practices that can help the cyclist gain more insight in his progress as a racer and to evaluate the effectiveness of the training methods used. Keeping track of the results and associated factors consciously and systematically is considered the essential foundation for racing and training effectively.

Specialization?

Here, as in other parts of the book, I assume that the vast majority of readers don't have boundless time and opportunity to devote to the practice of bicycle racing. For most of us it is a hobby, rather than either a profession or an obsession. Consequently, you will frequently be faced with the very mundane problem of having to decide how to fit racing and associated activities in with an already busy schedule. Here it may be tempting to economize by specializing in one particular type of racing, and trying to train specifically for that kind of work only.

However, it has long been universally agreed by successful coaches and bicycle racers, including those with very limited time schedules, that such specialization is not desirable in the long run. Prepare for all kinds of racing and participate in as many different types of events as you can, given other restraints, in order to

A Frenchman in America: Bernard Hinault at the 1985 Coors Classic. (Photo John Swanda)

develop most fully and to derive the greatest satisfaction from the sport. One reason for this is largely that each type of bicycle race includes some of the elements found mostly in one or more of the other forms of competition. To give an example, the criterium racer needs some of the skills that characterize time trialing and the other disciplines, as well as those elements that seem to primarily characterize his chosen form of competition.

The way to improve your performance in any one type of race is by sharpening all the skill and strength elements that make up this discipline. And the best way to do that is by also competing in and training for the types of races in which that particular skill forms the major element. So you participate in time trialing to improve your ability to handle a solo escape or to catch up with the pack after a mishap in a road race. It all boils down to every bicycle racer essentially having to be a 'universal' bicyclist, one who can compete in all forms of racing, even if he gains his greatest successes in only one field.

Consequently, all bicycle racers should not only participate in different events, but also train all the various aspects of cycling in quite similar training regimens. In addition to sharpening specific skills, the participation in other kinds of races is an objective control method to check your progress in the skills that are paramount in that type of race. For that reason, you should try to participate in a wide range of different competitive events. Even if you only have time or opportunity to race once a month, it will be better to do one criterium, one time trial, one road race, and if appropriate one cyclo-cross race, and one track race, rather than doing four or five races of the same type during the same period of time.

All this must be done with a purpose in mind, though. Even while the criterium racer largely follows a similar training schedule to that of the road racer or the time trialist, and participates in all forms of racing, he must see these other pursuits as methods to sharpen certain skills in his chosen field. Nothing said here about universality should be interpreted to contradict the need for specificity in training. It remains a fact that the best preparation for a particular discipline or skill is that form of exercise that most closely corresponds to the same conditions. Distances very close to those ridden in races, types of terrain and other extraneous conditions similar to those encountered in races, speeds, gears and intervals similar to those ridden in the actual races must be used to prepare properly. But as for developing the many specific skills used in your discipline, there the other forms of competition and training will be just as appropriate for you as they are for the person who specializes in the particular field.

You will of course be free to pay more attention to your favorite type of event, and you will be most concerned about selecting the important events in that field. In fact, it is very likely that some form of specialization will be forced on you, since one kind of racing may be offered so much more in the area where you live than the other kinds. In Britain you will get more opportunities to do time trialing, while in the US it will generally be hard to find races other than criteriums, whereas cyclo-cross is restricted both to certain areas and to certain times of the year, not to mention track racing, which can't be done in many areas for lack of facilities.

The various training methods recommended for general competitive cycling were covered in the chapters of Part II. All these should be followed as much as possible to become a universally competent cyclist. In the specific chapters that follow, I shall highlight the most important aspects that set the various forms of racing apart from the others. In each chapter you will find a description of the peculiarities of that kind of competition, as well as specific hints on equipment choice, training and competition that are most suitable for that discipline.

Also included in each of these chapters will be a brief section on peaking. That is the intensive and somewhat specialized training program to be followed during a period of several weeks immediately preceding a very important race, which was described in Chapter 19. The following chapters contain additional instructions to help you do this for particular events. As you may have gathered from the above remarks, this kind of peaking and specialized preparation should be approached rather carefully. When peaking for one event, you are at the same time neglecting some other aspects, and your overall training progress may actually suffer, especially if you have limited time. First determine which races really justify this drastic approach, and don't think there is something wrong if your list consists of only one or two races a year. In fact, chances are you'll never participate in any race for which peaking is justified. Don't do it just in the hope of moving from 50th to 40th placing.

Time to Race

Racing is a time consuming hobby, especially if you don't live in one of the few areas where bicycle racing is a really popular sport. In many of the major urban centers several races will be held almost each weekend during the season, but even there most races will take place far enough from your home to take up most of the day. And well they should, since a duration sport like bicycle racing requires essentially all your energy for the day. Be at the site of the race early for warm-up and to accustom yourself to the course, the surroundings and the competitors. Stay around after the race to socialize, which may well prove an excellent way of obtaining useful information about both your competitors and the sport in general.

If the race is held more than a two hours' journey from your home and if you have the time, I suggest you travel out the night before the race, especially if it takes place early in the day. Whatever you do, travelling together with others will usually make the trip less tiring and boring and provides an opportunity to socialize. A weekend trip to race in a major center at a greater distance from your home, for which you probably don't have the time too often, should probably be exploited to the fullest: try to leave early enough on Friday to participate in a short Friday night race as well as events on the Saturday and Sunday. Don't do that if one of these races is a very important one for you, though: in general, you should avoid hard racing on consecutive days.

Even if you live in one of the bike racing centers, it may not be a bad idea for your social life (especially your family life if you should be so blessed as to have one), not to devote every weekend to racing. Instead, you may occasionally exploit one weekend by racing all three days in exchange for the odd free weekend. For the same reason, other weekends should not be totally devoted to racing: one race per weekend is generally enough. A fulfilling social life probably affects your racing results positively by putting you at ease, feeling good about yourself and the rest of the world. Just avoid excesses of any kind.

For those who live further away from the action, the program may be made more enjoyable if they do other things as well. Perhaps a weekend trip to the race area should also allow you to do something else. Though I would not recommend you spend your time in nightclubs or discos, you may well use the trip to partake in some other social or cultural activity. I know racers who travelled all over the European continent, without ever seeing any of the things for which they would have made the same trip as tourists. Needless to say they regretted it once they returned.

These considerations are particularly important if you have a spouse or a partner. Even from a purely pragmatic standpoint, enjoying one another's company and staying on good terms may turn out to benefit your racing more than maximizing your training and racing time would have done. All this is merely a suggestion, assuming your are interested and your social life includes other things than cycling. Feel free to spend all your time riding bikes or talking about them, if that really is the only thing that interests you and those with whom you associate.

Preparing to Race

Most races can be seen as part of your regular training program. During the racing season they form the control method that helps you monitor progress. Of course, each race provides additional racing experience that helps you handle the next race with greater competence. In addition, they provide the best opportunity to ride beyond your previously presumed maximum: the challenge of competition often makes one push oneself further than one would do under the toughest training regimen. Finally, for those who are forced to do much of their training alone, races

provide the best opportunity to learn and improve group riding skills.

Specific training schedules should be designed individually as outlined in Chapter 19, on the basis of the training methods presented in chapters 16–18. Nevertheless, a few hints for the period immediately preceding a race may be given here in a more generalized form. This, then, is additional guidance for your schedule during the active racing season.

As an element in your training schedule, the race day is the one I have labelled *day 1* in Table 22–I. This day is generally followed by the rest day. It is not necessarily always the toughest day of the week. Though you should of course give all you can in a race, it may be less demanding than your toughest training day during the week, depending on the length of the course and the competition present. The toughest regular training day will be selected to put you in the best possible shape for the race: it should be the day that leaves two easier days before the race. If the race is on a Sunday, then the hardest training day must be the Thursday before.

Though it is easiest to keep a regular weekly schedule, you may have to vary it a little if the race is on another day. This is certainly worthwhile if it is a particularly important race. In that case you may even carry out a peaking program during the few weeks preceding that event. That program actually includes some racing on each of the two weekends before the major race. But most races are not that critical, and you'd do better adhering to a regular schedule than experimenting around too much. Only vary your schedule if you notice there seems to be something wrong with it, and then stick to the new schedule equally consistently.

Anyway, three days before the race will be your hardest training day, both

Table 22-I Example of a pre-race training schedule

day	designation	suggested training
1	race day	real or simulated race, warm-up, calisthenics and breathing exercises, massage
2	rest day	short aerobic ride or e.g. walk, calisthenics or stretching, breathing exercises
3	hard training day	long distance ride with aerobic or anaerobic intervals, calisthenics, breathing exercises, massage
4	light training day	shorter aerobic ride with or without aerobic intervals, calisthenics or stretching and breathing exercises
5	hard training day	similar to day 3, though with more emphasis on intervals and speed than on distance
6	light training day	similar to day 4
7	preparation day	short distance aerobic speed intervals, stretching or calisthenics and breathing exercises

in terms of speed and the number of high output workouts in interval method training. As on the racing day itself, careful warm-up and cooling down before and after the intensive work will avoid injury on this day. Don't waste this day riding very great distances in the LSD mode, even though that is what many people still think of as being the essence of a hard training day. LSD training is only useful for building endurance, and that must be done before the start of the racing season. By the time you are in the racing period, you should have all the endurance you need, so an LSD ride is only required once a week, and a long race will take care of that in some weeks.

After the hard training day, don't slack off completely, but avoid forcing yourself excessively during the two days immediately preceding the race. On the first of these, train quite extensively, doing both high speed intervals over increasing lengths and a continuous ride in which you pay particular attention to style, technique and pedalling speed, if you ever catch yourself falling below your set goal of anything above 90 RPM. Do some speed intervals, but avoid what I call force intervals (often erroneously referred to as power intervals), so always gear down to stay within the comfortable range with respect to pedal force. The last day before the race can be a little easier again, but must still include some high speed interval work of varying lengths. Fast group riding or motor pacing is considered very useful during these two days.

If it is at all possible, try to find out in advance what the course of the race will be. In case the race is in your own area, you should take the opportunity to ride the actual course there no later than the day before the race. A really important race a little further away from home may justify a trip the weekend before. That way you can ride the course over at least once, taking notice of its characteristics and important landmarks. Even if you can't get out there to ride it, at least study a map of the area and of the course to get as familiar with it as you can.

Check your equipment two days before the race. This way you can be sure to be able to buy any replacement parts that may be needed and have necessary adjustments or repairs carried out in time before the race. Make sure your equipment is set up to best handle the terrain encountered. Check to assure that the wheels are well tensioned, have smoothly running hubs and that the tires are suitable for the terrain. Gearing and brakes must operate optimally, and everything must be adjusted, lubricated and wiped clean. Ride the bike for about thirty minutes to make sure it really is in perfect order, and then leave it alone until the day of the race.

In addition to training, you also need rest and food. The most critical night for rest is not the final one, but the one before, i.e. the night between the two easier days. The best way to assure a good night's sleep is to get up early the morning before, to do enough physical work during the day, and not to get too involved in social activities in the evening. If nothing else works, you may take a mild sedative that one night. Don't get onto the medication carrousel: unless you make a habit of it, an aspirin or a glass of wine is enough to do the trick in most cases, and millions of people get by admirably without ever needing either, which is preferable anyway.

The most important thing to say about food is that you shouldn't race on a stomach full of hard to digest food. Table 20–II in Chapter 20 shows which kinds of food take longer or shorter to digest. Hardly any type of food will be of much help if taken less than two hours before intensive work like racing. Eating a heavy meal is one heck of a method to disrupt your normal digestive process, even though you will need meals like that. The time to eat your heavy meal, including anything high on proteins and fat as well as fibers, is the night before the race, preferably relatively early in the evening, rather than shortly before going to bed. If needed, you may then also take a light snack meal later in the evening.

The Day of the Race

There is nothing wrong with eating on the day of the race, and proteins need not be avoided altogether, providing easier to digest foods, such as starches and sugars, dominate and fats are avoided as much as possible. I have fruit and waffles with milk, but there are a thousand other acceptable breakfasts that can be eaten on race day. Breakfast must be completed at least two hours before the race starts or three hours before the really hard work begins, whichever comes first. This is one reason to get up early in the morning on race day – easiest to do if you didn't go to bed excessively late the night before. A thorough visit to the bathroom before going to bed and on the morning before the race (each time preferably after doing some light exercise) may help you sleep and ride better and keeps your weight down.

Breakfast may be skipped if the race is short and starts really early, providing you take some sugary food, such as fresh fruit before the start. If the race exceeds two hours, and especially if the weather is hot, you must count on liquid losses through perspiration. That means you will need to make up by starting to drink liquids before the race, continuing as the race progresses and indeed after completion. Plain water is fine if the duration is less than two to three hours.

If there is any chance of running low on blood sugar, it will be smarter to use the water simultaneously as a carrier of sugar. Most racers spend ridiculous sums of money on supposedly superior athletic drinks, but the essential ingredients are water, sugar and salt, which can be cheaply combined in your own kitchen, following the suggestions in Chapter 20 for an isotonic drink. Carrying two bottles, one with water and the other with fruit juice will be equally effective and tastes better.

Some racers prepare for certain events with carbohydrate loading, which was also covered briefly in Chapter 20. It only makes sense for 2–3 hour one-day races. A good reason to steer clear of such nutritional tricks is that they disturb your regular eating and training schedule. Effective though it may be for the occasional cyclist who only once in a blue moon wants to prepare for a really unusual high output effort of the appropriate duration, carbohydrate loading is more likely to negatively ef-

Cyclo Cross racing in California. Roy Knickman, now a professional road racer working in Europe, who placed second at the 1984 Nationals in Santa Cruz. (Photo Darryl Skrabak)

fect your wellbeing, and thus your performance, than improve it. Perhaps you want to try it – if it works for you, it may be in order to continue when the situation suggests it.

The last hour before the race should be used for warm-up, to bring the muscle temperature up to the level where the enzyme activity is high and maximum work can be delivered without risk of injury. If it is at all possible, you should already have ridden the course at least once before the race. If not, you may in some cases be able to combine the warm-up with a ride over the course or part of it, providing you are there early enough. Either during warm-up or before it, do some breathing exercises and light calisthenics to help you relax and become flexible.

Warm-up riding is not to be confused with last minute training, nor is it merely riding around leisurely. Proper warm-up takes at least 15 minutes and

up to 45 minutes. Wear warm clothing if the weather is cool. Start off in a low gear, pedalling at a gradually increasing speed. After at least five minutes, increase the speed enough to act as a light aerobic interval, slow down again and do a few more repetitions, each time keeping pedalling speed high and the force moderate. You should work up a sweat this way. Then gradually slow down again and unwind, riding at a relaxed pace for at least five minutes, to finish warm-up about 10–20 minutes before the start of the race. Wear a warm-up or track suit while waiting for the race to start, to avoid cooling off again when standing still.

The race itself, depending which type it is, will be ridden as described in the chapters that follow. Always prepare yourself mentally for the race, making a plan of action on the basis of your knowledge of the track, your condition, your future plans and your estimation of the other contestants. Once the race gets underway, be prepared to modify the plan, but in the heat of the competition it is not the right time

to figure out the various possibilities and considerations. So you may revise your plan, but you should have one ready made to start off with. Ride consciously or associatively, rather than dissociatively, for an optimal performance.

After the race, try to ride at least five minutes at a relaxed pace, to cool off and recover while still moving, which is more effective than passivity. Wear your track suit and try to take a warm shower, after which you wipe yourself thoroughly. If at all possible, get a massage, even if it is only the simple form of self massage described in Chapter 18. If there is no opportunity immediately after the race, massage may also be administered later in the day. Stick around to socialize with the other competitors for an additional chance to learn more about your chosen sport. At night, record your impressions of the day – racing and non-racing alike – in your training and racing log, which will be described in Chapter 30. In the long run this will help you identify what is the best way to race and train effectively.

23
The Practice of Time Trialing

The time trial has been referred to as the race of truth. It is indeed a test of cycling strength – a race against the clock in which each rider is on his own, started at intervals of (usually) one minute. Your nearest opponent will be half a mile down the road at the start, and competition rules forbid you from getting close enough to have any physical benefit if you do catch up. Riding a good time trial is considered one of the hardest things in cycling. Though some have a less difficult time of it than others, it is physically and mentally the most demanding discipline. The skills most needed are consistency and an accurate knowledge of your own capabilities. The most useful aid is comparative knowledge of your own and other riders' progress along the way.

Participation in time trials has distinct advantages for the beginning bicycle racer, as well as for those who live isolated from others. Not putting the rider at close range with other fast and mean riders, time trialing demands less in the way of handling skills, group riding experience and courage. It also serves well as a gauge of your own performance, which can be compared with the results of other riders and so used to decide when it is reasonable to compete in other forms of road racing. As time trials are generally ridden over modest distances, they require less in the way of duration training, thus fitting into a busy person's schedule more easily. On the other hand, it is psychologically difficult to concentrate on this isolated effort, but that is a problem for all time trialists, whether newcomers or not.

The skill of time trial riding is a useful one for other disciplines as well. It can be of paramount importance in all forms of bicycle road racing and of course in triathlon. In the latter, the cycling discipline is essentially a time trial, though without the strict time separation of riders at the start and with less rigorous rules. All other forms of road racing also require the skill of cycling alone at maximal duration speed, e.g. in a solo escape or when catching up with the pack after

Rebecca Twig held in place at the start of a time trial. Taken at the Olympic Velodrome in Dominguez, California. (Photo Dave Nelson)

losing time. Stage races generally include a time trial as a full stage or a prologue. That may be the most important stage: more often than not, the biggest overall time differences are achieved there, making the winner of the time trial also the overall winner.

Whereas most longer time trials are held on the open road, record attempts are ridden on the track. The track discipline of time trialing, usually combined with pursuit races, demands the same cycling skills, though these track events are always very much shorter than road time trials. Training for any kind of time trials and participating in them is obviously essential for any bicycle racer and triathlete.

Though real time trial work should be an element in your training program, it is also perhaps the least desirable one to spend too much time doing. It is almost impossible, certainly for the beginner, to maintain an adequate training intensity as well as to pay sufficient attention to pedalling rate and riding style, when plodding along by yourself. For that reason, I suggest you do not try to duplicate actual time trialing conditions while training too frequently, except perhaps once or twice a month as a control method. Better ways to train will be a variety of the exercises discussed in chapters 17 through 19. Often ride the distance of the time trial, but not necessarily alone. During the last few weeks preceding a particularly important time trial race, your training schedule should be geared more specifically towards the work involved in the peaking process. This subject was briefly described in Chapter 19 and covered in more detail as it applies to time trialing below.

Time trials may be held in any terrain and over any distance, yet in the English speaking world most individual time trials are ridden on mainly level roads over a distance of 25 miles or 40 km. This is also the most universally ridden distance in triathlon events, though the tougher triathlons may call for much longer distances and include hilly terrain. In stage races, time trials tend to be shorter, especially if they are ridden as a prologue. In addition to individual time trials, there are team trials for two or four man teams, though the former are unfortunately hardly ever held in the US. Sometimes time trials are ridden on a track. The most prestigious cycling record is the one hour time trial on the track: a ride that leads to exhaustion in exactly 3600 seconds,

In any kind of regular road time trialing the course will consist of a stretch of open road with a minimum of motor traffic and unguarded intersections. Most typically, one half the total distance will be marked off and a pylon will be placed as a turnaround at the end of this stretch. You ride out to this halfway point, round the pylon and return. At the start, you will usually be supported by an aid who releases you when it is time to start. Triathletes merely grab their machines and leap on.

Equipment

You can ride a good time trial on any racing bicycle. I doubt whether there is more than a few seconds' gain possible in a 25 mile ride when moving up from a simply acceptable bike to the ultimate time trial machine. There is thus no point in getting very special equipment, unless you are really a world class competitor. It is curious to observe the discrepancy between useful and illusory equipment selection techniques frequently recommended for time trial work. In fact, some of the things often proposed are actually counterproductive. I suggest taking a look at chapters 11 and 12 again for an understanding of what should matter in time trial work. Though there are exceptions, here are the peculiarities of most time trial racing as they should be reflected in the sensible selection of equipment:

☐ Air resistance is an important factor, since the rider is fully exposed, not being allowed to take shelter behind another rider. Consequently, one should minimize the frontal area and optimize the aerodynamic characteristics of equipment, clothing and posture. Place the handlebars as low as you can, while still allowing you to hold them at the drops. Remove unneeded protrusions such as the inner chainring and the front derailleur, as well as unnecessarily big sprockets in the back. Use smooth tires, referred to as slicks, on V-section rims and perhaps a radially spoked front wheel with 28 or 24 bladed spokes if you can afford such extravagances. Make sure your clothing fits tightly and is smooth. Wear a helmet without air scoops.

☐ Some of the measures taken in the hope of reducing air resistance are ineffective. Neither the use of oval frame tubing, nor shaving the hair off arms and legs helps one iota. Installing the front brake behind the fork actually exposes it to more air turbulence, resulting in greater resistance, though still so insignificant that you may never know the difference.

☐ Speed changes are no factor in time trialing; consequently, minimizing the weight or mass is of no significant benefit either. In fact, one of the reasons – in addition to the undisputed advantage of reduced air resistance – for which disc wheels are chosen by some, is their greater rotating mass. Though slightly slower to start, their greater

inertia gives them a gyroscopic tendency, helping the rider to maintain a constant speed. Plainly ridiculous for time trial work is therefore the common obsession with selecting the very lightest tires and filling them with helium. The frame and the other components need not be particularly light either.

☐ Though no more so than in other disciplines, minimizing rolling resistance and friction will be beneficial in a time trial. It helps to inflate the tires to the highest pressure they can bear and to make sure the entire bike is optimally lubricated with oil to minimize rolling resistance and friction, respectively. To reduce the resistance in the transmission, you may install a slightly longer chain that actually hangs slack in the highest gear used. You may wish to install an improvised chain guide at the front chainwheel to avoid dumping this loose chain.

☐ Power surges are avoided entirely in time trialing, smooth maintenance of speed and power being the key to consistent riding. Consequently, the frame need not be particularly rigid. For the same reason it will not be necessary to change gear often once you are on your way in a time trial. Fewer gears will probably suffice and many time trials can be ridden with a single front chainwheel and without the front derailleur.

☐ Cornering, sudden speed changes and really long term comfort are of less significance in time trials than these factors are in other disciplines. This means that the balance of gear selection and crank length may well be varied a little from what you would otherwise choose. Many riders find slightly (2.5–5mm) longer cranks for time trial use most beneficial. Since they reduce the pedal force required to develop the same power, though with a longer pedal stroke length, the longer cranks allow you to ride in a slightly higher gear. With a given pedal force and pedalling rate, this results in a correspondingly higher road speed.

☐ The terrain may be familiar, but the wind may change. Consequently, you will generally be able to get by with fewer gears, once you have established which gear you will probably need. Yet you must have at least one higher and one lower gear, to be prepared for unpredicted changes in the wind.

☐ In a short time trial, you will not need to drink along the way. So you can do without water bottle and bottle cage, which will at least in theory reduce air resistance and weight slightly.

☐ Especially in stage races and triathlon events, completing in a reasonable time is more important than risking failure due to the choice of excessively sensitive equipment in the hope of gaining just a slight or illusory advantage. Consequently, choose reliable equipment and carry a spare tubular tire (or tools and a spare tube if you have wired-ons). Though a tire change will take at least three minutes, and you will lose any chance of placing amongst the top, it's better than giving up altogether. For the same reason, carefully check and try out your equipment before the race, correcting anything that is even questionable.

☐ Hill climbing time trials, particularly popular in Great Britain during the autumn, pose slightly different demands, since weight and equipment rigidity will matter more and air resistance less. For those events, select a light but rigid bike with all the gears you may need. Since you will work very hard at a low riding speed, you will need a helmet with plenty of ventilation.

☐ Team time trials require the riders of the same team to stay very close together. Thus, special short bikes with smaller wheels (especially in the front) may be of benefit, wherever allowed by the racing rules.

Technique and Training

Certain technical elements are peculiar to time trialing and must be practiced consciously before engaging in this discipline. These include in particular the start, smooth and consistent aerodynamic riding at speed, and the turnaround. Just like the swimmer may benefit more from perfecting start and turn techniques than from doing any number of laps, the time trial cyclist should not waste many hours of training time on riding the very distance of the race, but practice each of these elements separately many times.

Time trial riding takes place at or close to the range of the anaerobic threshold. In addition to the specific skills described above, the best thing to train for is shifting this threshold upward. As we've seen, that is done by frequently riding at output levels that exceed the current aerobic maximum. That is done in intensive interval work, in which group riding and motor pacing may be used to advantage. You definitely do not need to absolve long distance training rides in the formerly popular LSD mode.

Critical to your performance is a detailed knowledge of the times needed to ride portions of the total distance. Though you must also train the actual distance of the typical time trial for specificity, practicing over shorter stretches in time trial mode may be more useful than doing only actual 25 mile bouts. Identify a couple of 5–15 km (3–10 mile) long loops along your regular training route that can be ridden continuously, i.e. with a minimum of intersections, driveways and pedestrian crossings. Select the route so that you can warm up for at least ten minutes before reaching such a loop.

After warm-up, ride this loop several times at least once a week. Alternate interval sessions with continuous constant (maximum) speed efforts. The interval style should start with a sub maximal pace, which over a period of several minutes is gradually increased to your absolute maximum, maintained for 10–15 seconds. Subsequently, reduce speed until a pulse of about 100–110 BPM has been reached. Keep a close record of your times for each entire training loop and for shorter sections of it.

To keep fatigue down, many riders have found a peculiar pedalling technique very beneficial in time trialing. It consists of drastically reducing the force with which one pedal is pushed down every fifth stroke, which will automatically alternate from one leg to the other. This will effectively rest each leg 10 % of the time, while still staying in motion. Relaxation in movement is known to be more effective in avoiding fatigue than immobile rest. Consequently, the reduction in output may well be more than offset by greater strength during the power phase.

Not every rider can learn to do this effectively, but it is worth practicing long enough to establish whether you can benefit from this technique. Whether or not this style of riding is used, make sure you don't rock sideways, and keep your speed as constant as possible, not only from one minute to the next, but also from one pedal revolution to the next, yes even within each pedal revolution. Breathe deeply and regularly from the diaphragm, rather than from the chest. Concentrate all your attention on producing a maximum effort.

The best way of preparing for any particular time trial is riding that course before the race if you can. No need to do it at a racing pace: it's not a training ride but an orientation ride. This will help you establish what is the optimal gearing and which landmarks correlate to what distances, to help you set up a time schedule. In addition, the time trialist must learn to estimate his reserves and to judge the best speed throughout the race. Remember, every bike racer will have to use the time trialing style of riding at one time or another, so it follows that you should practice most of these things, even if you don't plan to engage in many time trials for their own sake.

The Race

At the start of a time trial, the rider's bike will usually be held up by an aid. Practice this with a friend until you can move off easily in a straight line at the starting signal. If no helper is available during training, hold yourself upright on the bike at a tree, a post or a wall. The feet must be in the toeclips, the straps pulled taut. For triathlon racing, you will need to practice doing the running jump into the saddle, in which case you will also have to practice placing the feet in the toeclips and tightening the straps when riding without losing speed.

Either way, select a low gear, but preferably not the extreme one of a six or seven speed sprocket, since the chain may be twisted excessively in such a combination. Place your strongest leg in the two o'clock position and relax until the countdown starts. Tense up briefly and relax, holding the bike by the brakes once you feel sure.

When the starting command is given, release the brakes and dive into the forward pedal with all your weight.

The first couple of pedal strokes you should stay out of the saddle and pull the upward moving leg up, as well as pushing the other leg down. Keep a straight line and sit down when your speed allows. Now change into your chosen gear and quickly increase pedalling speed to at least 90 RPM until your desired speed in the correct gear is reached. Find the smoothest portion of the road surface, usually where the outside wheels of cars travel. When there is a cross wind, get as close to any wind shelter as rules permit: you must stay on your half of the road.

Since air resistance is your main opponent in a time trial or other solo ride, take on the aerodynamically optimal position. Practice riding this way consciously with the same lowered handlebar position. Make use of the slipstream of overtaking motor vehicles by accelerating just before they pass and staying in their wake as long as you can, without clearly pacing or drafting, which is not allowed. Beware of danger on the road, though: don't merely look at your front tire, but keep an eye out for things ahead and by the side of the road. Many a promising time trialist has finished his career by running into parked trucks, crossing traffic or stray dogs. As always in cycling, whatever paranoid fears the public has about fast overtaking traffic from behind, the gravest dangers loom ahead of you, and survival is largely in your own hands.

When you encounter a hill, your technique will depend on its height and steepness. Short rolling hills that can be climbed in less than 20 pedal revolutions can be mastered by getting off the saddle and storming up in a rather high gear. Though this requires some harder work, you can re-

cover again during the downhill portion. Don't recover without pedalling, though: pedal down in your highest gear with reduced pressure for a nearly constant speed.

Longer hills should be climbed in a low gear, staying in the saddle. Since the negative effect of slow portions on the overall time is markedly greater than the favorable effect of fast sections, you should try to maximize uphill speed as much as possible. The same applies to the effect of winds: choose a low enough gear to ride as fast as you can at your optimal pedalling rate against the wind, and change up to a higher gear for maximum speed at the same rate with a favorable wind.

At the turnabout, keep up your speed as long as possible, since there is a significant potential of time difference there. Keep close to the outside of the road right past the pylon, gearing and slowing down before turning. Check back to make sure there is no traffic behind you. Then go around the pylon along a path as shown in Fig. 23.1. This is better than a symmetrical turn, allowing you to turn sharply at low speed and to accelerate while regaining a straight course immediately out of the turn. Don't assume you must return in the same gear as on the first leg of the ride, but quickly evaluate the gear that allows maximum speed at your highest comfortable pedalling rate.

You may notice that the first half of the return leg, i.e. the third quarter of the race, is the toughest. Here it is especially important to find a comfortable cadence and riding position, while forcing yourself not to slack. Things will probably seem to get easier in the last quarter. That is the time to gradually pick up speed and get as close to your maximum as you can, right up to the finish. Don't save your power for a strong short finishing

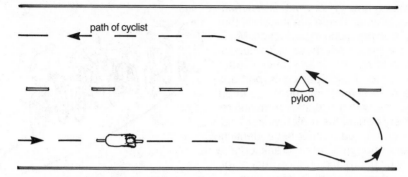

Fig. 23.1 Time trial turnaround (RH traffic)

dash. There's no need to gain a wheel length on a close competitor but seconds on a cruel clock, which can only be done by maximizing speed over a much longer distance. If you can sprint the last hundred meters or so, it means you haven't been going fast enough before.

If you manage to pass another rider, stay well behind him for some time, to adhere to the rule that forbids close following, mustering all your strength. Then accelerate gradually, maximizing your speed when passing. Pass with conviction, pretending you're not hurting a bit. Keep a lateral distance of at least 2 meters (7 ft) and don't relax your effort until after you have opened a gap of at least 25 meters.

If another rider catches up with you, try to avoid the same happening to you. You may never be able to pass him, but you may use him as a reference to pace yourself. Psychologically it is an enormous boost to have somebody whom you know to be fast (he would not have caught up with you otherwise) within reach in front of you. Don't let too big a gap open and try to maintain his speed. That may sometimes be easiest if you select the same gear, so you ride in the same cadence.

Team Time Trials

Both as a specific discipline and in stage races as one of the stages, team time trials have become increasingly popular. On the track and on the road there are races for two and four man teams, whereas the stage race may involve much larger teams. The usual distance for the four man team time trial is 100 km; two man teams generally ride shorter distances and team time trial stages in stage races may be any length. On the track the same riding principles are used in team pursuit races, whereas record attempts for the events usually ridden on the road are also ridden on a track.

The selection of the team is probably the trickiest thing a coach will be confronted with. Though the riders should preferably be strong, of similar body size and able to cooperate, neither selecting the club's strongest riders nor picking perfectly matched clones or good buddies will guarantee success. No doubt the strongest rider, i.e. the one who rides the fastest individual time trial, should be selected. He must be matched with people who have proven to ride well together with him in training rides and team time trials.

The most difficult skills in team time trialing are staying close together, judging when to change lead and knowing how to do it with a minimum loss of time. These are the skills that must be practiced to perfection. Much of the training of these skills can be done in smaller teams over shorter distances. Motor pacing is perhaps the most suitable method: ride effort intervals with the team in front and recovery behind the motorcycle. All riders on the team must have identical gears (though different crank lengths may be used) and change gear at the same time in order to keep mutually coordinated. Change as soon as you notice the lead is changing gear. The lead must know when to change: early enough and never near the crest of a hill, where a big gap and uncoordinated pedalling would result.

Whether in a race or a training ride, the efforts or pulls of the lead riders must be quite short. On a well balanced team each pull is 20–30 crank revolutions, though on a team with greater differences between riders the strongest rider may have to take longer pulls as long as he has the strength. All riders should try to ride their pulls as lead at the same speed; when one is weaker or more tired, he should reduce the length, not the speed of his efforts.

To change the lead, the ultimate way is for the lead rider to initiate it, moving slightly to the side, while the other riders stay in their original track. If the lead rider is insensitive to his decreasing power, the rider immediately behind is the one who must take the initiative for the change of lead, since he is the one who can best judge any slacking of speed. At that point he must move over to the side just far enough and move forward, while the riders behind him stay with him. Either way, the old lead moves over in the opposite direction but keeps up the pace until the new lead is right next to him. Only then does he fall back without really slacking too much. When his

Fig. 23.2 Team time trial lead change

front wheel is behind the third rider's rear axle he performs an acceleration and simultaneous sideways sweep to fall in place immediately behind, without creating a gap. Only in this position does he have a few seconds to get at ease or sip some beverage before the next person falls in line behind him.

Peaking for Time Trialing

Before a particularly important time trial, it may be beneficial to vary the regular training schedule for about three weeks in order to reach a peak performance. The general principle of peaking as described in Chapter 19 will be applied. During the first peaking week, about four weeks before the event, you may have to spend additional time practicing the skills peculiar to time trialing, as described in the preceding sections of this chapter. Even when you have mastered these, you may practice them again to become fully confident. Additionally, introduce longer effort intervals in your aerobic interval training rides twice a week. Build up the intervals for a higher speed in each subsequent effort. Concentrate more on speed than on duration, even during the LSD rides, which should be shortened to the length of the time trial to increase their specificity.

Two weekends before the event, participation in a real or simulated stage race (e.g. including motor pacing in the simulation) during three or even four days is very useful to deplete the body, so that overcompensation may set in. This is one of the toughest forms of training, sharpening both your competitive spirit and forcing you to do lots of high speed and anaerobic work, to deplete your system for subsequent recovery. The wrong thing to do here would be to ride actual or simulated time trials, since they don't provide a very useful training or depletion effect. If you do time trials at all, let them be short, encouraging high speed and giving more practice in technique. When riding these, concentrate on one of the various technique elements each

time: posture, pedalling style, pedalling rate, gearing and breathing.

After the high effort period, about two weeks before the critical race, a two-day recovery period should follow. Then you are ready for continued intensive training with an emphasis on speed. The weekend before the race is best spent in competition or motor paced training again. During the final week, resume the regular training program, with the same speed intensity but with a reduced total distance – about 75 % of your regular weekly training mileage, achieved by reducing the LSD rides to the time trial distance. The last intensive heavy training day should leave two relatively easy days with speed intervals before the race. On the day of the race, eat at least two hours before; warm up and wind down right up to your starting time. After completion, it will be best to cool off cycling at a reduced pace for at least five minutes.

Tandem racing on the track: Italy against France at the World Championships in Besançon. (Photo H. A. Roth)

24
The Practice of Criterium Racing

The great majority of all bicycle races, especially in the United States, take the form of the criterium: a mass start race of many fast laps around a short course. Although much of what was said in the two preceding chapters and the following one applies to all forms of road racing, and thus to criterium work as well, some techniques are peculiar specifically to this kind of racing. In this chapter we shall take a close look at the skills and training methods that will help you be a successful criterium racer. On the other hand, you are once more reminded that it is senseless to train and practice only one discipline. To excel in any one kind of racing, it is best to train for all disciplines.

Most typically, criteriums are rather short duration events as far as bicycle races go. Whereas regular road races usually cover distances of more than 160 km (100 miles), criteriums are never more than 100 km (65 miles) even for seniors. They may be significantly less, especially for the lower categories and age classes, as well as for women. The latter is rather unfortunate, since the typical female can handle longer distance work better than high speed efforts for shorter durations, due to various factors, including her usually greater fat metabolism. Just the same, these fast short races have their advantages, especially to the less developed racer. They are much less likely to cause muscle aches and unbearable fatigue. Certainly during the first two months of the season, criteriums are a very desirable form of competition for any racer.

Criteriums put a lot of fast riders at very close quarters on a circuit that is usually full of tight curves. In addition to speed, you will need a lot of nerve to do well under those conditions. For that reason, the beginning racer should prepare for this environment by participating in training rides in groups and perhaps by riding in fast city traffic. Even so, you may be excused if you don't ride out your first race of this kind, whether that is because you get involved in a spill or just fear you might. The experience needed comes with time, and indeed may well involve falling off the bike in the middle of a pack of cyclists once or twice, even though really serious accidents are surprisingly rare.

Equipment

A good criterium can be ridden on any respectable racing bicycle. If you can afford to equip yourself with special machines for different disciplines (something many world class racers don't even bother with), or if you want to set up your only competition bike to perform optimally in criterium races, here are some suggestions on how to choose frame and components. As in so many races, lightness and aerodynamic gimmickry will not do much for you at all in criterium racing: ruggedness and reliability will matter more.

Because speed and cornering are the primary characteristics of the criterium, the bike must handle nimbly, both when cornering and when accelerating. The tires must really be inflated to the maximum pressure consistent with the road surface encountered. This is especially important if the road should be wet, when many racers (fallaciously) think reducing pressure will improve adhesion. Neither will choosing an intricate tread pattern improve adhesion or other qualities in corners. More than in any other form of racing, tubular tires must be well glued in place, because the lateral forces when riding fast through sharp corners are likely to roll an improperly installed tire off the rim, which invariably leads to a spill.

To maintain stability when cornering and accelerating, the wheels must be tightly laced, and the frame itself must be as rigid as possible. The front wheel would best have 1-cross spoking, whereas the rear wheel should be spoked 3-cross or 4-cross, at least on the chain side. All the spokes must be under maximum tension within the limits of rim and hub strength. A rigid

Criterium stage of the 1985 Coors Classic in Old Sacramento. In the foreground is Greg LeMond, the eventual overall winner. (Photo John Swanda)

frame can be achieved by keeping its geometry short and upright, or by selecting tubing of slightly greater wall thickness. The latter is generally also necessary on bicycle frames of more exotic materials, to compensate for their inherently greater elasticity. The best frame is not necessarily the most expensive one, made of the very lightest and thinnest tubes. A cheaper frame, made of thicker wall tubing but with the right geometry, may well turn out to be better for criterium racing.

To allow pedalling around tight corners, the bike should ideally have both a slightly higher than normal bottom bracket, e.g. 27.5 cm (slightly less than 11 in), and pedals that are designed to take maximum banking without scraping the road surface. If your bike does not have the higher bottom bracket, the same effect is harder to achieve with shorter cranks, since the manageable variation in crank length is only 2.5–5 mm, whereas the difference in bottom bracket height may be significantly greater. If your bike is not set up that

way, you must stop pedalling in most corners. Though that is usually no big deal, a little continuity will be lost that way and the rider who keeps pedalling can attack in corners when others are barely keeping the pace.

Gearing for criterium races will be quite high with very small steps between individual gears, since hill climbing and strong headwinds are generally no considerations. Just the same, check out on the course of each race in advance and select your gears appropriately, because even a short incline that must be overcome every round adds up to enough total climbing to justify installing more widely spaced gears. As for shift levers, don't use bar-end models, since they are an open invitation to an opponent to put you in the wrong gear at a critical time. I recommend doing much of your criterium riding with the hands on the brake lever hoods, where bar-end shifters are impractical, rather than on the drops.

Choose a rather narrow handlebar model to minimize the room you need between other riders, and install the handlebars low enough to give you a reasonably low position, even when riding with the hands on the brake lever hoods. This posture allows you a better view of the field and, since wind resistance in the close pack is not quite as critical as it is in other forms of racing, there will not be a noticeable negative effect. You will not need to brake quite so suddenly and strongly as you may need accurate brake control most of the time. The higher position allows you to breathe more easily as well. It also puts the drops so low that you will have the aerodynamically and physiologically optimum position for a sprint.

Technique and Training

The essential technical elements for criterium racing are handling skill and continuous high-speed cycling in close groups. You will need some endurance too, but not as much as for longer point-to-point road races. You will need the ability to ride alone, but not for such long periods as is the case in time trialing or road racing. Most criteriums ridden these days take less than two hours in the saddle, and consequently they are less demanding in terms of distance than many training rides. But the high speed and fast cornering, which are the primary characteristics of criterium racing, can be very unnerving to the beginner.

I shall not try to teach you basic riding skills needed for criterium races here. To master these techniques at the level appropriate for criterium racing, practice all the techniques explained in chapters 8, 9 and 10, and get as much group riding experience as you can. For those who live far away from a cycling club, the only place to develop group riding skills will be by participating in many criterium races, and unfortunately these will also be mainly offered in the areas where the clubs are. But it is not impossible to become a competent criterium racer, even if you don't live in bicycle wonderland: you just need more talent, more training, or more concentration.

To develop the kind of high-speed riding strength appropriate for criterium racing, the training program must include exercises that emphasize these skills. Once more, LSD training, though required in the early season to achieve endurance, is not the best way to train for this discipline. I consider one weekly LSD ride of moderate distance – anything slightly in excess of the length of the longest criterium you'll be racing – adequate.

Even then it should also be used to practice some other technical elements, like pedalling style, pedalling speed, gear shifting and cornering.

Include at least two hard interval sessions and one or two less severe ones each week. A hard session will consist of five or more sets of repetitions over increasing and decreasing lengths, each emphasizing speed, rather than force. That means they must be ridden in a low enough gear to allow spinning fast. A recommended pattern for such a heavy set of repetitions would consist of a sequence with efforts like 25, 30, 35, 30 and 25 crank revolutions, each time recovering over two to three times those same distances. The pulse should be allowed to drop to about 100–110 BPM before the next set is ridden.

The secret of effective interval work is again to make sure you actually get to work as close to your maximum as possible. Generally, the time between sets should be spent riding at a fast clip, providing you are not fatigued excessively. There will be nothing gained by training at a reduced intensity when you are so fatigued that you can't reach a training level. If you tire that much, continue to ride at a relaxing pace in a low gear until you are fit enough to do another set of fast repetitions.

A light interval training period will consist of fewer sets of the same format, separated by longer and more relaxing recovery rides. Though the way you divide the various training exercises over the week will be up to you, there are a few points to consider. Firstly, hard training days should be followed by light days, to allow enough physical recovery for hard and effective work on the day that follows. Secondly, the easiest day of the week – often euphemistically referred to as the rest day – should follow the racing day, certainly if it was a hard race over a significant distance. Thirdly, the last hard training day must be the one that leaves two relatively easy days before the race. Finally, whatever you hear about easy days and rest days, they all require work: easy does not mean less speed, but less distance, and a rest day is not one spent in bed, but one with moderate exercise, requiring less force and distance.

Peaking for Criteriums

If the particularly critical race in which you want to perform as well as possible is a criterium, you may consider following a specific intensive training program aimed at peaking for that event. In general, the description of peaking in Chapter 19 applies here as well, though with some specific considerations, which will be discussed below. Evaluate your need for peaking about four weeks before that race, and spend the first week working on any skill or technique deficiencies you may have. The peaking process proper starts three weeks before the event.

At the beginning of the first week, do four or five days of particularly hard work under racing conditions. Participation in an actual stage race would be ideal, but two races at the weekend, followed by some very hard training days at high speed and distance, perhaps with motor pacing, is an excellent substitute. This series of hard days should be followed by two easy days to recover. After that, resume your regular training schedule, though with some modifications to emphasize the kind of work you most need, and avoiding less specific work.

Avoid long duration endurance cycling and hill climbing during this period, especially if the latter would be done at a low pedalling rate. If you live in a hilly area, you may not be able to avoid it altogether, so your bike must be geared to climb at a high pedalling rate and acceptable pedal force. This will avoid any undesirable conditioning to slow slugging and will prevent muscle aches that would inhibit training to your full potential.

The emphasis during this week should be on short duration speed, and LSD riding should be reduced to lower distances. Interval riding must consist of sets with quite short efforts, e.g. increasing and decreasing with efforts as follows: 15, 25, 35, 25 and 15 pedal revolutions, separated by recovery periods of two to three times those distances. If you can handle them, include more repetitions of the same distances within a set. How many sets you can ride in a day depends on your condition, but avoid interval work when you have become too fatigued to ride at maximum speed. Each training session should have at least one full intensity sprint over a distance of about 200 m, preceded by whatever kind of riding was typical for that session and followed by very low power winding down.

During the following weekend (and perhaps during the week, if available), enter one or two criterium races. If that is not possible, do some motor paced high speed training or fast group training. After that race, continue with this training schedule, but reduce the total distance ridden during the week by about 25 %. Again, don't reduce speed or intensity, but distance alone: at the end of the day you should perhaps be just as tired, having done as much really hard work as usually, but spread over fewer miles.

The last weekend before the critical race it will be good to ride in a criterium or to simulate one in motor pacing or group training at high speeds. After the rest day that follows, the first few days of the final week

should also adhere to the same schedule with fewer miles and fast riding. The last and hardest training day must fall on the day that leaves you two days before the race (i.e. Thursday if the race is on a Sunday). On the last two days, don't force yourself, but do relatively short distances with limited high speed intervals after very thoroughly warming up and followed by an equally thorough cooling off ride.

The Criterium Race

Whether this is the one highly important event for which the preceding peaking procedure was relevant or just any old criterium race, the preparation and participation procedures will be the same. One or preferably two days before the race, check out your race equipment and make any repairs or adjustment necessary, followed by a half hour's ride with it to make sure it operates perfectly. Try to find out the details of the course, to verify you have selected the right tires and the right gears. If at all possible, ride a few laps on the actual course to get acquainted with it ahead of time.

The most intensive training day should leave you two relatively easy days before the race, the last day being particularly light in terms of force and distance. On the day of the race, make sure you eat at least two hours before the start – for a short criterium you may be better off riding without breakfast than with a full stomach. Register in time, and spend the last 30–45 minutes before the start doing a thorough warm-up.

During the race, spend the first few laps quite attentively studying both the course and the other contestants. Find out how the various corners can best be ridden and where you may chance an escape later on. But also check which of the other riders are eager for sprints and escapes, and which are on the same team or otherwise seem to support one another, though this is generally less applicable in criterium racing than it is in other forms of mass start road racing. Size up the competition to find out who is a good bike handler and whom to avoid, who is a powerful puller and whom to fear in a sprint.

Nothing very significant that directly affects the result will take place during the first half of the race. If this is a points race (where points are awarded for placings at the end of certain laps) or if premiums are awarded, don't be tempted to run for these placings during the first half of the race. You don't want to be noticed too early, since it will make it that much harder to attack during the all important latter part of the race. Every other experienced racer is doing what I recommend above, and once they know you have the potential or the ambition to attack, there will be plenty of riders to make sure you don't succeed when the race heats up.

For the beginning racer, the biggest initial problem in criterium racing will be to stay close enough to the front, where the action is. It is also the safest place, where you'll be less likely to have dangerous things happening right in front of you. In the back you may be surrounded by incompetent riders, which is all too common in the less proficient categories. Finally, if you're near the back of the pack, you may lose touch with the essence of the race. In that case, you may find yourself lapped before long, though you seem to be working just as hard as the riders near the front.

Once you are behind the group you would like to be with in order to have a chance to place well, decide on your tactics to make the jump. Base your decision on your knowledge of the course, and take the riders around you by surprise. Try to pass by them from the back, preferably on the shel-

tered side. Don't draw any attention to yourself and accelerate from behind. Try to move about 3–4 km (2–3 miles) faster than the riders you want to pass, maintaining enough lateral distance to keep them off your rear wheel.

If you have not drawn attention to yourself as an ambitious rider before, chances are they will let you go, assuming you'll exhaust yourself and fall back again soon enough. If they want to catch you, they probably will, although you may have a teammate in that group who will help to keep down the pace of the chase. Once your gap is at least 25 meters, you can relax a little, still making sure to move slightly faster than the riders you hope to catch. This is obviously easier on the longer straight sections when the other riders are close enough to be seen. Once you manage to catch up with the group ahead, stay near the back and keep a low profile, since you have just worked a lot harder than they have.

Use the same style to escape ahead of the first group towards the end of the race, if you have a chance. If you are not a spectacular sprinter, a solo ride over the last lap or part of it may be your only hope of winning. Try not to get someone who is known to be a sprinter on your rear wheel, and give up on the whole venture if you do: the last thing you want to do is launch someone who will be sure to beat you into an unchallenged position. Nor do you want to take the risk of the rest of the group following in a chase to catch the two of you: you'll be the most tired rider of the lot, without any chance.

If a close group is together during the last lap, the race will be decided in the final 200 m sprint. The sprint will generally take place between the first group of up to ten riders, although on an open course with a long straight section, the group of contestants may be bigger. Decide well ahead of time how you hope to handle the situation. If you feel you stand a chance in a solo escape during the last lap, make sure you evaluate the course exactly and pick a landmark from where to start your escape. Do the same if you want to perform well in the brief final sprint: don't wait for another rider to take the initiative, but be prepared to start your sprint at a predetermined position along the track. Meanwhile, keep an eye out for what the others are doing, being ready to jump on the rear wheel of the first rider with a serious chance of escape, and try to pass him during the last 100 meters.

There are three ways to do well in this situation: simply being a good sprinter, who can work anaerobically; starting a much longer sprint, which will tire the real sprinters well before they can deliver their maximum, providing they don't get the advantage of your wind shelter; or by cheating. Though I don't suggest using the latter method, you must be warned that others may try doing it to you: when you are trying to pass a rider close to the edge of the road, especially on the sheltered side, he may suddenly move over to push you against the fence, which either forces you to brake or causes you to fall. Either way, you can give up all hope of finishing well, if at all. The moral is not to pass an opponent like that, though it will work fine if the other rider is your teammate and you agree on who has the better chance of winning.

25
The Practice of Road Racing

Curiously enough, the term road racing is used to describe not only all forms of bicycle racing on the open road, but also one particular kind of such race. In this sense, a road race is a one-day mass start event that takes place over a long course. Generally, road races are quite long: usually well in excess of 160 km (100 miles), at least for the senior men class. These are probably the toughest regular one-day events in any sport, comparable only to the few monster triathlons, which require similar endurance.

A road race may run from point to point, around a single big loop or several rounds of a circuit that is many times longer than that for a criterium. More often than not, the terrain over which such a race is held will be varied, including hills and level roads, towns and open countryside, straight roads and winding ones. As a rule, intersections along the course of the race will be guarded only while the major pack comes through, increasing the risks to stragglers, both in terms of traffic dangers and in terms of potential time losses. For this and other reasons, time differences between riders can get to be quite significant, though in many such races the bulk of the field comes through in one closed group. In that case a final sprint over the last few hundred meters may decide the outcome of a hundred mile race.

Although tactics have been called the key to success in road racing, endurance and other skills play an important role as well. Much more than time trials and criteriums, road racing requires universal cycling competence. To be successful in this discipline one must have both speed and handling skills, climbing power and endurance, tactical insight and determination. Obviously, there can not be just one particular kind of training that improves road racing performance. The road racer will also need a combination of all the different training methods. The way to find out what to work on most is to ride some road races attentively, and establish what your particular strengths and weaknesses are.

Work on both: concentrate on your strengths to find ways to exploit them, and on your weaknesses to try and overcome them. Having identified your personal qualities, you can avoid getting stuck in a hopeless situation, keeping your reserves up for those occasions in which your strong points can be applied fully. There are certain tricks to minimizing the detrimental impact of particular weaknesses. A poor time trialist can attempt a breakaway or a chase in the company of others, a poor climber will do it at a different point than a good one. A poor bike handler must make his escape well away from any curve and stay out of the way of the pack. Once you become aware of your particular qualities, you will also find ways to exploit them, just like you can learn to live with your weaknesses.

Equipment

If I mention equipment choice at all in this section, it is mainly to point out that there is little to say about the subject. Use any good racing bike with the most reliable components, and wear the most comfortable clothing. Since you'll be in the saddle a long time, make sure seat and handlebar adjustments are optimal for a relaxed riding style, as well as for strong pulls on hills and spurts.

Wheels and tires must be chosen to suit the worst section of the road in the particular race. If in doubt, choose 280 gram cotton tubulars, and make sure they are glued on properly and inflated as hard as you dare. Similarly, you should have gears to comfortably handle the toughest terrain encountered, especially if hills or areas with strong winds constitute a significant or decisive portion of the total distance.

It may be all right to sacrifice an out and out climbing gear or a really high top gear in favor of more closely spaced gears if climbs and descents are short. However, road races are generally too long and demanding to allow stomping up a longer hill anaerobically in too high a gear, hoping to make up for it on other sections of the route. In many races you will be required to carry a spare tire and a pump, while there may be an equipment van in other races. In the latter case, mark your spare wheels clearly with your name and number.

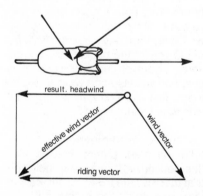

Fig. 25.1 Effective wind direction

Technique and Training

Most of the technical elements important for road racing are the same ones covered elsewhere for general riding or for the various other disciplines. Solo rides are described for time trialing in Chapter 23; group riding as required most frequently in criterium racing were covered in Chapter 24, and general handling skills in the various chapters of Part I. There is one technique that is used more in road racing than it is elsewhere: echelon riding. This is also referred to as bunching (in Great Britain) or drafting (in the US). The proper technique is rarely properly appreciated in English speaking countries, even amongst otherwise quite experienced riders.

The idea is to ride in a formation that gives each rider the maximum wind shelter most of the time. If the wind comes from straight ahead or if there is no wind, the best place to ride is right behind another racer, assuming you didn't pick the wrong wheel, i.e. follow a rider who is particularly slow or has an irregular riding style. Of course, any rider will tire after riding in the lead position for some time, so the ultimate is a formation in which riders take turns at the front.

If there is any kind of cross wind, the combined effect of riding speed and wind speed can be represented by a vector as shown in Fig. 25.1. To receive maximum shelter, ride in such a position relative to the person in front that corresponds to the orientation of that vector. Ride off-set to the right if the effective wind is from the left, and vice versa.

Easily said. But conditions change, and as the road curves, you will find the effective wind direction changes accordingly. So you should keep evaluating speed and direction of both the wind and the cyclists, to establish where you should be relative to the other riders. Experienced road racing

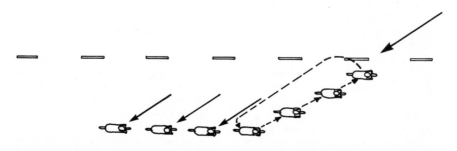

Fig. 25.2 Single echelon

cyclists almost unconsciously form into echelons whenever there is an effective cross wind, especially if they are attempting to escape from the pack or are trying to chase one or more riders who have escaped.

The echelon turns out to be the critical technical and tactical element in many road races. Since you need so much less power at the same speed (or can ride so much faster with the same power) when cycling in another rider's wind shelter, the skill to get in an echelon and stay with it may be crucial for your chances in a road race. Though the pure technical skill can easily be practiced in group training rides, the tactical elements must be understood as well. Only participa-

tion in road races gives you a chance to perfect this aspect of bicycling technique.

The illustrations Fig. 25.2 and Fig. 25.3 show the two types of echelons, referred to as single and double echelons, respectively. Only the lead rider, in what is called the 'point' position, is exposed to the wind for a brief period, after which he trades places, moving back as the second rider now moves into the point position.

Note how in Fig. 25.2 the entire lane width is taken up and the last few riders tag along behind. Though these stragglers are each immediately behind another rider, the cross wind will deprive them of any shelter in this situation. They have the same resistance

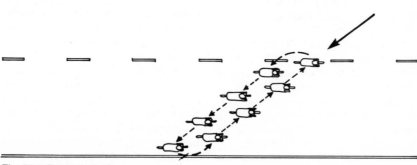

Fig. 25.3 Double echelon

as the lead rider, who is constantly rotating with the others in the echelon. If you are forced into this situation, quickly muster some other riders and form a second echelon to get the same benefits as those in the original one, who may well do all they can to keep you out of it if you are considered either a hindrance or a threat to their position.

The double echelon, shown in Fig. 25.3, is perhaps the most efficient method of riding in a cross wind, providing the riders quickly respond to orient the formation according to the effective wind direction as it changes, and take turns at the front with minimal loss of continuity. Here the lead position rotates either clockwise or counterclockwise, as the direction of the wind demands. After some time, the lead rider falls back only a little to take the position halfway behind the (new) lead. This results in a more constant pace and less disturbing movement within the echelon.

Though the second and other echelons will have the same wind cheating advantage as the first, it is almost impossible to win a race unless you find your way into the first echelon well before the finish. In addition to understanding the formation and maintenance of an echelon, you must develop three critical and largely contradictory skills to get into and stay in that first echelon. These are getting into an echelon, jumping from one group of riders to the one in front, and keeping others out of the echelon.

First appreciate that, though all other riders are potential opponents, many of them are also potential (though often limited) partners. Getting to know the subtleties of deciding whom to treat as a partner and whom as a opponent, and when during the same race certain partners and opponents change roles, is a tactical subtlety that can't be fully covered in a book like this. Try to comprehend how races are decided and ridden. Talk to others and read the reports in the cycling press of the events you have participated in yourself. You will learn the tricks of the trade as you develop racing experience. But it will suffice for now if in group training rides you practice the art of getting into an echelon. The essential skills for these techniques are covered below in the section entitled *The Road Race*.

By way of specific training for road racing, there are a few points to bear in mind. The interval training sessions most suitable for road racing preparation include sets consisting of fewer and longer repetitions then those used for e.g. criterium work. Whereas the kind of intervals typically ridden for criterium preparation may have jumps of only 15– 35 crank revolutions, road racing efforts should be more varied and longer. After warm-up, the first set of repetitions should perhaps have efforts of 20, 40, 60, 40 and 20 pedal revolutions in the appropriate gear, each time recovering over distances two to three times as long. After each set like that, first ride a considerable stretch aerobically until full recovery. Then you will be ready for a set consisting of repetitions with longer efforts, eg. 20, 40, 60, 80, 60, 40 and 20 crank revolutions during the efforts, two to three times that long for the recovery phases.

Ride several sets of each type, but avoid intervals when you are too tired to achieve your maximum. Between sets of repetitions your pulse should return to about 100–110 BPM, and you should have reached a feeling of relaxed fitness. The emphasis should be on quality, rather than on quantity. Don't punish yourself with an increased workload in the last few days before a race, since that may do more harm than good.

Climbs and Descents

Although other races may include hills too, they are more frequently an important element in road racing than in other disciplines. Success in mountainous terrain is not restricted to very strong riders who muscle their way up to the top, nor to very light ones, who have an easier time of it. Determination, riding style, self-knowledge, bike handling abilities and courage in descending are all factors that may influence the outcome of a race in hilly terrain.

Of course, the best way to develop the skill of successful mountain riding is to do it during your training. There is no substitute for the real thing, and that is the reason so many of the world's strongest climbers come from mountainous regions. Cyclists who think they can develop climbing skills doing weight training are fooling themselves. It may not hurt them if they are strong and talented anyway, but the same time spent doing actual mountain riding will be infinitely more effective for training and race preparation.

It will probably be tempting to select training routes so that they avoid the hills. Early in the season that is probably right most of the time, so you can concentrate on developing speed and endurance. But always include some climbing and descending work in your training schedule, even if you have to go out of your way to find a suitable hill, and even if you have to ride that same hill many times. When I lived in Holland, the closest thing to a hill within 70 miles was a 100 foot high bridge ramp, which the local racers who cared about this skill cycled up and down more often than I care to remember. Increase the proportion of hill riding as the season progresses to prepare for road racing.

In a race, hills often provide the best opportunities to make an escape from the pack. Depending on your particular qualities, that may be done during the climbing portion or on the descent. There is no great advantage to staying in a close formation on either an uphill or a downhill. When climbing, the air resistance will be negligible relative to the gravity effect, and on the descent you will be hindered more than helped by the close proximity of others. Even if you are not a particularly strong climber, you can often do well in a hilly race merely by hanging in there, without exhausting yourself excessively, providing you can make the most of the descent. Since many strong climbers relax the pace on the level, you may well catch up on the level stretches.

Peaking for Road Races

There may be one particularly important race of this type in which you want to do as well as possible, even if it takes an extra sacrifice. Your district or national championship may justify this kind of special training boost during the last three or four weeks. Basically, follow the hints on peaking as they were given in general terms in Chapter 19. Specifically for road racing, remember the peculiarities of that discipline, and emphasize them during the preparation period in the first few weeks of peaking: some solo rides, some climbing and some fast sprints as well as technique practice.

Despite the endurance requirement of road racing, there will be no point in emphasizing the duration aspect. Staying power should be well developed as late in the season as the road racing championships will be held. If you don't have it four weeks before the race, it is too late to make up for it in a crash program like this. Peaking must not be confused with compensatory basic training. Perhaps it is appropriate to spend a first week paying additional attention to pedalling, handling and gearing technique.

Once this has been taken care of, devote the next part of the program to fast long distance work that will exhaust you. An excellent way is to ride either a stage race or several long criterium races three weeks before the critical race, followed by one or two recovery days. The rest of the week is then devoted to intensive training, emphasizing speed and long-ish intervals. Throughout the peaking period, you should try to get at least two rides a week in that cover the same mileage as the actual critical race you are preparing for, preferably also in the kind of terrain typical for that race.

The next weekend should preferably include one or two races to sharpen your competitive edge. After a recovery day, resume the training program with longish intervals, followed by another weekend race. Then comes a week of regular training with a 25% reduction in total distance, but with a continued emphasis on speed intervals, preferably concluded with another race at the weekend. Your last hard training day should be timed to leave two easier days before the critical race. And don't forget to warm up properly on the day of the race.

The Road Race

In this section, only a few remarks that apply specifically to the road race will be covered. This does not only apply to the all important race for which peaking is justified, but for any road race. For general suggestions on the subject of racing, see the relevant remarks in Chapter 22. If it is at all possible, plan the race ahead of time. Either ride your bike along the route before the race, drive along it in a car, or at the very least study a map and the plan of the route very attentively to establish the features of this course.

It is preferable to get to the location of the start the night before if the start is early, as is usually the case. Get up at least two hours before the race starts, and spend your time preparing for it. Have an early breakfast. Your body takes about two hours to wake up, the same time being needed to digest even a light meal adequately, and such a race is too long to go without food in your belly. About 45 minutes before the start, begin your warm-up, as recommended and described in Chapter 22. Make sure you register in time and that your equipment is functioning properly.

At the start, arrive well on time and try to get a good position to reach the front. Experienced riders near the front of the pack are usually the first ones to form an echelon. You'll get the message if you are right there, but you may have to fight your way into an echelon if you are further to the back or were caught napping. Realize that the hardest place to join an echelon is at the rear. The last rider may well have the specific job of keeping opponents out, referred to as 'guarding the gate'. You will have to move closer to the front of the echelon and squeeze in just before the front rider falls back. You have to launch yourself in there quickly and decisively.

To bully your way into the echelon, muster all your strength, of which you need more than the riders already in there, who deal with less wind resistance. Dash for the position you want when a gap appears. Be confident and assertive. That only works if you can be sure of your bike handling skills, since you may have to literally fight to get in and stay in. Once in the echelon, take care not to lose your position, and do your fair share of the work. Not every rider's pull in the point position must be equally long. Like in the team time trial, described in Chapter 23, changes are made whenever necessary to keep the pace constant, and the strongest riders will naturally take longer pulls than weaker ones.

If a rider is obviously not doing his share of the work, or even reducing the pace when he is in the lead position, he is no use to the echelon and he should be dropped whenever possible. He may be stalling for tactical reasons to allow a team mate to catch up from behind, or to increase his lead ahead of it. There are permissible and improper ways to push a rider out. A weak rider can be dropped by sprinting away from him when he is in last position; once the gap is more than a few meters long, chances are you'll never see that rider again. A strong stalling rider is harder to drop and he may well find himself accosted physically.

Trying to stop a rider from joining the echelon is a matter of keeping a tight line and not budging in the rear position. A good bike handler is in his element in the rear position, and only an equally good bicycle acrobat, preferably with some resistance to extended elbows, is likely to get in unwanted. To stay in against the wish of the other riders is almost as difficult, so the best thing is to avoid making it obvious you may harm the others. If you look tired but basically cooperative, chances are you're not found out until it's too late to push you out.

To make the jump from one group of riders to an echelon or a solo rider ahead requires lots of strength and determination, as well as a very thorough knowledge of your own abilities. Timing is critical, as is the surprise effect. The jump is of course easiest when the benefit of the echelon is minimal and when the distance to be bridged is relatively short. On a steep climb the effect of wind resistance is minimized due to the reduced

In road racing the pack, referred to as the peleton, often stays close together for most of the race. Taken at the 1985 Redlands Bicycle Classic in Redlands California. (Photo Dave Nelson)

riding speed. Another opportunity is when a curve changes the required direction of the echelon. Make your jump from a position to the back, and keep pedalling at your absolute maximum output level until you have reached your initial goal, which is an almost unbridgeable gap of at least 25 meters (80 ft). Keep up an extended pace until you have caught up with the riders ahead. Once you are in their slipstream, relax briefly to regain your breath, but then start pulling your weight in the new echelon and avoid being dropped.

Road races take a lot of energy and generate a lot of sweat, so you will need food and drink before, as well as during the race. For a typical road race, carry at least one water bottle on the bike and perhaps one stuffed in your back pocket. That is the only place where a flat supposedly aerodynamic water bottle, which is more awkward to handle otherwise, makes any sense, since it follows the contours of the back more comfortably.

Replenish water and liquid food whenever you can, especially if the course is hot and dry or involves a lot of climbing. Also take some food along: cheese or ham sandwiches (without much butter or other fatty substances) and some fresh or dried fruit, providing it can be easily handled on the bike. Practice passing and receiving the musette (feed bag) and water bottle before the race. The helper should wear easily recognizable clothing and run along the road holding the article in an outstretched arm so it can be easily grabbed by the rider. The helper swings his arm forward at the same time as the rider swings his back while grabbing for it. Immediately put the item in place, rather than trying to eat or drink in the melee.

The feed zone is a likely place for an unobserved surprise attack or escape. Make sure you get your food early, and be ready either to attack or to catch any riders who try to get away. Being early also has the advantage that you are less likely to be involved in any falls, which often happen there, as a hundred riders are fighting for a position close to the side of the road, trying to pick out their supply person, and then have to regain their balance with bags and bottles. If you have learned to handle the bike and have practiced receiving the musette and bottle as well as consuming their contents, you will have one problem less to worry about during the race.

Should you have an equipment failure, raise an arm to let the other riders know where the problem is, so they can avoid running into you. If there is an equipment van, or other riders on your team are supposed to support you, raising the right hand will signify you need a new rear wheel, or the left hand for the front wheel. Whatever way you handle the repair – new wheel, replacement bike or exchanging the tire – ride like hell to catch up with the pack as soon as you can. If a team mate could stop to help you, so much the better, but if the supposed helper is not up to the task, you and the team might both be better served if you try to go it alone.

A tire change takes a minimum of three minutes; a wheel change only one minute. But first the helper with the new wheel must reach you, which may make the operation even more time consuming. Certainly if it happens early in the race, it may be entirely possible to catch up again. It is a lot easier to catch up from behind than to escape from the front of the pack. In the first case you are free to set your own fast pace and use riders in front for reference, whereas the latter situation merely results in a response from the other riders, who will speed up until you are brought into line again.

If you are not supported by a team, make your own arrangements ahead of time to be picked up by a friend in case of trouble. Even if you don't have a problem, there may be some planning involved. Often the start is some distance from the finish, and you will need either a car or at a minimum warm-up clothes brought to the finish, if you want to avoid a miserable ride back to the location where your gear is.

For a discussion of the techniques needed during the last dash or sprint, refer to the appropriate section at the end of Chapter 24, since the same

applies to road racing as to criteriums. It is not possible in the scope of this book to give you a complete rundown of how to ride a road race. Practice the various elements described above, keep your eyes open for opportunities, and learn to estimate your own potential, as well as other riders' strengths and weaknesses. Beyond that, it becomes a matter of experience, luck and the tactical advantages of support from other riders, as provided by a team of at least three members. Even if you are the strongest rider in the field, chances are you will never win a road race, since the number of factors that influence the outcome is so great and so unpredictable. But you can certainly improve your chances by following the above advice.

Fig. 25.4 A day's work in terms of elevation differences (bottom) and heart beat (top). Recorded during a 215 km (135 miles) road racing stage of the 1986 Tour de France for one of the participants (Bundue).

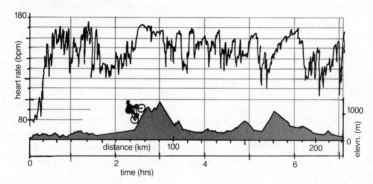

The Practice of Stage Racing

Essentially, the stage race is nothing but a sequence of separate races (each referred to as a stage) on consecutive days. Sometimes there may be two shorter stages on a single day, and conversely a longer stage race may include one or more rest days. The times and placings attained by the individual riders are cumulated after each stage. The riders' overall standing at any time during the race is expressed in the general classification (referred to as GC). The overall winner will be the rider with the best total time. In addition to the individual placings for the day's results and GC, there often are ratings for teams, as well as point ratings based on individual placings in sprints and for climbs.

The Elements of Stage Racing

The first and still the most spectacular international stage races, such as the Tour de France, originally included only point-to-point road racing stages, the race starting daily from the point where the previous day's stage had finished. But over the last 30 years this has changed. Two consecutive stages may now well be separated by a lengthy bus or plane journey, and stages representing other types of bicycle racing have been added.

Though many US stage races are little more than a short time trial and two or more flashy criteriums, the more traditional and longer ones have varied stages. They include individual and team time trials, criteriums, point-to-point road races and mountain stages. Time trials were added in order to introduce the possibility of greater time differences. This makes the whole affair more interesting than when day after day all the favorites arrive in the same group, and are thus awarded the same times. In addition, 'artificial' time differences are created by awarding time bonuses to the first finishers of each stage, as well as to the winners of certain sprints along the way.

If strength was the key to time trialing, handling skills and speed to criterium racing, endurance and tactics to road racing, then it can be said that team tactics are perhaps the most important factor in stage racing. That applies particularly to the famous international stage races. Since this book is mainly addressed to the individual rider, the team aspect can not be covered in excessive detail, and in consequence this chapter can be kept much shorter than those dealing with the various distinct types of one-day races. Though some remarks on tactics for cumulative events will not be lost on the individual racer, to him the problems of stage racing are much the same as those that apply to the various types of racing represented.

To be ready for stage racing, you have to be able to handle every kind of bicycle racing. To do really well in stage races, you have to be spectacularly good in at least one discipline: you must be either a fast sprinter, a consistent time trialist, a strong climber or an untiring endurance cyclist. And above all, you have to be able to do the one thing that is unknown in any other sport, and indeed seems to contradict recommended race preparation practice: you must be able to perform well in a punishing sport day after day. Clearly then, this is not a discipline for beginners.

Even so, to gain experience and as a training tool, there is no harm in starting early with stage racing. Try to enter one towards the end of your second season. The varied disciplines and the need to perform well several days in a row call into action the compensation effect referred to in Chapter 16, providing a peculiar kind of toughening. This is particularly beneficial during the last couple of weeks before a very important event in any of the other cycling disciplines. Besides, stage races are worth entering for their own sake. If you are not a member of a team, it will probably be hard to find stage races in which you can participate as an individual, since most of them are the exclusive domain of teams. Some of these races are indeed open to individual licensed racers of the appropriate category.

Road race, European style. Mario Beccia at the professional World Championship in Salanches. (Photo H. A. Roth)

Team Tactics

Even for the individual rider, team tactics are important in stage racing, whether he is racing as the member of a team or not. For the racer who is not participating as the member of a team, it is valuable to know how to do well against riders who collaborate on a team. And the rider who is on a team must appreciate that the tactics are not solely dictated by an omniscient and omnipresent coach, quietly pulling invisible strings. Instead, a good team is one in which the individual riders understand how to benefit the team's overall position and are willing to work towards that goal.

First of all, get to know the teams and their members, not just by their jerseys, but by their noses and their names. Associate the individuals with their team; know who else is on the team of the rider whose wheel you are hugging. If yesterday's stage was won by another member of his team, or if

one of his team mates has a favorable placing in GC, understand that he may not be working for himself, but mostly against you. He may be trying to hold you back or he may be working to pull the sprint for someone else behind you.

The latter is merely one of many different possible examples of the various ways team tactics may influence your personal racing tactics. In stage racing, occurrences like this will be forever present and you'll have to become alert to them. There's no point in running down all the various possibilities of either exploiting or frustrating team tactics. All I can do is warn you how important it is to be alert to this phenomenon in stage racing. It will be up to you to draw up (or modify) your own plan and, using the techniques described in preceding chapters, try to outwit the other teams.

Obviously, experience will be of great benefit. Both in terms of learning what to expect from others and what to do about it yourself, and in terms of how to apply technical and tactical skills to carry out your own plans. The technical skills to realize your own plans can be sharpened in almost any other kind of mass start race. The tactical aspect is of course best learned by participating in as many stage races as you can. However, team tactics may also be at work in a lot of criteriums and road races, so participating in these may benefit your progress in this respect as well.

The next best thing by way of preparation for this kind of racing to physical participation in many actual stage races is mental participation. Read about them, as reported in the cycling press. Talk to racers, coaches and journalists who follow such races, and make an effort to understand what is going on. Don't just talk, but listen: you're trying to learn something, not to impress others with what you know

yourself. For the individual racer who may never have raced under the supervision of a team coach, as well as for the minor team member, it is rewarding to know that team coaches make mistakes too. In fact, an informed and alert outsider may at times be able to outwit the smartest team strategians.

Training and Technique

Training for stage racing amounts to practicing all cycling skills, with an emphasis on group riding techniques and endurance. Since there are so many different aspects to this form of racing, you may be able to do well despite some weaknesses. You may be able to compensate for poor climbing abilities through superior bike handling in downhill and criterium stages, where many of the strongest climbers fall right back. You may even be able to compensate for poor time trialing ability through superior smartness, picking the right wheel and doing well in sprints.

Even so, the ability to ride alone for a longer period, as in time trialing, is perhaps what gives a moderately endowed rider the best chances in stage racing. Unfortunately, this is not a skill easily trained: you either have it or you don't. In fact, concentrating in training on the kind of solo riding typical for time trials may be self-defeating. You may be flogging a dead horse, meanwhile neglecting other more promising aspects of your training program.

Instead of trying to practice the physical skill of time trialing, you'd do better to improve your mental ability to handle this kind of solo performance. Don't spend hours each day plodding along, hoping to improve, but learn to set yourself goals along the way, as explained in Chapter 23. What distinguishes the successful time trialist and solo rider from others is generally not a greater trainable physical strength, but a state of mind that allows him to set himself a goal and work for it, despite the absence of visible competitors for reference and encouragement.

In addition to improving your time trialing attitude (rather than training alone), particular emphasis should probably be placed on whatever are your innate skills. Your natural talent is your greatest asset, and exploiting it to the fullest will help you along more than anything else. If you have climbing or sprinting abilities, exploit and develop them as much as possible. Even more important than increasing your skills in training, is developing an alertness to opportunities for exploiting them. While racing, look out for possibilities where your greatest strengths may be applied favorably, and make sure you get in a position to benefit from them. To give but one example, your superior sprinting skill is of little use in the back of the field. Instead, do all you can to tag along in a position to finish really high up.

But the sprinter may also apply his skill in many other places, in addition to the final dash. The sprinting ability may equally be used to gradually work towards the front of the pack, by bridging gaps and making minor escapes to get closer to a group or rider in front. The other side of the same coin is to avoid situations in which your weaknesses are of detriment. Thus, the sprinter should not try to aim at a solo finish and the time trialist must avoid approaching the finish with a strong sprinter hugging his rear wheel.

Additionally, you have to work on overcoming your weaknesses, if at all possible. That may not apply to such largely genetically determined things as described above. You either are a sprinter or you're not – it's all in your anaerobic power and fast twitch mus-

cle fibers. But nobody is a born bike handler, time trialist, descender or tactician. These are the skills to work on, since there is much more latitude for improvement there than in the strength aspects of cycling. Rather than plodding along for miles and miles, fine-tune your bike handling skills and develop your mental grasp of the intricacies of racing tactics.

Participation in any kind of racing is probably the best way to prepare for stage racing. Although this statement may be reversed too, the use of stage racing to prepare for other racing is solely in the toughening aspect, whereas the competitiveness of other races will benefit your performance in stage races in many more ways. For this reason, it will be advisable not to start with stage racing too early, nor to devote too much time to it early in your racing career. Other forms of racing are more specific and favorable to develop speed, technical skills and competitive edge. These are all aspects that will help you in stage racing as well, without being quite so easily learned there as they are in other disciplines.

It has long been established that a maximal performance two days in a row is harder to achieve and more detrimental to overall condition than on alternate days. This principle applies in stage racing as much as it does in training. For that reason, it will be smart not to try doing just that. Instead, find out in which stages you have the best chances, and take it a little easier on the intervening days. Once more, this makes thinking and awareness more important than simple physical ability. Of course, luck and opportunity are significant aspects too, and your fine plans may well be foiled in the heat of the battle. So be flexible enough to revise your plans along the way, basing your decisions on all the information you have stored in the mind, both concerning your own potential and concerning the development of the race.

Another reason not to force things two days in a row is the fact that you will have drawn attention to yourself if you perform conspicuously well. When everybody is watching you on the day after a success, your chances will deteriorate, even if you feel fine and ride well. If that is the case, stay a little further back and don't show aggressiveness, especially in the first two thirds of the stage. This way, your opponents will not suspect that you have something up your sleeve. They are not aware that you have the potential to do well again, which improves your chances for a surprise attack towards the end of the day's stage.

Of course, you may ride many races without being near the front or being dreaded and watched. Not everybody (or let's be more realistic: hardly anybody) can be a successful racer, despite the pathetic emphasis on success that modern society seems to demand of every participant. What to do if you're not the greatest is perhaps more relevant to the vast majority of readers. Participate, allocate your powers, think, and exploit those few opportunities that do appear to every rider once in a while. Don't hang in the back of the pack all the time, even though your limited ability may force you to be there some of the time. Avoid being discouraged, and keep an eye out for opportunities. This way, you too may experience an occasional success of some sort: you may win a sprint or even a stage, or you may be acknowledged as a particularly smart, helpful or reliable rider. There are many other ways of getting satisfaction.

27
The Practice of Cyclo-cross Racing

Cyclo-cross is a form of outdoor racing that differs quite a bit from any other discipline. As the name implies, it can't be regarded as a form of road racing, though it is practiced largely by the same people who participate in various forms of road racing during the main season. The brief introduction to this form of sport contained in Chapter 2 will give you a taste of it, and may help you determine whether you should consider participating in it. Mainly practiced in what is the off-season to most cyclists, it is not only an exciting and demanding sport in its own right, but also an excellent form of off-season conditioning to keep in shape and build up both strength, endurance and handling skills.

To the uninitiated, masochism would probably seem to be the key to all forms of off-road racing: stomping through mud, dust or snow, bouncing off rocks or logs, and carrying bikes over the most impossible and unpassable terrain is not everybody's idea of a good time. Those who participate are happy enough about it, and there is a certain rustic charm about the whole affair. In the first place you are closer to nature in this discipline than you will be in almost any other competitive sport.

Furthermore, it is a sport that keeps you active in many different ways, challenging both imagination and skills. You not only decide in which mode to best handle a certain stretch or a particular obstacle, but then you have to actually do it as well. In many cyclo-cross races the bikes are shouldered as much as they are ridden, and the art of handling the bike under these circumstances is a skill apart. Unfortunately, cyclo-cross is virtually restricted to men only in the US. Though USCF rules now allow for women's championships, women still find themselves excluded from most other races, since they are called off the track as soon as they are lapped by the fastest male contestants. I feel women should be given a fairer chance in this discipline.

Mud plugging, is what the English call cyclo-cross. Here you see how appropriate that name is. (Photo H. A. Roth)

Cyclo-Cross versus Off-Road

In addition to conventional cyclo-cross races, in which a relatively small but difficult course is traversed many times by each rider for a predetermined time, off-road cycle races with mountain bikes (also known as ATB's) have become popular in recent years. In the latter discipline a longer course is ridden and this is generally traversed only once. I have devoted an entire book to the subject of mountain bikes (*The Mountain Bike Book*, also published by Bicycle Books) and useful information on bike handling and racing for this discipline can be found there. In the present chapter those points particular to cyclo-cross and those common to all kinds of cross-country racing will be covered.

In fact, the distinction between the two disciplines may some day disappear altogether. Fat-tired mountain bikes have been successfully used in several regular cyclo-cross races, and cyclo-cross bikes with skinny tires have been used with equal success in certain mountain bike races. At present the main distinguishing features is that – at least in the US – racing equipment is frequently changed during the race in cyclo-cross, while it is either prohibited or discouraged (and generally impractical) in mountain bike racing. Still quite confusing is the questionable status of USCF licensed racers in the US who participate in mountain bike races sponsored by NORBA (National Off-Road Bicycle Association). It is to be hoped that some lasting agreement between the two organizations will eventually be worked out. Such an agreement should either transfers the responsibility for all racing to the USCF, or allow USCF license holders to race in events sponsored by by the off-road organization.

The two forms of racing could actually complement one another nicely, since cyclo-cross is a winter sport, whereas mountain bike racing is most intensively practiced in summer. This way, cyclo-cross could appeal to both regular road racers and those who participate in mountain bike races during the season. On the other hand, there is no good reason to restrict mountain bike racing to the summer, and even if that's practiced, mountain bike riding may be an excellent form of training – whether for its own sake, for cyclo-cross or for general conditioning.

The sport of cyclo-cross will almost certainly gain in popularity with the infusion of new blood and different equipment ideas as a result of the mountain biking development. A start has been made, and the introduction of more reliable equipment derived from mountain bike technology should be welcomed by cyclo-cross racers, since it could make their lives a lot easier.

Equipment

As mentioned above, the equipment question is still evolving. The conventional basic requirements are for a sturdy frame with a high bottom bracket (28 cm or 11 in minimum), wide-range gearing, handlebar-end shift levers, knobby tires and cantilever brakes. Though some riders like to use 15-speed gearing, others prefer the relative simplicity of ten-speeds, which eliminate some of the front derailleur alignment problems inherent in any 15-speed configuration.

Many riders use several different bikes, set up for different sections of terrain. More rugged mountain bikes and racing bikes inspired by these types are gradually entering the field. Using much more reliable equipment may help you avoid what I call the equipment trap. Relying on this kind of machine, a rider may not be faced with the (real or presumed) need to have several different machines and helpers to maintain and shuttle them back and forth during the race. On training rides there won't be people around to take care of one bike while you're out wrecking another one either, so there the more robust machine is the answer anyway.

As regards clothing, a helmet is a must, while long-sleeved woolen shirts, long pants and thick-soled, lined shoes (fitting high enough around the ankles not to be lost in the mud when walking the bike) and finger gloves may be appropriate if the weather condition suggests their use. Since most cyclo-cross races are relatively short, and the things will only get in your way, a water bottle and its cage are not recommended for racing. While training and as pre-race or after-race wear, make sure you have clothing that keeps you warm, since the high muscle forces often developed in this sport, combined with the low temperatures commonly prevailing during the cyclo-cross season, could only too easily cause muscle or tendon injuries.

Technique and Training

The techniques needed for successful participation in cyclo-cross racing include general bike handling, climbing and carrying the bike when running, as well as getting on and off. Pay particular attention to the discourse on bike handling in Chapter 8. Practice those skills under off-road conditions for the greatest specific improvement in cyclo-cross performance. Since technique will be the biggest factor once you have reached adequate strength and endurance, most of your training time should go into working on your bike-handling skills. Do that both in relatively smooth terrain, where you can more accurately establish what is happening, and in the off-road environment typical to this kind of racing.

The most important specific skill not encountered in other forms of racing involves getting on and off the bike to carry it over obstacles or through terrain where the tires of the bike would get stuck. In a race this must of course be done with a minimum delay, which requires the maintenance of

Bike carrying demonstrated by a mountain bike racer. In cyclo-cross the bike will look different, but the style is similar. (Photo David Eppersom)

momentum and a continuous flowing movement. Here is a brief description of the correct technique to master this curious element of bicycle handling.

Establish beforehand where you will want (or may be forced) to get off the bike. Shortly before that point, select the right gear and slow down for the speed you will be running. Before you've slowed down fully, place your weight on the left pedal, keeping it in bottom position. Swing the right leg over the seat and forward between your left leg and the bike. When you've reached the location and the speed at which you will be dismounting, hop onto the right foot, take the left foot off the pedal and start trotting. The first few times you try this, you may find your right calf in conflict with the left pedal. Overcome this painful problem by leaning the bike more to the left and perfecting your timing.

To carry the bike at this point, combine the act of dismounting with that of picking up the bike. The moment you hop onto the right foot, reach the right arm down under the top tube all the way until you can place it over the right shoulder, which will slide into the corner of the frame where the seat tube and the top tube join. Grab the handlebars with the right hand, so you have the left hand free for balancing and to clear your way. That will be essential if you will be passing through vegetation or have to keep other competitors at bay.

Carry the bike shouldered like this, holding the handlebars with the right hand until you approach the point to remount the bike. Just before you reach that location, lean forward and to the right, allowing the bike to slip off your shoulder, while grabbing the handlebars with the left hand instead. In one continuous movement, swing the right leg over the seat and pedal the first stroke with that same leg, then place the left foot on its pedal

when it is in top position, slipping it under the toeclip. After a few strokes, tip the RH pedal to turn it in the correct orientation. Finally, tighten first the one then the other toestrap.

With a little practice, you can do all this without stopping or slowing down below the speed at which you can run while carrying the bike. Practice is all it takes, and the first installment of it is best gained on an empty parking lot. Once you're familiar with it, proceed to more difficult terrain, after which you may finally do it in a race. Practice these and the various other bike handling techniques covered in Chapter 8 very consciously during the three or four week period preceding your first cyclo-cross race each season, and continue applying these skills, while training during the cyclo-cross season. You will soon find out how big an advantage full mastery of the correct techniques gives you in cyclo-cross races. That applies especially in the lower categories, where you may be one of very few riders to do it efficiently. Not only do proper handling skills speed you up, they also mean you tire less, so you keep valuable energy for actual cycling and running.

As for training to develop anything else than technique, the same applies to cyclo-cross as for the other forms of bicycle racing. Do any or all of the exercises recommended in chapters 17 and 18, selecting in particular those that suit the time of the year and the available time. In winter that may mean relatively short training sessions. The recommended forms of on the road and indoor training would be any that include many force and speed intervals of varying duration. Of course, actual off-road training sessions, using either a cyclo-cross machine or a mountain bike, would be most effective, since they will be very intensive and specific.

Off-road Cycling as Training

Not only is cyclo-cross a fine sport in its own right, it also lends itself superbly to stay fit during the cold season. Since riding speeds are relatively low, and seeing you may ride in a more sheltered environment than the open road, you will keep warm much better. Besides, this discipline requires high energy outputs even when riding at low speeds, due either to climbing or to high rolling resistance. As a result, the training effect is quite significant, providing a kind of natural interval work. You will find it simply less cold and miserable than a similarly beneficial training ride on the road.

In areas where late fall and winter cycling seems to be precluded on account of road and weather conditions, I highly recommend you practice this kind of work whenever possible. It should be no problem to do it once a week in addition to high speed wind-load-simulator work and the various other indoor exercises covered in Chapter 18. Half an hour's intensive off-road work twice a week will do more for your general and specific cycling fitness during the off-season than any kind of weight training. Use either a cyclo-cross machine or a mountain bike. On any kind of terrain and in any kind of weather, the latter would be useful as a means of transportation for many trips you might otherwise be tempted to do in the car, allowing you to combine some form of training with your regular affairs.

Peaking for Cyclo-Cross

In principle, this doesn't differ much from the recommendations given in the preceding chapters for optimizing your performance with one very important race in mind. The big difference is, though, that the kind of competitive events recommended during

Though the USCF now specifies cyclo-cross championships be organized for women as well as men, women's cyclo-cross racing is still a rare phenomenon. In far too many races women are not given a fair chance, since they are called back as soon as they are lapped by the fastest men. This photograph shows Beth van der Liet courageously defying the organizers at the 1984 Nationals, when the race rules effectively barred women from participating. (Photo Darryl Skrabak)

the two to three weeks before the important race will not be offered: no stage races and criteriums during the cyclo-cross season. Consequently, it will be up to you to do the kind of work that will stimulate the hard depletion and training effects required.

Three weeks before that crucial race, do any kind of vigorous long duration work several days in a row. Two weeks before, try to participate in at least one race, to sharpen your competitive edge. During the last two weeks increase speed and intensity, while reducing the distances covered during regular training if you are on a long distance schedule. But let me emphasize again that peaking only makes sense if the event really is so crucial that you can afford to sacrifice some overall training efficiency. Chances are that you never need to do this work, especially in the case of cyclo-cross, which usually falls in a period of relatively less intensive training.

Ice and snow at world championship cyclo-cross race. The Belgian multiple world champion Roland Liboton at work. (Photo H. A. Roth)

You may of course find that cyclo-cross is the discipline in which you do best of all. Though the temptation will be great to decide to specialize in that form of competition alone, its limited season suggests keeping in mind my earlier recommendation to train and race as a multi-discipline cyclist. It will be wise to do a lot of training that closely approximates cyclo-cross racing conditions to make it as specific as possible for the activity that suits you best. But in addition, it will be smart to train for every other form of cycling as well, and to enter races of all different kinds. That will almost certainly benefit your competitive and technical skills more than the somewhat blunting single-discipline approach. If you really find you don't enjoy road racing, still do mixed training and substitute mountain bike racing in summer.

The Race

Participation in a cyclo-cross race may seem like a mechanic's outing at first: bikes and people fiddling on them everywhere. Ignore all that. Just make sure your equipment is in order before you leave, and warm up right up to the start of the race by going for a fast ride or a brisk walk, dressed warmly. Get to the start on time and find a good place on the open stretch from where the race starts. This is where some of your chances can be affected: if you reach the first rough terrain behind someone who can't stay on the bike, you will lose time. Besides, you risk crashing yourself, which is particularly demoralizing so close to the start.

The race will last any number of rounds that can be completed in the time prescribed, followed by a last lap after the bell tolls. It's perhaps pointless to concentrate too much on finding out just how many laps you have completed. Just keep an eye out to avoid falling back by a whole lap or more (something that is not uncommon on the relatively short and difficult course). Certainly in the beginning of your cyclo-cross career, you may have this humiliating experience frequently. That is one reason it will be better to set your goals in terms of the achievable: catching up with this rider or getting to that tree quickly, riding through this patch where you might have been forced to dismount otherwise.

As you participate in more cyclo-cross races, you will notice that your skills develop to the point where you are not dropped, providing you have followed a general training program that includes enough interval work. By its nature, any off-road cycling involves frequent changes of speed and power and lots of force intervals, as well as endurance after a significant amount of anaerobic work. Since each race is very different, though it includes the same elements, only participation in many races will help you develop. Don't be discouraged by that first experience. At first you may find riders who are no stronger than you on the road literally running away from you in a cyclo-cross race, and continuing vigorously, long after you started to feel like giving up. However, if you pursue this discipline, you may soon be heartened by the quick improvement in your performance.

28
The Practice of Track Racing

The many disciplines carried out on the track were briefly described in Chapter 2. As could be seen there, the number of different track events is quite overwhelming, and each one requires some specific skills and preparation. For that reason, this chapter is arranged somewhat differently from the preceding ones dealing with particular types of racing. Here we shall take a look only at those groups of track events that are likely to be encountered by the beginning racer, and explain what must be considered in preparation or practice for those disciplines.

A good all-round bicycle training program should include enough different elements to handle all the required skills and tactics for track events, as well as those needed in the various forms of road racing. It will be wise to do some specific training over distances that correspond closely to those of the particular track races you will be participating in. Yet an integrative training program, quite similar to the one used for any kind of road racing, is probably the most satisfactory broad basis for track racing as well. To develop the specific skills needed for particular forms of track racing, certain aspects most typical for that discipline must be emphasized within that general training program. In addition, the very skill of riding on a track for any purpose must be learned, but this requires only a very modest amount of time on the track.

The problem with track racing is of course that it can only be done on a track, and the chances of having a velodrome nearby are slender. This is especially the case in the US and Canada, where the number of outdoor tracks is very small and indoor tracks are virtually non-existent. In Britain and many other countries there are at least quite a number of outdoor tracks, while in some parts of the world (usually temporary) indoor tracks may be accessible for limited winter training and racing. Clearly, if you don't live near a race track, you won't get an opportunity to train on one. However, that must not be too serious a handicap, since the techniques of track racing don't really differ all that much from those of road racing, and it is entirely possible to train primarily on the road to race on the track.

Consider, in this respect, that the early successes of the US track racers in the late seventies were achieved by riders who received their most intensive coaching a thousand miles away from the nearest velodrome. On the other hand, if you do live near such a facility, this is a really wonderful place to train – whether you are mainly a track racer or not. You can concentrate fully on bicycling, without distractions. You can do it in constant sight of a coach, who can easily follow the movements of all the riders under his care – something that's impossible on the road. Obviously, the benefit will be greatest for specific track racing work, but road racers may find the track a fine place to improve their style too. Besides benefitting in general cycling skills, you may find that the track offers you the potential environment that suits you better than the road.

Though many successful track racers are also strong road riders, others have such specific skills that they only pay off in those track events that are based primarily on that particular skill. To give an example, you may be a strong sprinter without the duration potential to get to the front in any road race. In that case you will never have an opportunity to benefit from your skill on the road, whereas the track match sprint may be just the ticket for you. Or you may be better at short solo rides of one to five minutes than at either fast dashes or long time trials. In that case, track time trials and pursuit events will be just up your alley.

Equipment

For track racing of any kind, you will need a special track bike, as illustrated in Fig. 28.1. No big problem, since the simplicity of these machines makes them surprisingly reasonable, and the quality of even the cheapest models is quite adequate. The track bike has a very rigid, steep and short frame with a high bottom bracket and special rear-facing rear dropouts. The handlebar stem is of steel, to with-

Fig. 28.1 Track bicycle

Olympic size bicycle racing track. This fast 333 m outdoor track at Munich is covered enough to allow competition in almost any kind of weather. (Photo H. A. Roth)

stand the high forces sometimes exerted on the handlebars. The wheel hubs are held in with axle nuts. The bike has neither brakes nor gears, the rear wheel being driven directly and slowed down by restraining from the pedals.

I recommend buying a completely set-up track bike, rather than just a frame and equipping it yourself. That's because it will be hard to get individual components for track bikes. Choose a frame that is small enough to allow a very deep handlebar position, so you can ride perfectly tucked. The cranks are often selected about 5–10 mm shorter than for a road bike, though there is neither an ergonomic nor mechanical justification for that custom. Since lateral forces can be quite significant in the curves, I suggest using wheels with at least 36 spokes. The custom of tying and soldering the spokes at their crossing seems to have no scientific justification, since the resulting wheel is not really more rigid. The tires can be of the lightest type, and they should be glued on with shellac, which holds better than rubber cement or double-sided tape.

The hub for the track bike's rear wheel has special screw threading to accept both a RH threaded single sprocket (without freewheel mechanism), and a lockring with LH thread, as shown in Fig. 28.2. The front chainwheel has only a single chainring. I suggest setting up your first track bike with gearing in the mid sixties (development about 5.5 m) – e.g. 51 X 20.

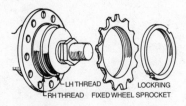

LH THREAD   LOCKRING
RH THREAD   FIXED WHEEL SPROCKET

Fig. 28.2 Track sprocket installation

Get chainrings with 49 and 53 teeth and sprockets with 19, 18, 17, 16 and 15-teeth as well, but don't be light-hearted about installing higher gears, especially in your first year on the track, nor in the first month of any year's training.

Even after some practice, it will be best not to gear higher than about 80 inches (development 6.4 m). That is not only because you must learn to spin, but also to improve control over your speed. Besides, remember that this will be your only gear, and it will be potentially harmful to start off with high muscle forces in a higher gear. Do most of your training in relatively low gears, but select the gear that maximizes your performance in particular disciplines when racing: higher for time trials than for any race involving fast acceleration or real endurance work.

Clothing will be as for the road, except that most people prefer thin slick jerseys without pockets. An energy-absorbing crash helmet is as important in track racing as it is on the road: your head will hit the track just as hard as it will hit the road if you are involved in a spill, which is not too uncommon on the track. Special outfits may be used for certain events and for at least one track discipline (motor-paced racing) a special bike is used, but by the time you get round to participating there, you'll have a coach and a sponsor to take care of things like that.

Starting out on the Track

If you have never ridden on a track before, the environment of the velodrome may be a little intimidating, so you may need some preparation. Though the track may seem a nice safe place to start off cycling to the naive, it is by no means a place for beginners. Start off your cycling on the road and don't shift to the track until you are reasonably confident handling the bike in any

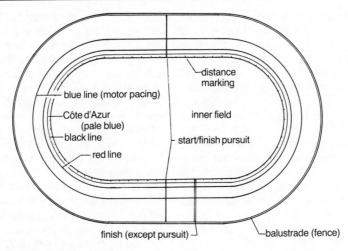

Fig. 28.3 The bicycle racing track

situation. Once you have your track equipment, first try it out on level ground – an empty parking lot or even a level grassy field will allow you to get familiar with the machine more easily than is possible on a banked track with racing cyclists swirling by every few seconds.

First get familiar with the track, on the basis of the terms in Fig. 28.3. When you finally get to the track, first observe the other riders for a while. Watch how they ride in the curves, and observe how they seem to be quite at ease near the top of the banking. That is the point where the curve radius is most generous, and it is the place where you will probably be most comfortable too, once you have the nerve to ride up the precipitous banking. Especially the small indoor tracks are very steep (45 degrees and more), whereas the more generous 333 m and longer tracks are banked by only about 25–30 degrees, which is a lot easier to handle psychologically.

For your own first ride, pick a time when there are not many other riders on the track. Start off near the beginning of a straight section, riding in counterclockwise direction. Stay either well on the inside or well on the outside. At first, the inside will seem best, since you can always move up further out if you can't handle a curve, providing you've made sure you don't get in someone else's way. Once you have gained experience riding around and following a consistent path, try to ride near the top, again retaining a constant distance from the edge.

The first few days it will suffice to merely turn your rounds and become at ease on the track, without trying to do any real training. Use your time on the track to observe other more experienced riders, and to modestly talk to them. You will find out that other regular track riders invariably belong to a team, and observing the way they get along with one another and their coach will probably show you whom to approach to get accepted on a team that appeals to you. Only that way can you get the benefit of competent track coaching. You may of course decide to train alone, but that does not seem to make much sense if you have the choice.

In the following sections, the various disciplines have been grouped by what is common to them. Only those events suitable for beginning track racers shall be covered here, since these are the events at the level where you are going to participate, whereas the other kinds of races will probably remain things to watch as a spectator. Included are some hints on racing. The most important one of these will be to prepare for the track race by following the same general advice given in the preceding chapters for road racing. That includes the need to do some kind of warm-up (cycling outside on the road if necessary) up to about ten minutes before your start, protecting the muscle temperature in the interim wearing a warm-up suit.

Individual Time Trialing and Pursuit
For the beginning track racer, this is the kind of work to start off with, even though it is less spectacular than the match sprint and several other track events. Unlike similar races on the road, these tend to be short duration events. Virtually all track time trials are either 1000 or 4000 m for senior men (instead of 4000 m, professionals ride 5000 m, women and juniors 3000 m). There are other time trial distances, such as 10 km and the hour, but these are not regularly scheduled races, but really only record events.

Pursuit races are held over 4000 m (3000 m or 5000 m for the other categories) and a racer qualifies for the pursuit race by riding a good time in a series of elimination time trials over the same distance. The difference between time trial and pursuit is that the time trialist rides alone, while the pursuiter competes with an opponent who starts at the opposite side of the track. The race ends if one of the riders makes up the half lap that separates the two before the total distance is covered.

Since the 4000 m time trials are qualifying rides for the pursuit race, a

fast rider who is confident of being amongst the 8 or 16 fastest may save his strength in the time trial. That is based on the presumption that there will be more energy left for the pursuit race if you don't exert yourself in the time trial. It will be smart to experiment around a little to establish whether that really applies in your case or not. Though this event calls heavily on anaerobic power, the compensation effect may be stronger than the exhaustion effect. If that is the case, you will be better advised going all out in the qualifying time trial and so ride stronger in the pursuit. As a beginning rider, you will probably not qualify, so it will be smarter to go for the best possible time in the time trial anyway, even if you establish that your second run is faster after taking it easy in the first.

The 1000 m time trial is a really dramatic event that takes only slightly over one minute. It is very tough, being dominated by anaerobic work. Here you may well select the highest gear in which you know you can handle the initial move from standstill to maximum speed. Start off with an explosive pull, trying to reach top speed as soon as you can. Most riders drop off significantly in their second lap, and some come limping in.

Especially for the 1000 m trial, few riders to date take the trouble to keep a schedule to follow, merely riding as fast as they think they can go after the start, and then falling off. I feel there may be a wealth of potential for improvement by keeping a more constant speed. Experiment with different schedules, using your subjective impressions of pedalling speed and fatigue to guide you, comparing the overall results of differently ridden races and training rides to select the style that suits you best. In the longer time trials this technique has been successfully used by some, but especially in the often inconsistently ridden 1000 m, there is even more to be gained by setting up a good schedule, based on control training practices.

Pursuit presents another problem, since the rider also has to avoid being caught by his opponent. Even on a large track, the 4000 m race will cover 10–13 laps, and starting off in the speed that results in an optimal time may get you into trouble before you get halfway. Your opponent may well catch up with you during the first 6–8 laps, even if you'd be able to run away from him beyond that point. Just the same, it will be best if you have the kind of unperturbable attitude not to panic when you see the other guy getting closer and closer, providing you know you can stay ahead and have enough energy left to regain territory in the latter part of the race.

Madison racing. Patric Sercu of Belgium, the world's most successful six-day racer, with partner Gregor Braun. (Photo H. A. Roth)

Mass-Start Racing

This discipline, more familiar perhaps from road racing, is the other kind of event suitable for many developing track racers. The term is really a catch-all for various different disciplines, including points races, elimination rides and scratch races over distances ranging from five to 20 km. These events, especially the longer ones, have something for everybody, and seem especially suitable for those who don't have any particular strengths, but are good all-round riders.

The general skills and training methods are all very similar to those used in preparation for criterium or road racing, except that the shorter distances dictate higher speeds and more intervals. In fact, mass start track races of all kinds, and their simulation during training, may be amongst the most intensive methods of preparation for road or criterium racing. Especially the elimination

race and the points race require frequent short sprints, which have the effect of speed intervals.

In the points race, the placings at the end of every so many rounds are tallied and cumulated. One popular tactic is to try and stay up front during the early part of the race to gain points which nobody can take away from you. Alternatively, you may save your energy in the beginning by not participating in any sprints, only to take a decisive lead, which you try to maintain for several laps around the middle of the event, when the riders who sprinted for the early points are too tired to catch you.

In the elimination race the last rider to cross the line after every round (or every other round) is taken out of the contest, until only two remain to race one another for first place. Here it will be useful if you can somehow manage to drop the strongest sprinter early in the race, which can sometimes be done due to the playful atmosphere that develops in this kind of contest. The most successful elimination riders seem to be those who can keep close to the back without going off the end. And as a defense against arbitrary decisions, you may be well advised to never be anywhere near the very end in a big pack.

Match Sprint

This is no doubt the most track-specific bicycle discipline, being unlike anything else performed in any other sport, cycling or otherwise. The distance ridden is 1000 m, but only the last 200 m are timed, and that is – oddly enough – usually the point where the decision has been made. That decision is generally made when the first rider loses his nerve and starts the sprint, only to be passed by his opponent. This is not a discipline for beginners. Watch some good sprinting during your first two sea-

sons, and start to participate after that, if you have established your qualities are in anaerobic work, which is the sole motor in the match sprint.

The fist eliminations may be ridden between groups of three or four contestants, and only the winners move on to the next round. Starting with the quarter finals, only two contestants compete against one another. The trick is to stay at the top of the track in the banking, so as to be able to benefit from the downhill effect in the final sprint. Since both riders have to watch each other to avoid missing the boat, the rear position has the advantage. When the other rider starts on his sprint, try to pass him on the high side, giving you the greater advantage.

That's the textbook sprint, shown many times at major championships. But when you start participating yourself, you will find out that the secret to most sprinting is not so much shrewd tactics as exemplified by long surplaces (standing still on the bike while guarding the opponent, also referred to as track stop), but speed. The vast majority of all sprints are ridden more or less continuously, although a sudden slowing is common around the point just before those last 200 m, after which there'll be a burning dash for the line.

Whatever gear you used in most of your training, you will find that gears of 88–92 inches (development 6.9–7.2 m) are about right for a strong rider in the sprint. Weaker riders, junior and women should probably choose a slightly lower gear. As for the rest of the equipment, sprinting is where mass or weight savings pays off most, providing you don't sacrifice strength or rigidity. Essentially, that is another way of saying it will be impossible to gain anything due to more sophisticated equipment. Just use your sturdy track bike and mount the lightest tires you can afford.

Teaching a cyclist to become a successful sprinter is not possible in any book. The track is the place to learn it, and your opponents are the folks to learn from, though an experienced coach can be a great boon. If you don't live near a track, chances are you will never be able to develop your full potential as a track sprinter. Near the top of the sport, tactics, which only actual experience and exposure can teach, begin to play such an important role that you can't be expected to improve by speed or force training alone. In fact, sprinting and the 1000 m time trial are perhaps the skills that can hardly be trained beyond a very basic level. That is due to the fact that these disciplines require such an overwhelming proportion of anaerobic work: either you have it or you don't. If you do have it, you may develop it more fully by understanding the game and participating in many contests than by any kind of training.

29
The Practice of Triathlon Cycling

This chapter is of course not a full introduction to triathlon. Nor does it contain all the advice on cycling that this book has to offer the triathlete. For successful general participation in that sport, you will have to adhere to some of the recommendations given in specific triathlon manuals. For effective cycling as an element of triathlon, you will do well to read the rest of this book as well, save perhaps some of the specific discipline-oriented chapters just preceding this one. This chapter merely contains some additional observations that seem to apply particularly to the triathlete concerning the activity of cycling, both in competition and in training.

Clearly, there can't be too much difference between riding a bike in a triathlon or doing the same thing for its own sake. By and large, the cycling leg of triathlon competition is a time trial, ridden on the open road. Consequently, most of the advice on time trial cycling given elsewhere in this book, particularly in Chapter 23, applies here too. The few additional things to be considered by triathletes shall be covered in this chapter.

Though in essence a time trial, the triathlon cycling discipline has several elements that set it apart. Depending on the particular event, the length of this time trial may well be quite a bit shorter or longer than what is typical for most forms of established regular time trials for racing cyclists. The fact that the participant comes out of the water and will be doing some tough running afterwards is of course reflected in the style adopted. And, not to be ignored, most triathletes are less competent as cyclists, though this book attempts to change that.

Equipment

Triathlon rules on cycling equipment are less restrictive than those the UCI and the various national cycling organizations administer for regular bicycle racing. Thus, almost any kind of clothing can be worn (or left off). Also the bike itself can be quite unconventional, sporting disc wheels and other gizmos purportedly to reduce air resistance or provide other intangible benefits. Just the same, I feel you can do admirably well riding a very ordinary racing bike and wearing regular cycling garb. Heretical perhaps, but I suggest you try it before you equip yourself and your bike with expensive items that do more harm than good.

The suggestion to follow bicycle racing custom applies particularly to training rides. There it is more important to stay comfortable when periods of high and low work output follow one another. Under such conditions cycling clothing actually works to prevent discomfort, sickness and injury. And using things like disc wheels on the bike may be acceptable to minimize wind resistance in a race on a day without wind and on smooth roads. But they would probably make your training a lot less comfortable and effective.

It will also be of some importance whether you are participating in the relatively short races offered regularly, or in one of the spectacular events based on the Ironman schedule. The latter include such a long time on the bike that you'd better do all you can to remain comfortable. The top contestants in these events may be extremely tough and independently wealthy, so they can afford to take risks the other contestants should avoid. Even if the winners have skimped on showering or changing before the bike event, and though they ride bikes with disk wheels, that does not mean every contestant will benefit doing the same.

Technique and Training

Not every triathlon is an Ironman, and the thing to train for primarily is the kind of event offered most. Though triathlons vary greatly, most of the ones regularly offered all over the US, and slowly finding their way into other societies as well, are relatively short ones. These include cycling distances not exceeding 40 km or 25 miles. The thing to train for, though, is not only the length of the bike ride, but also the total duration. As mentioned in Chap-

ter 1, it is an excellent practice to do most of your regular cardio-respiratory or aerobic duration training for the entire event on the bike.

This approach has the potential drawback of making you slow. If the total race lasts say two hours, half of the time being spent on the bike, a two hour regular bicycle training session in the form of LSD riding is more than adequate to build up both endurance and aerobic potential. But it doesn't do much for either your ability to handle increased loads under aerobic and anaerobic conditions, nor particularly for your cycling performance. And, since bicycling is the key event, for which training can improve your overall time most significantly, your training program should also emphasize whatever exercises will improve specific cycling speed.

Consequently, triathlon training on the bike should distinguish clearly between sessions for overall aerobic strength and endurance on the one

Triathlon: bikers become runners at a Chicago USTS race. (Photo courtesy Bud Light – USTS)

hand and those to improve cycling speed and power in the region of the anaerobic threshold on the other hand. The former should be carried out over distances that take at least as long as the duration of the typical complete triathlon in competition, and must include a weekly ride of really long duration if you intend to ever participate in one of those monster triathlons. The latter should consist of shorter high-intensity sessions with an emphasis on speed and force intervals and other forms of high and variable speed training as outlined in chapters 17 and 18.

Triathlete Scott Molina riding a bicycle with a disk rear wheel. (Photo courtesy Bud Light – USTS)

In your yearly training schedule, aerobic work and endurance should come first to build up overall fitness. The more intensive (and less time consuming) interval work can start once basic fitness and endurance has been reached. Depending on your initial condition and your ultimate ambition, it may be acceptable to train at a low aerobic level only during the first year. In that case, do not introduce interval work until you have become familiar enough with the sport and have developed a smooth riding technique, some time into the second training year.

The first and most critical point to train for, as well as the thing to watch most while competing, is cycling technique. Pay particular attention to the skill of spinning the pedals fast in a relatively low gear. That might sound like a superfluous warning to anyone who has read most of this book or any other bicycle racing manual. However, this advice is still all too often lost on triathletes. Spend the first six weeks of each pre-race training season, and even longer in your first year, paying particular attention to pedalling speed. Choose a lower gear if you can't keep the speed up above 90 RPM essentially all the time.

The next things to work on for the triathlete who does not have a strict cycling background are body position, pedalling style and bike handling. These items were all covered in the chapters of Part I, to which you are referred again here. Practice these aspects to improve your performance and comfort at a given level of strength and output. The resulting initial improvement in cycling speed and endurance will be greater than that of training in the conventional sense of the word. This will even pay off in your performance during the running that follows, since you can run a lot better when you come off the bike without feeling shot. Start to train for strength, speed and endurance only after you have achieved good technical skills.

One thing that distinguishes some triathlon events is that the course of the bicycle ride may include hills, which are not encountered in most regular time trials. For that reason, you may be well advised to pay more attention to the hill climbing techniques as outlined in chapters 7, 14 and 25. The other distinguishing feature is the presence of so many other contestants of varying ability. You will be surrounded by all those folks who are about as good at swimming as you are, though their cycling abilities may vary quite a bit. Don't become too confident you are doing well if you are passing participants that came out of the water ahead of you. An other aspect of the presence of all these other athletes is the potential danger of crashing. Learn to handle your bike really well, as outlined in chapters 8 through 10, and try to steer clear of unpredictable bike handlers – preferably by cycling so fast that you stay well ahead of them.

All the other training techniques that apply to cycling can also be used in preparation for triathlon events. But always keep in mind that technique and style are prerequisites for effective cycling in training and competition, and that a good cycling performance is the key to good overall performance in triathlon. Suggestions like warming up (on the bike if you can, but any other way if you can't) also apply to triathlons, whether in training or competition. That applies to pre-race conditioning as well: though it may not be what others are doing shortly before they hit the cold (or not so cold) water, you should be warming up and keep covered enough to avoid excessive cooling off before the race. After any training session or race it will be smartest not to just lie back and watch your body stiffen up. Continue moving at a reduced output, to unwind and to allow your muscles and cardio-respiratory system to recover.

30
Keeping Track of Your Performance

This final chapter contains some suggestions to help you keep track of your progress in racing, as well as in training. We've seen in Chapter 21 how knowledge of results (KOR) can improve an athlete's performance in a particular race. There is a good case to be made for the assumption that knowledge of progress – let's call it KOP – may have a similarly positive effect on long-term performance, from one race to the next and from one season to the next.

Doing this in a systematic manner will make you a more conscious participant in the sport, one who is more aware of his own strengths and weaknesses. Even if it does nothing else for you, it will at least help you determine whether you are progressing at all, and in what fields your potential is greatest. Though this chapter deals primarily with your results in competition, there should be a feedback from competition results to training input, as suggested by the diagram Fig. 19.1 in Chapter 19.

Planning Calendar

The first step in keeping track of anything is planning the items to monitor. So your first tool should be a simple schedule of events to be followed as you continue planning and scheduling. Do that with a large calendar that shows the entire year on one sheet. Use a poster-size sheet of blank paper and divide it up into weeks and days as shown in Fig. 30.1. Some people divide it into months, but you will find the breakdown by weeks more useful, because the days of the week are more significant and regular to your overall time schedule.

On this sheet, enter any events offered in which you might want to participate as soon as they are announced. Write them in pencil in the top of the box for the appropriate day. Only very brief descriptions will be possible, such as 'Santa Cruz – 70 km crit.'. Cross out or erase the information if an event is cancelled (many are announced but never ridden). Any race that you do not want to miss can be written in more clearly with a red felt tip pen. These may be district championships or other events of some greater importance. Once both the race itself and your participation in it are confirmed, write it in ink (in the case of the ones written out in pencil first) and put a circle around it. Go over this sheet regularly to update it, considering also whether particular events will fit into your general schedule.

You now have a personal racing calendar that will always be up to date and easy to read. This schedule at any time shows you the current status of events offered, emphasizing those you will participate in and highlighting in particular those that you consider most important. But this sheet still has a lot of blank space: all the boxes for days without races are completely free, as are the lower halves of the ones corresponding to the racing days.

Leave the lower halves of all boxes free for subsequent entries, but use the top parts and the margins of the sheet to make notes to yourself. Write what you intend to do in those spaces, especially by way of pre-race preparation. That may include some races as well: if you ride a criterium in preparation for a later more important race,

	week No.	Sunday	Monday	Tuesday	Wednesday	Thursday	Friday	Saturday
January	1					1	2	3
	2	4	5	6	7	8	9	10
	3	11						
	4							
	5							
February	6							
	7							
	8							
	9							
March	10							
	11							
	12							

Fig. 30.1 Yearly planning calendar

write in how you intend to ride that one. Similarly, write down for each training day what you want to watch out for during your training that day, especially if it differs from your regular routine. This sheet should be kept in some highly visible place, and must be pondered each day before you start out.

Training and Racing Log

The overall planning calendar just described is very useful for a quick overview, but it is not enough for detailed planning and record keeping. You must also have more precise information in a more portable form. For that purpose, use a note book in the 4 x 6 inch format (or the international standard size A6). This is small enough to be carried along, and big enough to accept all the essential information. Take a two-page spread for each weekly period, and at the top of each appropriate page record all the additional information about the races you intend to enter: date, time, contact person with phone number, starting point, category, type of event, distance, terrain, and so on.

The larger part of each page should remain available for notes about your physical condition and training as well as the races. Some people use a separate (and perhaps more detailed) training diary, but I feel all the information that has to do with preparation and progress, training and racing, can be kept together. It will be more useful and less confusing if only one book is used. This will force you to be brief in the notes you take. It will improve the chances of them being concentrated on the really significant things and makes it easier to gain a quick but complete overview when you consult the book to gain insight into what has happened afterwards.

You can divide the remaining space on the page spread up into roughly equal blocks for the days of the week. Enter the training you do each day in there. Notes about the training you plan to do may be entered first, followed by what you actually did, how you feel, and each day's vital information: resting pulse rate, weight and any other comments on your health and wellbeing, particularly anything out of the ordinary. All the information entered must be brief, easily legible and systematic. If necessary, develop a kind of private shorthand and use it consistently, maintaining the same format and the same abbreviations throughout.

After the race briefly describe the event in terms of your placing, time, average speed etc. in the appropriate space on the page. Then comment on the way the race was ridden, both by you and the other participants. If you made a particular mistake, analyze it in simple terms, including the effect it had on your overall performance. Do this conscientiously the day of the race, and supplement it the day after with comments on the way you feel, and with the benefit of the hindsight that makes you evaluate the race better after some time has elapsed.

Since the results of the race, together with the other comments about it, are more important than many other details on the page, draw a box around this information. Later, when leafing through this note book, you will be able to pick out everything pertinent to race performance and progress at a glance. At the same time, and always on the same page spread, you will have a convenient recall reference of the information about the training you did during the week before, as well as the way you felt. Consult this booklet frequently to compare the results over time.

You should of course fill in important other details about your racing career in this booklet as well, taking care to make the facts that have a significant impact stand out. These other comments may for instance include notes about such diverse things as a period in which you can't train due to sickness or injury, the transition to another category, or the participation in a training camp. Whatever the nature of the special events, they should be highlighted if they have a significant impact on your training and racing life, so you can recognize them later when going through the booklet.

In addition to actual racing results, you can also include the times achieved in the various tests you may have set up in connection with what I call control method training in Chapter 17. The most important results of races and these tests can be entered on your large planning calendar, but I suggest you don't clutter that big sheet with too much detailed information, even though it provides a quick overview. It should be more a planning tool, while your little booklet will be your reference.

Some people like to do things like this record keeping on computer. Sounds professional, but it will be far more practical to use the old paper and pencil technique. Unlike a computer, little booklets can be taken along to be pondered or updated at will, and, unlike computers, big planning sheets may be conveniently hung on a wall or a door, where they will inform you and invite you to update the information whenever you pass.

Appendix

Gear table – gear number in inches

number of teeth chainwheel

		24	26	28	30	32	34	36	38	40	42	44	45	46	47	48	49	50	52	53	54	55	56
number of teeth sprocket	12	54.1	58.5	63	67.5	72	76.5	81.1	85.5	90	94.5	99	101.2	103.5	105.7	108	110.2	112.3	117	119.3	121.5	123.7	126
	13	49.8	54	58.1	62.3	66.4	70.6	74.7	78.9	83.1	87.2	91.4	93.4	95.5	97.6	99.7	101.8	103.9	108	110	112.1	114.2	116.3
	14	46.2	50.1	54	57.8	61.7	65.5	69.5	73.3	77.1	81	84.9	86.7	88.7	90.6	92.6	94.5	96.4	100.3	102.2	104.1	106	108
	15	43.2	46.8	50.4	54	57.6	61.1	64.8	68.4	72	75.6	79.2	80.9	82.8	84.6	86.4	88.2	90	93.6	95.4	97.2	99	100.8
	16	40.5	43.7	47.2	50.6	54	57.2	60.9	64.1	67.5	70.9	74.3	76	77.6	79.3	81	82.7	84.4	87.8	89.4	91.1	92.8	94.5
	17	38.1	41.2	44.4	47.6	50.8	54	57.2	60.3	63.5	66.7	69.9	71.5	73.1	74.6	76.2	77.8	79.4	82.6	84.1	85.7	87.3	88.9
	18	36	39	42	45	48	51	54	57	60	63	66	67.5	69	70.5	72	73.5	75	78	79.5	81	82.5	84
	19	34.1	36.8	39.7	42.6	45.5	48.2	51.1	54	56.8	59.7	62.5	64	65.3	66.6	68	69.4	71.1	73.9	75.3	76.7	78.1	79.5
	20	32.4	35.1	37.8	40.5	43.2	45.9	48.7	51.3	54	56.7	59.4	60.8	62.1	63.4	64.8	66.2	67.5	70.2	71.5	72.9	74.5	75.6
	21	30.8	33.4	36	38.6	41.1	43.7	46.4	48.9	51.4	54	56.6	57.9	59.1	60.4	61.7	63	64.3	66.9	68.1	69.4	70.7	72
	22	29.4	31.9	34.3	36.8	39.2	41.6	44.2	46.6	49.1	51.5	54	55.2	56.5	57.6	58.9	60.1	61.4	63.8	65	66.2	67.5	68.7
	23	28.1	30.5	32.8	35.2	37.5	39.9	42.4	44.6	47	49.3	51.6	52.8	54	55.2	56.3	57.5	58.7	61	62.2	63.6	64.5	65.7
	24	27	29.2	31.5	33.7	36	38.2	40.5	42.8	45	47.3	49.5	50.7	51.8	52.9	54	55.1	56.3	58.5	59.6	60.7	61.8	63
	25	25.9	28	30.2	32.4	34.6	36.7	38.9	41	43.2	45.4	47.5	48.6	49.7	50.8	51.8	52.9	54	56.2	57.2	58.3	59.4	60.4
	26	24.9	27	29	31.2	33.2	35.3	37.4	39.5	41.5	43.6	45.7	46.7	47.8	48.8	49.9	50.9	51.9	54	55	56	57.1	58.1
	28	23.1	25	27	28.9	30.8	32.8	34.8	36.6	38.6	40.5	42.4	43.7	44.4	45.3	46.3	47.2	48.2	50	51.1	52	53	54
	30	21.6	23.2	25.1	27	28.6	30.6	32.4	34.2	36	37.5	39.6	40.5	41.4	42.1	43.2	44	45	46.8	47.5	48.6	49.4	50.2

Addresses of Bicycle Racing Organizations

AACF (Australian Amateur Cycling Federation)
20 Paterson Crescent,
5043 Morphettville

BCF (British Cycling Federation)
16 Upper Woburn Place,
London WC1H 0QE

CCA (Canadian Cycling Association)
333 River Road, Vanier,
Ottawa KIL 8B9

FIAC (Federation Internationale Amateur de Cylisme)
Via dei Campi Sportivi 48,
00197 Rome, Italy

FICP (Federation Internationale de Cyclisme Professionelle)
26 rue de Cessange, Leudelange, Luxembourg

ICF (Irish Cycling Federation)
5 St. Christopher's Road, Montenotte, Cork.

NICF (Northern Ireland Cycling Federation)
3 Rosemount, Lurgan, Co. Armagh

NZACA (New Zealand Amateur Cycling Association)
P.O. Box 3104, Wellington

UCI (Union Cycliste Internationale)
6 rue Armat, Geneva, Switzerland

USCF (United States Cycling Federation)
1750 East Boulder Street,
Colorado Springs, CO 80909

Bibliography

Ambrosini, G., *Ciclismo*. Sperling and Kupfer, Milan (Italy), 1974.

Åstrand, P.O., and Rodahl, K., *Textbook of Work Physiology*. McGraw-Hill, New York, 1977.

Bakker, R., *Voeding en verzorging van een wielrenner*. Sport Expres, Amsterdam (Netherlands).

Borysewicz, E. and Pavelka, E., *Bicycle Road Racing*. Velo-News, Brattleboro (USA), 1985.

Burke, J. (Ed.), *Towards an Understanding of Human Performance*. Movement Publications, Ithaca (USA), 1977.

Carlson, F.D. and Wilkie, D.R., *Muscle Physiology*. Prentice Hall, Englewood Cliffs (USA), 1977.

Clarijs, J.P. and Ingen-Schenau, G.J. van (Eds.), *Wielrennen*, De Tijdstroom, Ghent (Belgium), 1985.

Daniels, G., *Trainen voor wielrenners*. Het Volk, Antwerpen (Belgium), 1979.

Darden, E., *Nutrition and Athletic Performance*. Athletic Press, Pasadena (USA), 1976.

DeLong, F., *DeLong's Guide to Bicycles and Bicycling*. Chilton Books, Radnor (USA), 1976.

Donath, R. and Schuler, K.P., *Ernährung des Sportlers*. Sportverlag, Berlin (GDR), 1979.

Faria, I.E., *Cycling Physiology for the Serious Cyclist*. Thomas, Springfield (USA), 1978.

Faria, I.E. and Cavanagh, P.R., *The Physiology and Biomechanics of Cycling*. Wiley, New York, 1978.

Forester, J., *Effective Cycling*. MIT-Press, Cambridge (USA), 1984.

Fox, E.L., *Sports Physiology*. Saunders, Philadelphia, 1979.

Fox, E.L., and Mathews, D.K., *The Physiological Basis of Physical Education in Athletics*. Saunders, Philadelphia, 1981.

Harre D. (Ed.), *Trainingslehre*, Sportverlag, Berlin (GDR), 1979.

Inside the Cyclist, Velo-news, Brattleboro (USA), 1984.

Israel, S. and Weber, J., *Probleme der Langzeitausdauer im Sport*. Barth Verlag, Leipzig (GDR), 1972.

Konopka, P., *Cycling Sports Guide*. A&C Black, London, 1983.

Matheny, F., *Beginning Bicycle Racing*. Velo-news, Brattleboro USA), 1983.

Matwejew, L.P. *The problem of periodization in sports training*. Moscow (USSR), 1965

Mellerowicz, H. and Meller, W., *Training*. Springer Verlag, Heidelberg (GFR), 1975.

Mondenard, J.P. de, *La Consultation Médicinale du Cycliste*. SLOCAM, Paris (France), 1981.

Nijs, P. (Ed.), *Sport and Doping*. De Sikkel, Malle (Belgium), 1978.

Pernow, B., Salting B., *Muscle Metabolism During Exercise*. Plenum, New York, 1971.

Plas, R. van der, *The Penguin Bicycle Handbook*. Penguin, Harmondsworth (GB), 1983.

Racker, E., *Mechanisms in Bio-energetics*. Academic Press, New York, 1975.

Tricker, R.A.R. and Tricker, G.J.K., *The Science of Movement*. American Elsevier, New York, 1976.

Van der Plas, R., *The Mountain Bike Book*. Bicycle Books, San Francisco, 1984.

–, *The Bicycle Repair Book*. Bicycle Books, San Francisco, 1985.

Whitt, F.R. and Wilson, D.G., *Bicycling Science*. MIT-Press, Cambridge (USA), 1982.

Zorn, H., *Wielersport*. Elmar, Rijswijk (Netherlands), 1984.

Note:

To keep the length of this bibliography down, individual articles are not included. On the other hand, several important books in foreign languages are listed. This should be seen as a suggestion to English language publishers: each one of these foreign titles deserves to be translated into English.

Index

About the Author

Rob Van der Plas is a professional engineer and a former bicycle racer and coach. For many years he has closely followed the biomechanical research and the development of both practical and scientific training methods. Since 1975 he has devoted most of his interest to the technical and scientific aspects of the bicycle and the research on what makes the cyclist tick. In this book he shares with his readers the knowledge gained from first hand experience and extensive literature search on the subject of effective training practices.

Though he gave up active racing himself long ago, he still cycles a lot and follows the international bicycle racing scene with a keen interest. In addition to this book, he has written *The Mountain Bike Book*, *The Bicycle Repair Book* (both published by Bicycle Books) and *The Penguin Bicycle Handbook,* as well as many other books that have been published in

Holland, Germany and Denmark. His contributions on all aspects of bicycles and bicycling appear regularly in cycling periodicals both sides of the Atlantic.

Other books by Rob Van der Plas, published by Bicycle Books, Inc.

The Mountain Bike Book
ISBN 0-933201-10-9
6 x 9 inches, soft cover, 144 pages
with 150 line drawings and 50 black
and white photographs
US price $ 7.95

The first and still the most authoritative
book ever published on the new breed of
fat-tired bicycle. Shows how to choose,
equip, ride and maintain the mountain bike
or ATB.

The Bicycle Repair Book
ISBN 0-933201-11-7
6 x 9 inches, soft cover, 140 pages
with 300 line drawings
US price: $ 7.95

The most thorough and systematic bicycle
repair manual on the market today, covering all repairs on any kind of bicycle. Complete with step-by-step instructions and
troubleshooting guide.

All books published by Bicycle Books, Inc. may be obtained through the book
or bike trade. If not available locally, use the coupon below to order directly from
the publisher:

Bicycle Books, Inc.
1282 a – 7th Avenue
San Francisco, CA 94122
Tel.: (415) 665 8214

Please send the following book(s):

_____ copies *The Bicycle Repair Guide* _____ x $ 7.95 = $ _____
_____ copies *The Mountain Bike Book* _____ x $ 7.95 = $ _____
_____ copies *The Bicycle Racing Guide* _____ x $ 9.95 = $ _____

Sub total $ _____
California residents add 6 % tax $ _____
Postage and handling _____ books x $ 1.00 = $ _____

Total amount (check or money order enclosed) $ _____

Name: _____

Address: _____

City, state, zip: _____

Telephone: (____) _____

Signature: _____ Date: _____

Payment in full must accompany order. California residents add 6 % tax. Enclose check
or money order for full price of order, including $ 1.00 postage and handling for each copy
ordered. Allow three weeks for delivery. Mail coupon with payment to Bicycle Books, Inc.,
1282a – 7th Ave., San Francisco, CA 94122.